The Selected Letters of Mark Van Doren

The Selected Letters of
Mark Van Doren

Edited, and with an Introduction, by
George Hendrick

With a Foreword by
Dorothy Van Doren

Louisiana State University Press
Baton Rouge and London

Library of Congress Cataloging-in-Publication Data

Van Doren, Mark, 1894–1972.
  The selected letters of Mark Van Doren.

  Bibliography: p.
  Includes index.
    1. Van Doren, Mark, 1894–1972—Correspondence.
  2. Authors, American—20th century—Correspondence.
  3. Critics—United States—Correspondence.   I. Hendrick,
  George.   II. Title.
  PS3543.A557Z48   1986   811'.52 [B]   86-7456
  ISBN 0-8071-1317-4

Frontispiece courtesy Dorothy Van Doren

Contents

Preface and Acknowledgments

Dorothy Van Doren had originally planned to edit her husband's letters, and she collected a large number of them, mostly those written to his friends. After she asked me to take over the editorial duties, she passed on to me the letters she had collected and also gave me the names of additional friends of theirs to contact. I did attempt to locate all possible Mark Van Doren letters in private hands, but I was unable to locate several sets of letters. In some cases, letters no longer exist: almost all of his early letters to his close friend Joseph Wood Krutch were destroyed in a fire, and Van Doren's letters to his parents have not survived.

I contacted over sixty libraries with holdings of Mark Van Doren manuscript collections, and from these libraries I had access to hundreds of additional letters. Many of them were brief notes to confirm a time for a poetry reading or thank you notes to people who had entertained him during his reading tours, but important sets of letters were found also. His letters to Allen Tate and Carl Van Doren were at Princeton, those to John Gould Fletcher were at the University of Arkansas, those to John Berryman were at the University of Minnesota, and those to Thomas Merton at Bellarmine College.

This collection would undoubtedly have been quite different had all of Van Doren's letters been preserved and been available. I have included in this collection about one-fourth of the letters available to me. I have used the significant letters to Berryman, Fletcher, Merton, and Tate. I have included a sampling of letters to his students, to writers who turned to him for advice, to his publishers and editors, and to his family. Within the limits set by a one-volume format for these letters, it has been my intention to suggest the range of Van Doren's interests.

I am indebted to many people and libraries for their help during the years this volume was under preparation. Many people furnished Van

Doren letters still in private collections. I have included correspondence furnished me by Mortimer Adler, Howard Baker, Margaret Clark, Edward Davidson, Gladys Ely, John Haffenden, Sholom J. Kahn, Donald L. Keene, Ernest Kroll, James Laughlin, James McCartin, Sarah Singer, Mrs. James Thurber, Charles Van Doren, John Van Doren, Dorothy Graffe Van Doren, and Arthur Wang. William Claire gave me permission to quote passages from *Voyages*, V (Numbers 1–4, 1973), the Mark Van Doren issue. A large number of libraries provided me with letters in their collections, and I drew from the libraries cited in the list of abbreviations herein.

Willene and Sarah Hendrick and Peggy Harris helped with typing and encouraged this project. Librarians have been extremely generous with their time, particularly Dr. Robert Daggy of the Thomas Merton Center, Bellarmine College; Samuel A. Sizer, Curator of Special Collections, University of Arkansas Library, Fayetteville; the staff of Butler Library, Columbia University (where Mark Van Doren's own papers are deposited); and the staff of the University of Illinois Library. Dr. John Haffenden and Eileen Simpson helped with John Berryman annotations, and Robert Buffington helped with Allen Tate annotations.

I am especially indebted to Dorothy, Charles, and John Van Doren. They provided me with letters in their possession, helped me locate others, and gave me information which helped identify people and places mentioned in the letters.

A Note on the Text

In order to conserve space, I have standardized the dateline of each letter to contain the name of the person to whom the letter is addressed, the date (in brackets if conjectural), and the place from which the letter was written. The notations ALS (autograph letter signed), TLS (typed letter signed), or APS (autograph postcard signed) show document type. Abbreviations such as NjP and MnU indicate where the letter is to be found, and a list of these abbreviations follows this note.

When pertinent, a short explanatory note precedes the body of the letter. These general remarks are brief and are in italics. Identifications of names, places, or events are to be found in the notes following individual letters.

To save additional space, I have omitted formal salutations and closings. Mark Van Doren was informal and addressed his friends by their first names. Mark Van Doren is abbreviated to MVD in the notes, and Carl Van Doren is often shortened to CVD.

The letters offer few problems in the way of legibility. I have attempted to present a text identical to the original letters without reproducing obvious scribal errors. I have retained abbreviations, set superscripts on the line, and have included all editorial additions within brackets. All postscripts have been placed at the end of the letter, whether the material originally appeared there, or, as is sometimes the case, at the top of the page. In the case of struck-over words or phrases, the author's revisions are followed.

Individual letters in this volume have been edited, and many repetitions have been omitted; if Van Doren recounts the same incident to two or more people, I have used only one account. Many strictly personal items are also omitted. I have used the following methods to indicate elision: Three asterisks centered on the page mean the omission of one or more full paragraphs at the beginning of a letter. To indicate omissions within

sentences three-point ellipses are used; a three-point ellipsis at the beginning of a paragraph indicates that the opening word, words, sentence, or
sentences have been deleted. Four-point ellipses signify deletion of the last
part of the sentence, the first part of the next sentence, a whole sentence
or more, or a whole paragraph or more. Omission of only the compli-
mentary close and the signature is not indicated.

I have used the chapter headings from Mark Van Doren's *Autobiography,* adding a final one for the years not covered by the memoirs.

Abbreviations

ArU	Special Collections, University of Arkansas Library, Fayetteville
CSmH	Henry E. Huntington Library, San Marino, California
CSt	Stanford University, Stanford, California
DLC	Library of Congress (Manuscript Division), Washington, D.C.
ICN	Newberry Library, Chicago, Illinois
IU–Ar	University of Illinois Archives, Urbana (S. P. Sherman and Russell Miles collections)
IU–R	Rare Book Room, University of Illinois, Urbana
KyLoB–M	Thomas Merton Studies Center, Bellarmine College, Louisville, Kentucky
MH	Houghton Library, Harvard University, Cambridge, Massachusetts
MnU	University of Minnesota Library (Manuscripts Division), Minneapolis, Minnesota
NNAL	Archives of the American Academy and Institute of Arts and Letters, New York, N.Y.
NNC	Rare Book and Manuscript Library, Columbia University, New York, N.Y.
NNHB	Harcourt Brace Jovanovich
NhD	Dartmouth College Library, Hanover, N.H.
NjP	Princeton University Library, Princeton, N.J.
OkU	University of Oklahoma Library, Norman, Oklahoma
P	Letters in private hands
TxU	Harry Ransom Humanities Research Center, The University of Texas at Austin
ViU	Clifton Waller Barrett Library, University of Virginia, Charlottesville (Elizabeth Shepley Sergeant Collection)

The Selected Letters of Mark Van Doren

Foreword

by Dorothy Van Doren

The bulk of these letters from my husband are directed to a few people with whom he had a personal relationship. As the reader is likely to be curious about the sort of persons those correspondents were, it seems worthwhile for me to say something about them from my own recollection. My remarks, however, merely supplement what some of them have said about themselves, and what is remembered by others.

Carl Van Doren went to study and to teach at Columbia in 1908. His relationship to Mark, the fourth of five brothers of which Carl was the eldest, has been described by both in their autobiographies as singularly loving and close, with Carl acting as father and teacher, blazing the trail that Mark, not without independence, was to follow. Shortly after World War I, Carl was living with his wife, Irita, and presently his three daughters, near Columbia. He became literary editor of the *Nation* in 1920 and had already made a name for himself as a scholar, critic, and man of letters who was particularly interested in American literature. More than any other person, he, who had read everything in English and American letters worth reading (and much more besides), was responsible for my husband's conviction that wide reading in the works of any author was the prerequisite to having a worthwhile opinion of him, not the analyses of single letters or other men's interpretations.

Before my husband began his teaching career at Columbia, he spent a year and a half in the army, from the summer of 1917 to Christmas 1918. Then, too, his letters to Carl were numerous and revealing of all his interests. Later still, when he went to England and France on a Columbia traveling fellowship with Joseph Wood Krutch, a fellow student and lifelong friend, Mark wrote to Carl about what they saw, the books they read, the plays they went to in London and Paris, and the friends they met. After both brothers took up residence in New York, meeting often at Columbia or the offices of the *Nation,* the correspondence naturally declined, but there were other friends to write to.

Shortly after Mark became literary editor of the *Nation* in 1924, he met Allen Tate. Mark had published a poem of his and Tate was very happy about it and in his letter of thanks he suggested a luncheon meeting. He said diffidently, "I am twenty-five years old," as though that were juvenile beyond consideration. Mark at that time was thirty, so he could assure Tate that twenty-five was not too young to be Mark's friend. Their correspondence dealt with matters that were close to both of them. They wanted to talk about poetry, the poems they had written or might write, and various literary friends. But the friendship soon included their wives and children. Because Caroline Gordon, Tate's wife, was an accomplished novelist, and I, too, was writing novels, we had a shared interest. And the Tates' daughter, Nancy, became a close friend of our sons.

Beyond his concern for poetry, Allen Tate, as a southerner, was deeply learned about the Civil War. I remember an occasion when the Tates were visiting us in Connecticut that the boys got out the blackboard from their playhouse and Tate, in his gentle southern voice, gave us a blow-by-blow description of the Battle of Gettysburg that held us completely fascinated. The Wheat Field, the Devil's Den, Little Round Top, Pickett's Charge— he took us all from one place to another and made us see, as if we had been there, how desperate, how bloody, or how triumphant the fighting had been.

As his letters indicate, there was no one to whom Mark felt a closer rapprochement with regard to poetry than Tate. Mark's letters to John Berryman were, on the other hand, always those of a teacher to a gifted student. The discussions of poetry were not generalized, but had reference to Berryman's own poems. Mark was best man at Berryman's first marriage in St. Patrick's Cathedral, and our family and Berryman's soon became friends. Throughout his life, Berryman was beset by problems, personal and poetical, and he poured them out to Mark and doubtless to other friends. Since he was a great traveler—to the South, to Europe, finally to settle at the University of Minnesota—the correspondence flourished, though long and often deeply disturbed telephone conversations also took place when he was particularly unhappy.

Joseph Wood Krutch was my husband's oldest and closest friend. After their European tour, they were teaching colleagues at Columbia for a time, until Krutch retired to the Arizona desert and became the naturalist he probably always should have been. Most of Krutch's correspondence was destroyed by fire, but the letter in this collection about his biography of Samuel Johnson was saved. Krutch declared it the finest critique of one friend to another that he had ever read. Mark explained that he had just finished the book while on a trip to Harvard. In his hotel room that night, he wrote the letter, eight handwritten pages of it, and put it in the mail before he went to bed.

Besides being a distinguished writer, Krutch was an incomparable storyteller, always pausing at just the right time for the proper effect, and never hurrying through an anecdote. His stories of Tennessee, where he grew up, were the marvel and delight of his listeners. Until he moved to the desert, he was plagued with bronchitis, but at every crisis of health or other distress, his wife, Marcelle Leguia, a French Basque and a trained nurse, took over and saw the patient through his problems. As with the Tates, our friendship was long lasting.

Another student of my husband's, Thomas Merton, was also a cherished friend. At college he had been teased by the idea of communism, but he turned to the church instead, became a member of the Trappist Order at Gethsemani in Kentucky, and eventually was ordained as a priest. In spite of his serious vocation, Merton was never solemn, and the two visits I made to the monastery (my husband was there at other times, as well) showed him to be the merry and wise fellow he had always been. Although the Trappists are a silent order, Merton, as teacher of the novices, was permitted to speak, and when we saw him he had evidently received a special dispensation, so that when he took us over the abbey farm he talked along as he always had. The church had left him his own man.

From Scott Buchanan my husband came to know, as he never had, the works of the great philosophers—Plato, Aristotle, Aquinas—and the other medieval writers that were to make up a large part of the curriculum at St. John's College. Buchanan, before he became Dean of St. John's, was already a philosopher. To our surprise, he and his wife and son had already made a visit to Hope, where Mark was born, and which is now the ghost of a small village—the church, a few houses, and some fine trees. "What shall I say about Hope," Buchanan wrote in a long letter to Mark. "Those little towns are so eloquent with only a suggestion of their history, the groves that your grandfather planted, the house that burned down after your mother left it, the schoolhouse that Carl's book had already made familiar, the little church, and the real Van Doren house on another bulge in the hill. . . . May I say that I now know very vividly why you once wanted to be and are now a poet."

Other poets are included in this collection, one at least less merry than Merton, less witty than Tate. John Gould Fletcher came to visit us in Connecticut on several occasions and he was always sad. He always felt that he had not achieved what he was meant to achieve and that as a writer he was neglected. It is pleasant to record that his second wife, a sensible, happy person, was able to dispel much of his gloom.

Another friend with whom my husband corresponded was Mortimer Adler. Mark knew Adler slightly as a student, but shortly after Adler graduated, they shared a section of the General Honors course, the forerunner of the humanities series. Adler was lively, enormously energetic, a great talker, and incomparably intelligent. They had a great time together, and my husband felt that he had to work his hardest to keep up with this volatile, yet deadly serious student. In his *Autobiography,* Mark writes, "he would talk so fast that his tongue, as I told him, fell over itself." Soon they began to see each other away from the university, and as with so many of Mark's friends, the wives were included. After the General Honors class, on Wednesday evenings as I remember, I would meet the two men at the Adler apartment and Helen Adler would make muffins for us. I particularly remember the four flights of stairs I had to climb, as our son Charles was born that winter. My husband has always said that he learned everything he knew about philosophy from Adler and Buchanan, and a great deal from Adler about poetry, which Adler denies. At any rate, the friendship flourished for more than forty years.

Although there was a warm feeling between Mark and Robert Frost, not many letters were exchanged and they did not meet often. We did visit Frost at his farm in Vermont, and we saw him at several celebrations, but I remember one evening particularly. Frost had read his poems at the New School in New York. He never ate dinner before a reading but afterwards he usually went to the apartment of his friend, Joseph Blumenthal, accompanied by people who had heard the reading. That evening, Mark was sitting next to Frost, who suddenly put a hand on his knee. "Why don't we see more of each other?" Frost asked. Mark smiled. "I don't know, Robert," he answered. "Maybe it's better as it is." Mark was perhaps thinking of the many friends, particularly other poets, with whom Frost had quarreled. He never quarreled with Mark, and I am told he had never been heard to speak disparagingly of him. Frost nodded. "Maybe you are right," he said.

There were times when I felt my husband's voluminous correspondence, which kept him up so late, was wearing him out. But reading these letters I realize what a valuable part of his life that correspondence was.

Introduction

Mark Van Doren was born in 1894 in Hope, Illinois, son of a country doctor. In 1900 Dr. Van Doren moved his family to Urbana, where the state university was located, in order to give his children better educational opportunities. Dr. Van Doren reestablished his medical practice, continued his interest in farming, and over the years became involved in various speculative ventures. The five Van Doren boys attended Urbana public schools and then Carl, soon followed by Mark, entered the University of Illinios. Both were influenced by Stuart Pratt Sherman, one of the most distinguished members of the English department. Many years after he had studied with Sherman, Mark wrote that Sherman "thought while he talked. And since his mind was rich, he was always discovering new depths in his own understanding. . . . But the main thing was Sherman's mind, at once a critical and creative instrument; he gave it all to Shakespeare, and Shakespeare responded as he ever will to those who bring him their whole selves."[1] Shakespeare, Matthew Arnold, Carlyle, Emerson, whichever writer Sherman taught interested him personally. The young Mark had seen a master teacher at work, and he was to apply much of Sherman's method in his own distinguished teaching.

After writing a master's thesis on Thoreau, Mark Van Doren followed Carl to Columbia University for additional graduate work, which was interrupted by World War I and a period of service in the army. After his discharge, he received a fellowship for research in England to complete his doctoral dissertation on Dryden. He wrote almost weekly to Carl during his army service and during the year he was in England and France on a fellowship; space limitations have necessitated the omission of these early letters, but Van Doren himself has covered these early years of his life in his evocative autobiography.

Upon completion of his doctoral work, Van Doren received an appointment to the English department at Columbia, and he settled into an active intellectual and professional life: teaching, editorial work for the *Nation*, panelist on "Invitation to Learning," and his own critical and creative writing. He married Dorothy Graffe, a *Nation* staff member, and they had two sons, Charles and John. The marriage was a long and happy one; Dorothy, also a writer, was a shrewd critic of her husband's work. The Van Dorens bought a farm in Connecticut where they lived during the summers away from the city. During those summer months, Mark Van Doren spent his mornings writing, his afternoons and evenings working on the farm and with his family and with friends who came to visit. He largely escaped writing blocks, and over the years he published a large body of poetry, criticism, fiction, and plays.

In New York he began to make literary friends and to gather around him talented students. He was comfortable with his literary colleagues, both in and out of the academy. He did not feel threatened by them. Instead, he encouraged and supported the work of his fellow professors and a large number of students, young poets, and critics.

Mark Van Doren was known to generations of students as a kind and generous man and an intellectually stimulating teacher. Thomas Merton once wrote to him, "With you it was never a matter of trying to use poetry and all that is called English literature as a means to make people admire your gifts; on the contrary you always used your gifts to make people admire and understand poetry and good writing and truth." In *The Seven Storey Mountain* Merton pointed out a quality other students were to see and feel: "his mind looked directly for the quiddities of things, and sought being and substance under the cover of accident and appearances." Eileen Simpson in *Poets in Their Youth* has described Mark's influence on her husband John Berryman. "It was as Mark's student that John had developed his lifelong passion for Shakespeare. It was Mark who introduced him to Stephen Crane, Mark who encouraged him to become a poet, Mark who tried to keep him in line during his unruly undergraduate days. . . . And it was Mark, when John settled down to become a serious student, who recommended him for the Kellett Fellowship to Clare College, Cambridge."[2] Mark Van Doren was one of the most respected and popular teachers at Columbia, for he had a well-stocked mind, a poet's imagination, and a desire to know and understand and to teach what he knew.

As an editor, reviewer, and critic, he was also much admired, for his mature critical readings are characterized by an unusual breadth of vision. As his philosopher friend Mortimer Adler has noted, Van Doren had the ability to submit himself "without reservation to the poet's fancy." He "surrendered himself completely" to the vision offered by the work he was studying. His readings of Dryden, Cervantes, Hawthorne,

Shakespeare, and many other writers consistently expand the perceptions of the reader.[3]

It was his poetry, however, that most engaged him, and he published over a thousand poems. He was influenced by Dryden, Yeats, Hardy, Emily Dickinson, Edwin Arlington Robinson, Frost, and undoubtedly other poets, but as Allen Tate remarked, they added up to "Mark Van Doren who is not like anybody else." William Claire in the volume *Poets* in the Great Writers of the English Language series perceptively noted about Van Doren: "He treated his principal subjects, the cosmos, love, finality, family matters, and particularly children, animals, paradox, and knowledge in a lucid manner that transcends simplistic notions of modernity and personal sensibilities. There is a passionate intelligence lurking behind many of the poems that somehow never intrudes." In spite of the Pulitzer Prize, which he received in 1940, he was never accorded the same kind of critical attention given to his contemporary, Robert Frost, or to his students John Berryman and Thomas Merton. The reader who submits himself "without reservations to the poet's fancy" will discover that Mark Van Doren had a unique voice.[4] He also brought his poetical insights to bear in his critical studies, and his Shakespeare and Hawthorne books (to name just two) are rare achievements.

He was a man with many friends. He remained on cordial terms with his parents, his brothers, his children, and with his childhood friends; with several reviewers and contributors from his *Nation* days; with contemporaries such as Joseph Wood Krutch, John Gould Fletcher, Lionel Trilling, Allen Tate, Robert Frost, Archibald MacLeish, and Carl Sandburg; and with former students John Berryman, Thomas Merton, Robert Lax, and many others. In his letters he emerges as a dedicated writer, as a devoted family man (no less so during his son Charles's difficulties), as a teacher able to bring out the best abilities of his students, as a critic able to bring readers to a fuller understanding of a work of art, and as a friend to his many correspondents.

These letters give us an insight into the literary and cultural world in which he lived and provide new information about Allen Tate, John Berryman, Thomas Merton, John Gould Fletcher, and others. They also allow us to know a gentle man of letters, a dedicated poet, and a distinguished critic.

1. Mark Van Doren, *Autobiography* (New York, 1958), 66.

2. MVD, *Autobiography*, 276; Thomas Merton, *The Seven Storey Mountain* (New York, 1948), 140; Eileen Simpson, *Poets in Their Youth* (New York, 1982), 23.

3. Mortimer Adler, "Mortimer Adler on Mark Van Doren," *Voyages*, V (1973), 45.

4. Adler, "Mortimer Adler on Mark Van Doren," 24, 45; James Vinson (ed.), *Poets*, Great Writers of the English Language Ser. (New York, 1979), 1026; Tate, "Very Much at Ease in Formal Attire," *Voyages* (1973), 24.

Hope
1894–1900

No letters of Mark Van Doren's exist for the period of his early childhood. For accounts of the Van Dorens in Hope, Illinois, where Van Doren's father was a country physician, one should look to two sources: Mark Van Doren's *Autobiography* (New York, 1958) and Carl Van Doren's *Three Worlds* (New York, 1936). From quite different perspectives, the brothers recalled life in an Illinois village. Their mother, the former Dora Butz, was the daughter of Hope pioneers. Dr. Van Doren was a man who loved to tell stories; he was interested in language, and he obviously was a major influence on the later literary careers of his sons Carl and Mark. Dr. Van Doren owned a large farm (he was to acquire others), and Mark Van Doren early on developed a passion for country living, a passion often reflected in his poetry.

Urbana
1900–1915

Dr. Van Doren moved his family to Urbana in 1900. Hope had only a one-room school; Urbana had a fully developed public school system and was the seat of the state university. The Van Dorens built a large house on Oregon Street in Urbana, and the Van Doren boys were caught up in school affairs. Again, both Mark and Carl have written of these years in their memoirs. Mark Van Doren often spent his summers at the family farm at Hope or at another farm near Villa Grove. He entered the University of Illinois in 1910 and received a bachelor of arts in English in 1914 and a master of arts in 1915.

To Carl Van Doren
ALS/NjP

May 30, 1910   *Urbana, Illinois*

In late May, 1910, Carl Van Doren and Stuart Pratt Sherman sailed to Europe, where Van Doren was to remain for six months, traveling and revising his manuscript on Thomas Love Peacock. Carl Van Doren gives an extended account of the trip in Three Worlds *(New York, 1936).*

Well, Carl, you will of course be churning the high seas when this bulky envelope is brought to you. At least I feel now, at the beginning, that our letter will be a corpulent scamp—probably too much so for you. If it tires you very much, don't hesitate to heave it out into "vasto gurgite" along with the rest of your contributions to the vigilant denizens of the deep. Now I suppose all your letters have had some mention of such philanthropic situations, but I *must* make you miserable by leading you to reflect on that inevitable visitation as well as the rest.

A little blank space is herewith provided for reflection. (This with apologies to Mark Twain.)

I suppose your plans all worked smoothly for your voyage. It must have been quite an exciting time. Mr. Sherman told me Saturday that he supposed two people never contemplated traveling together with as little fore-planning and mutual knowledge of each other's wishes as you two. He had thot [*sic*] but very little about the trip, he said, and I assured him, tho I doubted myself, that you were all in readiness. Here's to your trip, at any rate, and may you reap both weighty and intellectual benefits from it! . . .

I See the World
1915–1920

Mark Van Doren left Urbana to enroll in the doctoral program in English at Columbia University in 1915, and his first book, on Thoreau, was published while he was still a graduate student. Letters concerning his early years in New York are generally not available, for his correspondence with his parents was destroyed after the death of his mother. For this period, his *Autobiography* (New York, 1958), is indispensable. His most important friend was a fellow student, Joseph Wood Krutch. After the United States entered the European conflict in 1917, Van Doren was drafted; he was not sent to France but saw stateside service in Iowa and Arkansas.

He wrote regularly to his brother Carl, describing his new life. The integrity and character of a regular-army man greatly impressed Mark Van Doren, who wrote Carl on August 18, 1918: "People do not begin to prize any man's words until they have been impressed by some sort of character behind them—some pointedness about the writer's personality, some determination about his attitude, some extremity either of weight or lightness about him." Carl wrote asking about religion among soldiers, and Mark responded on October 3, 1918: "I have observed none at all. Of course I am far from the seat of the war, and have seen none of the stress which is supposed to bring religion to the surface. I don't believe all I read about its operation in the field, however. In civil life it was always the poorest souls which became the most Xian. Why should this not hold true under fire—the weakest search most desperately for consolation?" He made extended comments about his reading, but most of his letters from the army camps are shrewd observations about life as he was observing it.

After the armistice, Mark Van Doren returned to Columbia, and for the year 1919–1920 received a traveling fellowship which allowed him to complete his doctoral dissertation on Dryden in London. His thesis was almost completed before he left New York, and he was unable to find anything significantly new about the poet in England. He did read widely during the year and prepared the final copy of his thesis. Joseph Wood Krutch also received a fellowship that year. The adventures of the two young men in England and on the continent are recounted in Van Doren's *Autobiography*. During this year abroad, he was in doubt about his future; he thought he would soon be choosing between life in the city and life in the country, between teaching at Columbia and at the University of Illinois. He wrote Carl Van Doren on December 19, 1919, "With that damned coolness which you used to observe, and which I am aware is the opposite of virtue, I am letting the dilemma slide over me without actually worrying very much."

His thesis completed, he went to Paris in 1920 and began to write poetry; his "Simple Cymon" (never published) was based in part on Dryden's story of Cymon and Iphigenia in the *Fables*. His dilemma about his immediate future was solved: Illinois did not call and Columbia offered him an instructorship in the English department. He had written Carl on January 20, 1920, that "Grub Street sounds better," but he decided to accept the offer from Columbia.

To Stuart P. Sherman
ALS/IU-Ar

November 11, 1915   *New York*

Mark Van Doren had some doubts about publishing his revised master's thesis on Thoreau. Stuart Pratt Sherman, however, advised him to accept the favorable verdict of the Houghton Mifflin readers, though Sherman did suggest some additional revisions.

I come to you again for advice. I heard from Houghton Mifflin's yesterday that they will publish the essay on Thoreau on more or less satisfactory terms, and I was glad to hear it—they having been silent three months.

But I cannot decide whether it will do to publish the essay at all now. In the first place, Mr. Sanborn of Concord, who wrote the *Life* for the American Men of Letters series forty years ago, is now engaged (at 84) in writing what he calls a "final" *Life*. Carl thinks it might not be wise to bring my essay out before Mr. Sanborn says his last word.

I am not so much concerned over that (for the two books would scarcely rub each other) as I am over the downright worth of my essay. I am wondering whether I said anything in it, and whether a few years from now I should not be ashamed to have it behind me.

Carl, fearing that (though he has not seen the essay), suggests that I might get the manuscript back and develop it into a dissertation for my Ph.D., and then bring it out after Sanborn.[1] But I am not sure that I care to stay two years longer in Thoreau's company. As it is, I can amend the manuscript in a few weeks right now and have it off my hands forever. I have made a few interesting discoveries in an important collection here in New York.[2]

If you can recall the essay, and can write me a few words expressing your present opinion of it and your opinion of the whole situation, I shall be more grateful to you than I can say. I am perfectly willing to throw the whole thing over if that is wise. I hope you will not bother yourself too much about it, in any event. . . .

1. This plan was abandoned, and MVD's doctoral thesis was on Dryden.

2. MVD had access to George S. Hellman's Thoreau collection.

To Carl Van Doren
ALS/NjP

May 8, 1918   *Camp Dodge, Iowa*

After spending the summer of 1917 on the family farms in Villa Grove and Hope, Van Doren was drafted on September 6. He was sent first to Camp Dodge, Iowa. During his army service and during his fellowship year in Europe immediately after the war, he wrote frequently to Carl Van Doren. This period of Mark Van Doren's life is thoroughly described in his autobiography, and only one of his letters is included here.

I am ashamed to consider how much I have on hand to tell you. The accumulation convicts me of neglect, ingratitude, etc. The truth is, that the disruption of my flawless T. S. regimen involved in going home, returning, and taking up new duties at these Headquarters has destroyed the spiritual equilibrium which I have always found necessary for correspondence.[1] Now that a new routine is beginning I can with a new conscience interpose a little ease, and dally once again with false surmise. Which brings me to say that I have enjoyed nothing so much in these whole 8 months as I have your letters and cards, and the patient ear into which you have let me pour the rubbish of my thoughts. A good many of my letters must have seemed foolish, ill considered, and long. That has been because I have had no other forbearing (I can't assume it has been forgiving) ear to dump my eloquence in. Sherman asked me when I went to see him in Urbana if I were writing anything—meaning, if I were keeping a journal. I told him I disapproved of journals, and preferred letters. . . . I suppose I have not written enough these 8 months. But I hardly know where I could have got the time to write. And I have a notion that these fellows who send copy back from the front (with the exception of Norman Hall and one or two others) are not the most useful soldiers.[2] If I have written anything which I really and carefully meant this winter, it has been in an occasional letter to you. Too bad I sent so much trash with it.

No one was commissioned from the T. S., as I warned you. But about ⅔ of the students were recommended for commissions as 2nd Lts "as soon as suitable vacancies should occur." I came 17th on this list of 350, so if there is any commissioning to be done, I suppose I shall not have to wait until the last.

My 10 days in Urbana were some of the happiest I have ever seen. The family, and my friends in town, were so good to me that I was almost spoiled for military purposes. I received there for the first time any notion of how the war is going on among the civilians. I had been told, but had not understood before, that it was being waged no less thoroughly there than here, or at the front. . . .

1. MVD had entered Officer's Training School in January of 1918, had graduated in April, and had been given a ten-day leave, which was spent in Urbana.

2. He is probably referring to accounts of James Norman Hall included in *Kitch-*ener's Mob: The Adventures of an American in the British Army* (Boston and New York, 1916) and *High Adventure: A Narrative of Air Fighting in France* (Boston and New York, 1918).

I Start to Work
1920–1928

Mark Van Doren accepted an instructorship in the English department at Columbia in the spring of 1920 while he was still in Paris. He returned to New York to take his final doctoral examination, and that summer, before beginning to teach, he filled in for Carl Van Doren as literary editor of the *Nation*. During the early years of the 1920s, Mark Van Doren worked hard at his teaching, married Dorothy Graffe, bought a farm in Falls Village, Connecticut, where they spent their summers, and became literary editor of the *Nation*. His work on Grub Street was not entirely congenial; one of his frustrations was that Oswald Garrison Villard, owner of the *Nation*, often objected to the poetry that Van Doren selected for publication. While he was at the *Nation*, he did meet and correspond with many writers. He reviewed modern poetry extensively and worked at his own poetry, which began to be published. During the later years of this period, he met Allen Tate, who was to become a close literary friend.

To Dorothy Graffe
ALS/P

July 4, 1921   *Urbana, Illinois*

Van Doren was writing a poem, in heroic couplets, about his Butz grandparents. The long poem was to be called "Agatha."

Here it is. Your plaintive little sentence, "This week will end it, won't it?" has come true, and you have another job on your hands. Take your time, and when you are done ship the sheets to me in the enclosed strong envelope. After all, I *will* revise at Oxley. We leave Wednesday morning[1]. . . .

My grandparents will not recognize themselves for two reasons:
(1) They will never read the piece, published or unpublished.
(2) They are not recognizable in it. They changed into entirely different creatures from about the fifteenth line on—why, I can't say. . . .

1. The Van Dorens were going to Canada for a vacation.

To Dorothy Graffe
ALS/P
July 21, 1921   *Urbana, Illinois*

Van Doren was in Urbana with his parents and was preparing to visit his brother in Detroit and then vacation in Canada. The long poem "Agatha," which he was then writing, was never published.

Your nice letter this morning makes me eager for your marginal mastications on the fourth instalment. I'm sure they will be drastic—I hope cutting. When I am all through there will be about 200 lines to cut, I think. If you still are willing to undertake the manuscript as a whole then, I shall expect you to designate those 200 lines—or more—or fewer.[1]

1. MVD wrote in his *Autobiography* (New York, 1958), 134: "I sent it to Dorothy, who wrote me that she thought it good, though there were 'a few little things'—the phrase has since become familiar between us—she supposed might be changed or made clearer. She was the only reader the poem ever had; I wanted her opinion, for I had become dependent upon her opinion by and large; but in the end I gathered from her as well as from myself that it was not good enough."

To Dorothy Graffe
ALS/P
August 3, 1921   *Harrow, Ontario, Canada*

*   *   *

Your strictures on this part of the poem are as necessary and good as ever, but I am going to make one large, general objection to your remarks about Agatha. The objection doubtless is grounded in indolence. I should like to think it was the work of my judgment. You say Agatha isn't clear. I say the kind of clarity you insist on for her is an inferior kind. . . .

Joe [Krutch] writes from Silver Mine, Connecticut . . . where he is spending a couple of weeks with Raymond Weaver. Weaver is finishing his book . . . on Herman Melville, and as might have been expected is using a very precious, labored style. Joe's advice to him after he had heard a chapter should become classic, and will almost certainly be used in any review that he writes: "Absent thee from felicity awhile." . . .

To Dorothy Graffe
ALS/P

August 20, 1921   *Urbana, Illinois*

During the summer of 1921, Van Doren also worked on another long poem. As he wrote in his Autobiography: *"One was about Hephaestus, the Greek god in whom both Homer and Milton had got me deeply interested long ago—I liked him because he worked and limped, and I took his side because the other Olympians condescended to him and made him the butt of jokes."* [1]

*   *   *

I never read so fast before as I now am reading on Hephaestus. He seems to fall very naturally into place, and I feel myself growing really pretty full. He is a subject I have been fond of for several months—since I taught Homer last winter, to be exact—but never thought of for a poem until now. I think him wonderful material—for someone who can handle him. I am almost afraid. I have been reading magnificent articles in German and French, and a few superficial ones in English, as well as going through Homer, Pindar, Hesiod, Pausanias, Herodotus, Plato, and Plutarch for references. I think I shall have the poem a blank verse monologue (a la Browning, I fear) spoken by a rather cracked old Athenian smith who, displeased with Athens and the perfunctory worship of the smith-god there, has gone over on Lemnos and set up his forge in a place where he fancies fire from Hephaestus thrusts through the ground. There he will celebrate the deity of his choice with as rich a string of legend and epithet as I can command. . . .

1. MVD, *Autobiography* (New York, 1958), 135.

To Dorothy Graffe
ALS/P

August 26, 1921   *Urbana, Illinois*

---

*   *   *

Hephaestus hasn't begun yet. I am sorting out the material I have on paper and in mind. I figured out several beginnings, and several settings, none of which has cleared itself up sufficiently yet. I should begin tomorrow or Monday, and then I'll tell you more about it. I know you are interested, Dot. . . .

To Dorothy Graffe
ALS/P

September 9, 1921   *Urbana, Illinois*

---

*   *   *

You were sweet, and completely convincing, by the way, about "Hephaestus." To tell the truth, I liked it too, bow-wow as it is, though I was perfectly aware that it was literary, derivative, youthful, and wholly unsuited to the present day.[1] I did it, you know, in reaction to the realism of "Agatha and Larry." It had been so much work in that to render life in terms of art that I wanted to play a while in a world that was purely art— made for me centuries ago. I read both pieces to Stuart Sherman last night, at his invitation, and "A. & L." was the only one he took seriously (he *said* he liked it). "Hephaestus" finished, he grimaced and said: "A very pretty piece of pagan mythology, Mr. Van Doren." Wordsworth, you probably don't remember, said that to Mr. Keats after he had been read the Ode to Pan. . . .

1. "Hephaestus" was never published.

To Carl Van Doren
ALS/NjP

September 4, 1922   *Towaco, New Jersey*

Mark Van Doren and Dorothy Graffe were married September 1, 1922.

If you did not decide on Friday that a man so recently married would be incapacitated for an article, let me still do Hudson.[1] I have read most of him, and when I am in town tomorrow can get up some biographical stuff. I want very much to write about him, and if I do not hear from you to the contrary within a week, I shall do it, and count no labor lost even if I do hear.

Dot and I drove over pretty nearly all the country between West Point and the Sound, but we can tell you whatever you care to know about that when we see you. Make no plans about seeing us until Dot talks to Irita at the office. She has some ideas, it seems, which she will communicate tomorrow. Thank you for asking us up. I don't think we can depend on Dad's coming. Better make no arrangements whatever, and when there is need see what occasion is left.

My telegram to the folks, which Mother has just returned, read "Worried today." Did yours lie so? We had a very happy wedding trip and expect to get on nicely at 43 Barrow Street if poor Joe can find another place for the winter. He is to marry Marcelle in April, if not before—and now it may be before. He says he is relieved that I did the thing first. . . .

1. W. H. Hudson's *Afoot in England* had just appeared in the United States. MVD does not seem to have written the article he was proposing.

To Sherwood Anderson
TLS/ICN

January 2, 1924   *New York City*

In addition to his English department duties at Columbia, Mark Van Doren replaced Carl as literary editor of the Nation, *a position with many frustrations since some of the writers he dealt with were difficult or not scrupulous about meeting deadlines.*

As the rest of *The Nation* staff are punching me up about the series for which you are writing us an article, I have promised them that it will begin in the next book number, for which copy must be on hand by January 21st. I don't like to bother you with too many letters about this, but this letter will at least suggest a date by which I should like to have the article. I hope three weeks time will not press you too hard. Good luck with it, and a Happy New Year!

To Charles Erskine Scott Wood
ALS/CSmH

November 2, 1925   *New York City*

Colonel Wood (1852–1944), Indian fighter, lawyer, and writer, is now best remembered for Heavenly Discourse *(1927). Van Doren met Colonel Wood at the* Nation *office.*

"1601" is here at last, and a great piece of work it is. . . .[1]

Your association with Mark Twain in the enterprise is most interesting, and you should be proud of it.[2] As I read your preface I was inclined to quarrel with you for refusing to praise "1601" without qualification. I thought your distinction between pure and forced obscurity rather finely drawn. But when I got over into the document itself I found you were right. It is first-rate, and several times I laughed aloud—but the impression is of a man, or boy, saying certain words for their own illicit sakes. If those words were not taboo, I imagine there would be very little left of "1601", and I am not sure that it would be funny. However, let us not pick on almost my favorite author. And by no means let it be suspected that I object to any English word at any time.

On looking over your card of ten days or so ago, I recall that you were to send me your own copy of "1601" and wait for another one from the Grabhorns. That was particularly generous. . . . I certainly should like to see those Heavenly Discourses[3]—yes, they antedate me. . . . Could Mencken stand them, I wonder?[4] I read your long poem before I mailed it to the *Mercury* and liked it for the way it knocked most of our props from under us—as well as for its running strength. . . .

1. Mark Twain's "1601" was long suppressed. MVD had received a 1925 private edition of "1601" with introduction by Colonel Wood.

2. Colonel Wood had originally had "1601" printed in book form for Mark Twain.

3. Parts of *Heavenly Discourse* had appeared earlier in the *Masses.*

4. Mencken was apparently not impressed; he did not publish sections of *Heavenly Discourse* or Colonel Wood's poetry in the *American Mercury.*

To Allen Tate
TLS/NjP

March 22, 1926   *New York City*

Allen Tate was to be an important literary friend. The two met at a time when Tate and his wife, Caroline Gordon, were sharing a house with Hart Crane near Patterson, New York. Tate's first letter to Van Doren is quoted in Van Doren's autobiography.

As you suggest I had better wait till I see you to talk over this whole matter in detail.

"Causerie" is of course interesting, but you don't know *The Nation* as well as I do if you think for a minute that anything of the sort would get by.[1] I'll explain that also when I see you.

[P.S.] I haven't touched T.S. [Eliot] yet.

1. The epigraph of the poem read ". . . party on the stage of the Earl Carroll Theatre on Feb. 23. At this party Joyce Hawley, a chorus-girl, bathed in the nude in a bathtub filled with alleged wine.—The New York Times." After the poem was rejected at the *Nation*, it appeared in *Calen-dar of Modern Letters*, III (October, 1926), 205–206. A different version of "Causerie" appeared in *Transition* (June, 1927), 139–42; the poem published in *Calendar of Modern Letters* now appears under the title "Retroduction to American History"; the epigraph is not used.

To Allen Tate
ALS/NjP

April 15, 1926   *New York City*

I am letting some examinations lie unread while I write to assure you that it will be a pleasure to lunch with you whenever the occasion offers. Please don't hesitate to call me the next time you are in, as I probably shall not be busy. As to the incompleteness of our conversation, I had thought all conversations, at least good ones, incomplete. I like them when, as in this case, they start many ideas. It doesn't matter so much perhaps if these never get finished. You started several dozen in an hour and a half, which surely is enough.

But you will finish something in the essay you spoke of, and I hope I have a chance to read that some time.[1] You certainly are right about these categories—will you not become the Einstein of modern criticism if you go on? I usually shy at abstract words applied to my favorite art, but I have always felt the need of a defender of poetry against dogmas as to what it must do and be. People forget that poetry *says*, not *sees*, that it *talks*, not *does*, that ultimately, even, it *is* not anything at all. Or is that dogmatic?

I was told by philosophers here today that your review of Santayana was awfully good—much better, they added, than the long and very ambitious one in the current issue of the *American Philosophical Review*.[2] That may give you fresh courage with Spengler. Query: Is Spengler really any more considerable than Keyserling?[3] But I mustn't keep slurring a book I haven't read. Somehow I have begun to doubt the man. And I can give no reasons, naturally. You will know what you think.

Twenty-five or any other age would be relatively immaterial. It happens I did think you about my age—31!—but why not be younger? I can't see what is signified.

1. Tate had been writing a long essay entitled "Poetry and the Absolute," which was to appear in *Sewanee Review*, XXXV (January, 1927), 41–52.

2. The review of George Santayana's *Dialogues in Limbo* appeared in the *Nation*, April 14, 1926, pp. 416, 418.

3. Oswald Spengler (1880–1936) was a German philosopher whose *The Decline of the West* had recently appeared. Hermann Keyserling (1880–1946) was also a German philosopher. His *The Travel Diary of a Philosopher* had appeared in 1925.

To Allen Tate
ALS/NjP

March 30, 1927   *[New York City]*

The Tates had left the farmhouse near Patterson, New York, and were living on Bank Street in New York City.

God bless your Southern soul for such a letter. In the first place I hadn't expected you to look at those poems for a month or so, and in the second place I wasn't prepared for criticism that should be at once so careful and so pleasing to my great vanity. I am so vain, indeed, about my poems that I have never been able to think about them, and so have believed what anybody said they were or were not. This is only true, of course, within limits—the remark does not apply to your remarks, which come from a critic who has made me do a good deal of thinking about poetry this last year. As a matter of fact it was thinking of you—and perhaps fearing you—that made me sit down two months ago and try to write poems that would have more in them than I had formerly put in. Hence in part my pleasure at hearing you say not only that "Above the Battle" and other pieces are complex but that they interest you. I had hoped quite definitely that they would. It was good, too, to hear that [John Gould] Fletcher liked "7 p.m."—Dorothy and I both thought him a charming man. It was a nice evening.

You are welcome, naturally, to as many pieces as will fit in—if any will—to the anthology. The copies you have there were specially made for the purpose, so you needn't handle them with undue care.

I wonder if you have changed your mind about a review for the *Nation* of "7 p.m." [1] I hesitate to bring the matter up again, but the other editors have, and I apparently don't need to worry now lest you find nothing to say. You could say simply, and briefly, that the book is not simple-minded; that would be much, and doubtless enough. No need to express an embarrassing judgment—one that would embarrass you either now or later. Please do as you like. If it would be quite easy to write such a column, go ahead; if not, ignore this with a good conscience.

Do you know that I have defended you often lately against the charge that you are serious? The nerve of anyone saying so!

1. Tate's review of *7 P.M. and Other Poems* appeared in the *Nation*, April 27, 1927, pp. 482–83. He praised MVD as "one of the most ambitious poets now writing," whose chief defect was "his technical virtuosity." He continued: "Mr. Van Doren's rhythmical skill occasionally blinds him to the internal direction of the poem itself; we get a poem perfectly rounded out on the surface, but somewhat obscured internally."

To Charles Erskine Scott Wood and Sara Field
ALS/CSmH

July 11, 1927   *Falls Village, Connecticut*

The Van Dorens bought a farm near Cornwall, Connecticut, in 1923. "To me it was an earthly paradise," Van Doren said of it, and it became their summer home and, finally, their permanent home. [1]

*   *   *

The way I live up here is this. I get up with Dorothy and Charlie fairly early in the morning, watch him eat breakfast in his bathrobe and red slippers, take him out to his pen or his sand pile to play while we eat breakfast, get wood for the fire if it is a cold morning or ice for the icebox if it is a hot one, walk around a while over my grass or along the borders of Dorothy's flower beds, go down and talk to Charlie, call Sandy the big Airedale that we are keeping this summer while Glen Mullin is in

Europe, and wade the wet grass to my study across the meadow.[2] This study is a long, low, grey-brown, sway-backed hay barn and saw mill shed, with a small room partitioned off at one end within hearing of the water that overflows our ice pond and spills into a little jungle of ferns, mint, moss, forget-me-not, willow shoots, and columbine. There, with the door open aback on the meadow, I write a poem—always write one, good or bad. Then back for Charlie's dinner and ours, and an afternoon devoted to very serious chores—mowing the lawn, scything the orchard, mending something, making something for Charlie, tending the garden, going to town, or anything whatever that is good and hot and hard. Then supper—crackers and milk and cheese—and a short evening of talk or sitting or reading. Almost no letters at all except to C.E.S.W. and S.B.F.[3] Indeed a life lived altogether for me and mine, and all saved up and centered on three things: Dorothy, Charlie, and the sawmill house. The *Nation*, of course, goes hang. So does Columbia. So does New York. . . .

And do you really want me to let the sonnets lie? I read them again just before I left on vacation, and they are certainly too beautiful to lie in a drawer. I was terribly moved and impressed. Maybe I'll disobey you and try once more anyway. It never has been any trouble to send them around—don't think so for a minute.

Have you read Jeffers's latest? I hope you see my review of it in the *Nation*, and tell me whether you agree. Powerful and beautiful, of course, but over the line I think. The question is, though, what is the line?[4]

Dot is tapping away daily on her third novel, which is at its hundredth page and going well. For the first time in any of the three she is concentrating on a man (he is only 18 so far), and she finds him difficult. But she isn't too much worried about the supposed differences between men and women, and goes right ahead—and goes beautifully. . . .

1. MVD, *Autobiography*, 142.

2. Glen Mullin was a friend of CVD's who had been a student at Columbia when MVD was working on his doctorate.

3. Sara Field was Colonel Wood's second wife.

4. MVD wrote of Robinson Jeffers' *Women at Point Sur* in the *Nation*, July 27, 1927, p. 88: "I have read it with thrills of pleasure at its power and beauty, and I shall read everything else Mr. Jeffers writes. But I may be brought to wonder whether there is need of his trying further in this direction. He seems to be knocking his head to pieces against the night."

To John Gould Fletcher
ALS/ArU

August 7, 1927   *Falls Village, Connecticut*

John Gould Fletcher (1886–1950), was the imagist poet from Arkansas then living in England. Fletcher was a friend of Allen Tate's.

I have had your letters in my pocket for a month. I have read Salt's "Thomson," and more recently I have read "Branches of Adam."[1] So there has been much to write about, but I have rather deliberately not written until July, my vacation, was up. The month I have free up here each summer I devote purely to poetry and idleness—my own poetry, that is to say, and idleness is always one's own. I have found I work best in verse when I have nothing else to do or think about.

I had sworn to start a long poem this summer. Our conversation at André's had stirred an old impulse.[2] But I found myself still unready, and had to be content with doing a number of shorter pieces which will round out the third volume I expect to publish in about a year.

This is one of the reasons for the pleasure I have taken in "Branches of Adam," which is a noble work truly. It was good to see vast purposes outlined in the preface of a contemporary poem, and even better of course to see a style taking form which admitted of all manner of flexibility and freedom yet which could give the impression, when the poet chose, that he remembered the essential gravity of his greatest predecessors. It is both contemporary and classical—"Branches of Adam"—and I am sure we shall hear of it a long time from now. I read it first on the train coming up here from New York, and I remember very distinctly the shock of pleasure I got from the last page of Book III—particularly, I suppose, the last line. Noah is my man, as I take it he is yours. Those who still call you "imagist" should make the acquaintance of Noah!

I am not sure that your thesis is convincing—or even that it would be clear without the preface. As a matter of fact, I seem not to have reached the age when the metaphysical terms you use would mean the most to me. They would have meant much when I was younger, and they will undoubtedly mean more when I am older. I still am in that stage, doubtless, where concreteness is all—images if you like, or at any rate bits of "reality," being all I can take stock in with any satisfaction. The time of gathering up is still to come, I hope. But even then I am struck with the notion that "Branches of Adam" should have been longer. The theme of good and evil, if it is important at all, is *very* important, and deserves perhaps more argument, more filling in, than you have given it. But perhaps we have here only the groundwork for a poem which will eventually be as long as "Paradise Lost."

I was of course greatly interested in your mention of another long poem waiting to be written. Can you say yet what it will be like, or about? How I envy you these visitations!

Best luck to the American book and to the critical work, if you ever write it, on poetry since 1900. We need a good one. . . .

I am glad to hear that you don't care for Humbert Wolfe.[3] He seems to have little or nothing in him, and it is serious indeed if he is all there is for the critics to get excited about.

Tate writes me that he has been touring the land of his ancestors (Tennessee and Virginia) in an old Ford. You know, do you, that he has started work on the Stonewall Jackson? And by the way, one of the poems I wrote last month had something to do with the Civil War, and would not have been written without our conversation at André's. . . .

1. James Thomson (1834–82), was author of "The City of Dreadful Night." Thomson's pessimism appealed to Fletcher, who had sent a copy of H. S. Salt's critical study of Thomson to MVD. Fletcher's *Branches of Adam* had appeared in England in 1926.

2. André's was a restaurant near the *Nation* office.

3. Humbert Wolfe (1885–1940), was an English poet who served, at one time, as Deputy Secretary of the Ministry of Labour. He had just published *Requiem* in 1927.

City and Country
1928–1933

Dorothy and Mark Van Doren and their two young sons, Charles and John, established a pattern for their lives that was to endure for many years: winters lived at 393 Bleecker Street in New York and summers at their farm in Falls Village, Connecticut. Van Doren gave up his editorial work at the *Nation* and largely gave up reviewing. He devoted himself to his teaching, his poetry, his family, and his friends. The Van Dorens spent his first Columbia sabbatical (1932–1933) at the farm.

The letters of these years are largely concerned with poetry (*Jonathan Gentry* and *A Winter Diary* especially) and family and friends. Columbia University and the state of the country and the world hardly ever intrude. He had found his two worlds, and Hoover and Roosevelt and the worldwide depression and emerging fascism were pushed aside, at least in surviving letters. Letters to his parents, which have been destroyed, must have been concerned with the collapse of Dr. Van Doren's various speculative ventures.

To John Gould Fletcher
ALS/ArU

January 8, 1928   *New York City*

*   *   *

How are your poems going, and do you keep yourself engaged with a long one? I hope so. I have hopes of hitting upon a larger subject some day, but meanwhile am busy with a series of stories and accounts of character that I like to think will grow into a book. I realize well enough that the larger subject will not occur to me without effort, as the smaller ones do, but at the same time I know from two sad experiences that it will not do to force the major muse (is one allowed to speak thus unprofessionally?). It is a delicate dilemma. For a time I am quite willing, however, to wait.

Didn't Tate read some poems by Phelps Putnam to us here one afternoon?[1] They are out now in a small book, "Trinc," which contains little else worth mentioning. But I am convinced that they are good. Have you got the book? If you haven't I'll send you a copy.

Tate is finishing his life of Stonewall Jackson and becoming even more of a Southerner in the process. . . .

1. Phelps Putnam (1894–1948) published his first collection of poems under the title of *Trinc* in 1927.

To Robert Frost
TLS/NhD

May 23, 1928   *New York City*

Mark Van Doren had asked for permission to publish two Frost poems in Anthology of World Poetry. *Frost responded, "I confess a choice so perfunctory and slighting hurts my feelings."*[1]

I am very sorry that I did not explain the scale on which I was constructing my anthology.

It is to consist for the most part of translations from about fifteen languages from Chinese to Russian, and there was room for only a small and highly selective section of original poems in English. No one is represented there by more than a few pieces. My choice in this case was not perfunctory, since the "Runaway" is one of my favorite poems, and since I thought "Mending Wall" could not be left out. But I am most anxious to have you in, and I am really glad of this opportunity to ask for more poems.

Could you tell me, for instance, which two of the following you would most like to see in—or there might be three of these if I left out "Mending Wall"?—

The Oven Bird
Mowing
An Old Man's Winter Night

The Tuft of Flowers
The Pasture.

I think these come in the order of my preference, but I won't stick to that.

1. MVD, *Autobiography* (New York, 1958), 170.

To Robert Frost
TLS/NhD

May 29, 1928   *New York City*

To Van Doren's letter of May 23, Frost responded: "I'm too touchy—particularly with friends. Treat me well and you'll be expected to treat me better. That's all the pay you'll get for treating me well. Such I am, though I don't usually give myself away or get found out because I live too far off in the country to speak on impulse and I'm too lazy to write."[1]

Not at all. I should have explained. And anyway I got a very nice letter from you as a result.

Let's make it, then, the four you agree on—and I too shall be relieved to find you represented in an anthology by something besides Mending Wall. Still, it is a mighty good poem.[2]

1. MVD, *Autobiography*, 170–71.
2. The following Frost poems were included in the anthology: "The Runaway," "An Old Man's Winter Night," "The Oven Bird," and "The Tuft of Flowers."

To Allen Tate
ALS/NjP

November 21, 1928   *New York City*

Tate had received a Guggenheim Fellowship, and the Tates were in England.

I am sending this through the American Express Company instead of to Oxford on the theory that you might soon be moving from there, and I don't want to lose any time in telling you that the review, which came this morning, overwhelmed me.[1] Not merely, either, for what it said, but for the evidence it gave that you had read the book with generous—no, lavish—care. Both of us are used to having our poems read carelessly if at all, and of course you know how grateful I am—not merely for the praise, which in itself excites me because it comes from you, but even more for the work of attention and analysis.

As to the things you say I have been thinking, I believe you. To admit that they were not clear to me before is only to say that you are an excellent critic, which you are anyway. The only time you go wrong is when you call me "conscious" and "intelligent." If that is your impression, so much the better, but God's truth is that I have never been conscious of being intelligent while I wrote a poem. Not that I wish to suggest the ineffable—only that I went rather casually along, trying many things that did not succeed and (to be sure) refusing to try them again. There may be an item of intelligence in the recognition that one is through with an idea or a form forever. But beyond that I cannot take the credit you give me. As to the processes themselves, I am convinced you are right. And nothing has ever given me so much pleasure as your pointing them out.

Meanwhile I wonder when Freda Kirchwey is going to use Fletcher's review of your book.[2] It came after I left the *Nation* and I have not seen it, but Dorothy tells me you will like it. And what about Fletcher? Was he still in London when you got there? If he is here I haven't heard of it. Eliot I do want to hear all about. As I think I told you this summer, he is the one man in England I would want to see. Joe Krutch's account of his self-burial in the Greek and Latin Fathers—I wonder how much of a legend that is?

I hadn't known how seriously to take your postal card from the ship, but your letter yesterday made it clear that the trip was devilish. What a pity—and more so that you have been sick on land. Do get well and see some of the country. I give you my word it is worth seeing, though I never saw it in a better capacity than that of a tourist. I liked Cambridge more than Oxford, and liked Ely more than anything for some reason. To walk westward into Ely and see that bull of a church rising out of what was once a marsh is to know something about religion—or at any rate about bishops. I really suspect that the best people in the Middle Ages took their cathedral-building bishops about as we take Manning.[3]

I was reading Villard's "John Brown" for a purpose the other day and found, I must say, more disapproval of Pottowatomie than you had led me to expect.[4] Or is it merely that you were offended by his being able to distinguish between the politics and the ethics of the massacre? He seems to think he can do that, and to think so is to be absurd. But I had got the notion that he whitewashed the whole affair, which in his way he doesn't. Not that I am for defending him. I am heartily glad to have him at his distance. You will be amused, by the way, to know that for several weeks after I quit down there I didn't know how to spend my time up here. The retired executive, you know.

Doubtless there is no hurry about beginning the Poem, but I am telling you there is a necessity for finishing it. Will you do that edition of Skelton, or was the project chiefly for Guggenheim eyes? Which would have been proper.

My anthology is out, and you are put down for a copy, but you may not get it until you are home again, and that is doubtless well since it is long and heavy—but a pretty good-looking book at that.[5] It is a great relief to see it done at last, and beyond change or improvement. . . .

Charlie rhythms right along at 165 West 12.[6] I can't see any difference between this year's curriculum and last except that they are learning this month to "sleep like bears"—curl up on the floor and become semicircles. The chief thing about it that interests Charlie is that "the two ladies" (teachers) do it too. John, the baby, flourishes and is said to look like me. . . .

1. Tate reviewed MVD's *Now the Sky* in the *Nation,* December 19, 1928, pp. 691–92. Tate praised the poetry, though he did find some obscurities. In the use of imagery, Tate wrote that MVD should be spoken of with Wallace Stevens and Hart Crane. He saw a symbolist influence in the poems, as well as a "macabre ferocity in some of his images."

2. Freda Kirchwey had become literary editor of the *Nation.* Fletcher's highly favorable review of *Mr. Pope and Other*

Poems appeared in the *Nation,* April 3, 1929, pp. 404–405.

3. Henry Edward Manning (1808–1892) followed John Henry Newman into the Roman Catholic Church, and was created a cardinal in 1875.

4. Oswald Garrison Villard, *John Brown, 1800–1859: A Biography Fifty Years After* (Boston, 1910).

5. *An Anthology of World Poetry* (New York, 1928).

6. Charles Van Doren was attending the City and Country School.

To Allen Tate
ALS/NjP

March 12, 1929   *New York City*

*   *   *

[Ford Madox] Ford did give Dorothy and me your message. It was at a party given by Hal Smith and Jonathan Cape at their new publishing house, and Ford was more than friendly, he was affectionate. Being a little drunk, he pressed my arm at least fifteen times as he was leaving and begged that we manage to see a great deal of each other this winter—he is at 30 West 9th, as you must know. Well, his kindness to you is a big point in his favor, but don't you think I should set that down in the book and volume of my brain and be done?[1] Nice as he is, I seem to get along beautifully without him. I fidget in his presence. Don't let Carolyn [*sic*] see this if you think she shouldn't.

Malcolm Cowley was at the same party, and his wife got about as drunk as they make 'em this side of Walpurgis.[2] She staggered from one wall to another, clawed her hair down around her face, got sick, and in general served as symbol for a regular American literary party. Cowley talked to me about your *Bookman* article.[3] He liked it, but said it had too many superlatives in it—called too many guys the best in their respective lines. Under eternity this is probably true, though you did make it clear that you were discussing a period of 9 years. It was a bold attempt, really, and if it erred it did so on the side of generosity. Have you ever been told your critical weakness—if any—was generosity?

Cowley is publishing a volume with Smith and Cape in June, and Smith seems to be doing all he can to let the world know about it.[4]

The 24 poems I wrote are not 24 poems I shall publish. I see that now after a cold reading—but such is always the case, and it is strange that I can never foresee it. My motto anyway now is: No more short ones till the long one is begun. The long one is about the Ohio River. Does that mean anything to you? I take the O.R. simply as something around which—or along which—to tell how once on this continent our fathers streamed into Canaan, talking of the Golden Age and remembering Rousseau. I have been working this winter at a compilation for Boni of American autobiographical documents telling our history in the first person so to speak,[5] and I have been moved by nothing so much as the spectacle of those birds flying West a hundred years ago. I may or may not moralize my song—probably not—but I shall tell some kind of story or lose a lung.

I don't expect you to talk at length about yours. You gave me the idea of it last summer, and doubtless you have enough to do now writing it. Therefore I do not probe you; but I do give it my most sanctified good wishes, and beg you not to let it lapse. If you have a number of new short poems now, and would like to send them to certain editors over here, let me have them, with directions, and I'll try to be a good agent. It might save time and bother, and I promise not to sell any to Cowley or the *Cosmopolitan.*

Thanks for suggestions as to how I can improve the Anthology, and thanks for liking it. You know better than most how imperfect it is of course. There will be a new edition some day, and when that time comes I'll go after these things by Winters and Crane.[6] The misprint in Beardsley will be corrected still sooner I hope.[7] . . .

1. At the end of January, 1929, Ford lent his Paris apartment to the Tates for six months, rent free.

2. MVD is speaking of Peggy Cowley.

3. "American Poetry Since 1920," *Bookman*, LXVIII (January, 1929), 503–508.

4. *Blue Juniata* (Norwood, Massachusetts, 1929).

5. Albert Boni was a New York publisher.

6. Yvor Winters (1900–1968) was an American poet and critic. Poems by Hart Crane were added to later editions.

7. Aubrey Beardsley (1872–98) was an English writer and illustrator. The misprint in his translation "On the Burial of His Brother" was corrected in later editions: "hopeless brother" should read "hapless brother."

To Allen Tate
ALS/NjP

May 5, 1929   *New York City*

Tate, living in Paris, had received many kindnesses from Ford Madox Ford. Tate also thought well of Peggy Cowley.

* * *

That was a noble letter of yours, if only for the sketches it contained of Ford and Mrs. Cowley. I read them both more or less as rebukes—but believe me, I was prepared to hear something of the sort about Mrs. Cowley, and was quite without prejudice. Didn't I confine myself to a description of her exterior, and could I have been wrong there? You make her tremendously interesting—and Ford too, though what I *see* of him still puzzles me. Yet I must believe anyone who writes so well about him. . . .

I think I told you about the compilation of personal narratives called "The Autobiography of America" which I am doing for the Boni's.[1] That has kept me very busy and interested. But it will be done I hope next week, and then I shall do practically nothing for a month except get ready to start the poem—which really means that I shall do nothing for a month. Idleness is all I need for the business. I used to try to think poems out—would sit down or walk around and say "Now I will arrange my ideas"—but I long ago discovered that such virtue is worse than useless. The only necessity is that there be nothing *else* to think about.

Or else I get my friends to think for me. I simply wait until they are in foreign lands and send them an announcement of my theme. When lo! I get from them magnificent perspectives on the work I am about to do. Which is really a serious way of saying that your remarks on the Mississippi Valley, and on East and West have given me the start I wanted. Not that you will ever recognize your thoughts in my poem, but I assure you that without them I might never have had knowledge of where to begin. My original feeling was strong but vague—a feeling that all those people who poured along the Ohio were doing both more (which was comic) and less (which was tragic) than they realized. Your analysis seems to me awfully good. You may be sure I am grateful for it.

So far as I know I haven't offended Fletcher yet—by the way, another brilliant sketch of yours. He has been here for a long and very good evening, and I spent several hours with him in the reception room of his hotel on 28th street, sitting on a gilded sofa under bright lights and talking of such different things as Eliot and religion (I defended Eliot), Aiken and Fletcher, oysters and gin (the sole diet of Aiken, he insists), Irving Babbitt, Hoover, Prime Minister Baldwin, Herbert Read, and Allen Tate.[2] He is extremely fond of you, let me say, though he is puzzled by some of your poetry (he admires the rest), and he didn't so much as mention Descartes and Spinoza. He is a good old boy.

Eliot's "For Launcelot Andrewes" was about 1000 times better than I expected it would be. In fact it almost converted me to the belief, not necessarily that the Church is useful or even interesting, but certainly that all of our intellectual troubles in the past five centuries have followed upon our loss of God—and our supposed necessity then of proving Man to be something other than the blind, permanently imperfect creature that he is. This disposes of democracy, sociology, psychology, and such questions as "Whither Mankind" and "Whither Marriage," doesn't it. And *much* poetry. It is in fact the only kind of dualism that interests me. Not Babbitt's certainly—which Eliot sufficiently damns. So you see you were right about Descartes.

Oh yes, Fletcher took me to his room to see the pictures of the house in Little Rock, his father, his mother, and Uncle Tom. . . .

1. Published in 1929.
2. MVD is referring to Conrad Aiken (1889–1973), who received the Pulitzer Prize for his *Selected Poems* (1929); Irving Babbitt (1865–1933), the American critic; Herbert Hoover (1874–1964), thirty-first president of the United States; Stanley Baldwin (1867–1947), British prime minister, 1923–24 and 1924–29; and Sir Herbert Read (1893–1968), English poet and critic.

To Allen Tate
TLS/NjP

November 8, 1929   *New York City*

***

I haven't read your *Davis* yet.[1] I have been wanting to, not merely because it is yours but because I have heard it highly praised; I even note that it has gone into a second printing. But your letter confronted me this evening; I seemed at last to be free to write you; and so herewith.

Speaking of poetry and compilations, I have this afternoon given my final word—No—to Albert Boni, who has been after me for months to edit a big American anthology, a Stedman up to date.[2] I never wanted to do it, but Boni seemed not to believe that until today—it would have been profitable to him and me. Don't you think I am right? I should really like to do a slender collection of American poems I care greatly for, from Poe and Emerson to Allen Tate, but this other thing would have been most noxious. There simply isn't enough stuff to bother about on that scale. Also, I am off poetry henceforth unless it is written by my friends or by myself. Life and art are both too short. Don't you think so? The business of being catholic and impartial and of "representing" nonentities—no!

How has the year started as to health? Tugwell of Columbia, who says he met you during the winter, gave me so dismal an account of the diseases you all suffered one after another that I am anxious about this coming winter.[3] Could you possibly, after waiting there long enough to get this letter, move into the country? It hardly seems worth while to spend so much time being sick. God knows you may have done all this long ago, and anyhow I am not lecturing you. The main thing is that I like to think you will all be well, for many reasons, poetry being only one of them.

The long poem, how is it?[4] Mine was finished in September,[5] but I am still not satisfied with it, though I have been sending it to magazines—the Forum, the New Republic, Scribner's, and now the Bookman—so far without success. It tells its story well enough, perhaps, to make a magazine piece, but when I think of what you probably expect from it I am ashamed. It has so few of the ideas you immediately, and so generously, attributed to me and supposed me capable of handling. It turned out to be merely a story of an Englishman who came over here in 1800, full of 18th century notions of America as the perfect world, and floated down the Ohio with a raft load of nondescripts until he became aware that no one else on board thought like him, and until he surrendered, or suspended, his vision. There I stop in mid air, or rather mid stream. I thought it too obvious to point the irony of the situation. If America today is not the perfect world my hero thought it would be, it is hardly my business to say so. And maybe it is. So much for the "idea." The rest is costume stuff, scenery, etc., with songs interspersed and with the free or blank verse breaking occasionally into long rhymed lines which I rather like. I would send you a copy but wish to save myself a while—at least till you say that *this* might be interesting.

I got today from Fletcher the saddest of all the letters I ever got from him. Discouragement issues from every sentence and even from the hand-writing. He speaks of his last visit here as being full of disgraceful and painful disappointments, most of which I know nothing about. But I do seem to know that the man is about at the bottom of despair. And furthermore I am sure that nothing can save him. Nothing but success, and either he won't get any of that at all or he won't get the kind his imagination has been elaborating.

Tell Nancy that if she met Charlie tomorrow and were reintroduced he would probably have only one word to say—Cuckoo.[6] I don't know where he got it, but that is what he replies to practically everything we tell him these days, and believe me it seems to me a lot. It means go to hell, all right all right all right, yes you are a very nice old fellow but what after all does one's father know about one and what right has he coming around to fawn on one or reprove one, ho hum, skedaddle, ha ha, and welladay— all these rolled up together. And the whole message very gently and sweetly delivered, yet with that cool firmness which I suppose one must grow accustomed to as time runs on. Nancy, of course, is better behaved than this. I remember your saying that you would see to it that she did behave, and I don't doubt for a moment that you have succeeded. Note: I am as devoted to Charlie as I ever was, and in addition now I find myself terribly attracted to John, who is said to look like me, but who doesn't talk yet and so can't prove that he has any of his father's great gifts. . . .

1. *Jefferson Davis, His Rise and Fall: A Biographical Narrative* (New York, 1929).

2. E. C. Stedman (1833–1908), a minor American poet and critic.

3. Rexford Guy Tugwell was a member of the economics faculty at Columbia.

4. Tate's long poem was never finished.

5. *Jonathan Gentry* (New York, 1931).

6. Nancy was the Tates' daughter.

To Allen Tate
TLS/NjP

December 16, 1929   *New York City*

*   *   *

In my general ignorance of the future I don't pretend to fathom the whitherness of the two poems you sent me, but I must testify that I see you going somewhere in them.[1] I like them, I think, better than any other things you have done in the same length, and you must remember that that is saying much. "The Pit" I have read many times, and always with a sense that you do better things with death in it than you ever did before. I like the larger symbolism here, the symbolism which goes not merely back to nineteenth-century France but all the way, and very directly, along the line of Blake and Dante—rather absurd names to pair, but they occurred to me. Yet the seven lines between the dashes confuse me a bit; whereas I am perfectly at home, or think I am, in "Message from Abroad," which I am inclined to call your best poem to date. It has all your old precision and intelligence, and even more of it; but it has in addition a warm suffusion of recognizable autobiography, and I approve of that. I don't mean at all that it is a "personal" poem in the obnoxious sense; as far back as I knew your work you were beyond that; I mean simply that you have put your art very ably to work at the business of saying what you as a creature feel, and being a creature ought not to conceal behind any kind of sophistication. In a word, I both admire and am moved. May you bring back more of the same.

I finally turned down the big anthology for the best of reasons: namely, that it would have bored me. Also for the reason that I want to start, to-morrow morning if God so allows, part 2 of my long poem; for I have discovered that the thing I wrote this summer was only one third of a whole, the whole being a history of something or other American, and, apparently, Middle Western.[2] But more of that when you get here. You may *have* to go through Part I, vain or no. . . .

1. "The Pit" and "Message from Abroad" were sent from Paris. The title of "The Pit" was changed to "The Cross."

2. He is referring to his poem *Jonathan Gentry.*

To Robinson Jeffers
ALS/TxU

February 13, 1930   *New York City*

James Rorty, the journalist, brought Jeffers' Tamar to Mark Van Doren's attention, and Van Doren then reviewed Roan Stallion, Tamar and Other Poems *in the* Nation, *November 25, 1925. Jeffers wrote Van Doren praising 7 P.M. and later that year wrote at length about Van Doren's review of* The Women at Point Sur.[1] *Van Doren began his letter "Dear Jeffers."*

That, by the way, is not how I should prefer to address you. If you have another name by which you allow yourself to be called, and if I may use it in our occasional correspondence, won't you let me know the next time you write?[2] Of course this is not necessary, and you may disregard the request. But Robinson sounds as much like a first name as Jeffers does, and I somehow don't take to it. Yet if it is what your friends call you, it is what I want to call you.

Of course I am sorry I didn't see you, but I have a great deal of sympathy with your desire to see no one. I have it myself, and though, as my wife points out, I have never really been sorry for any given encounter, I still have it. Fools and knaves are quite worth seeing, even. I know that perfectly from experience; yet whenever a new occasion for seeing one arises I run the other way—possibly for fear he will be a wise man, who is equally hard to endure.

England "wearily fluffy with trees." I like the phrase but don't accept the sentiment, for it is my peculiarity to love the imprisonment of common trees. You escape to the hard coast, and I can see why, but I take a perverse delight in staying where green is like a wilderness, and where the people all around me rot in peace, all like to one another and all, I suppose, damned. Yet I am never sure, and anyhow I haven't the dislike of damnation you probably have. You must have had a very good summer and winter, by and large, and I am sure you won't regret so lovely an encounter with the world.

As for reviews of poetry, and particularly yours, I have about decided never to write them again. For several years it has made me uncomfortable to do so, and now there is a bit of shame mixed in. I never, for instance, say what I set out to say about your poems. I always return to the absurd notion that I must not add another note to the monotony of my praise, and so concentrate on something to say which will not be praise.[3] I think I shall merely read you henceforth, and admire you, and perhaps write you letters to that effect. Why not?

Yet I did mean what I said about ideas in poetry. I suspect they don't belong there, at least on the surface, and I really should prefer that you didn't offer them as handles by which the poems are to be grasped. It makes the grasping at once too easy and too difficult. At least this is true for me, who have no mind of a certain sort—I admit it. I am much more interested in a poem's being good—i.e., absorbing—than in its being true. As soon as I have to think about its truth I lose sight of its life. For I am convinced of what my philosopher friends tell me—that every statement is true. Whereas every poem is not good—though every one of yours is.

I didn't mean to go on like this.

1. See Ann N. Ridgeway (ed.), *The Selected Letters of Robinson Jeffers* (Baltimore, 1968), 115–17.

2. Jeffers responded on March 14, 1930, "I'm familiarly called by the name of a little red-breasted bird." In later letters, MVD did address him as "Robin." Ridgeway (ed.), *The Selected Letters of Robinson Jeffers*, 168.

3. In his review of *Cawdor, and Other Poems* (*Nation*, January 9, 1929, p. 50), MVD said that Jeffers, like Euripides, Sophocles, and Shakespeare "dredges, as they dredged, too deep in the mud of mor-tality not to come up with images and rhythms terrible in their force and beautiful in their explainable strangeness." In his review of *Dear Judas and Other Poems* (*Nation*, January 1, 1930, p. 20), MVD said of the title poem, in which Judas' act is presented as an act of love, that it was not one of Jeffers' successes. MVD found that the poet's "long lines forget most of the time to be poetry." For Jeffers' thoughtful and gentle response to MVD's criticism, see Jeffers to MVD, March 14, 1930, in Ridgeway (ed.), *The Selected Letters of Robinson Jeffers*, 168–70.

To John Gould Fletcher
ALS/ArU

March 9, 1930   *New York City*

Coward-McCann have sent me a copy of "The Two Frontiers," I suppose at your suggestion, and I have been reading it, slowly and at intervals, but with constant wonder at the powers you display in it.[1] I finished it last night in bed, where I had been several days with a cold, and got up today, Sunday, to write you about it.

It is one of the most exciting books I have read in years. I haven't the slightest idea whether it is true, really, or the equipment to criticize your numerous parallels and generalizations but I don't know that that matters. Whenever I was acquainted with the pertinent facts I found you making use of all I knew and more—and what was better, establishing or suggesting fascinating new relationships. The literary parallels were certainly interesting, but I found even more so the social and intellectual ones, and the political. Doom is written over the final chapters, and I like that—not necessarily because I agree with your prophecy, though I don't know enough to disagree with it, but because it is so fine a tragic finish to a tale told in the grand style. I congratulate you—and wonder how the book is being received in England. I wonder if Shaw, for instance, has read it. He ought to. I have seen only a few notices here, but they have been interested ones. Malcolm Cowley attacked some of your generalizations—being rather beside the point, I think, in doing so. . . .

1. *The Two Frontiers: A Study in Historical Psychology* (New York, 1930).

To Ernest Kroll
ALS/P[1]

March 19, 1930

Ernest Kroll, a high school sophomore, wrote Van Doren and other writers to ask about learning how to write. Several years later, Kroll took Van Doren's Shakespeare course at Columbia, and again Van Doren urged him to read widely. Kroll was working as a reporter at night, and Van Doren told him not to worry about writing, since he was doing journalism for a living and "to keep in mind that those who wanted deeply enough to write would do so, anyway."[2]

I am afraid I can't give you adequate advice about the matter you mention, and I suspect no one else could—except possibly some one who knew you very well, and even he couldn't tell you everything. Most of the secret is within yourself—and it is a secret for you, too, at present, as indeed it may always be.

The point is that nobody knows what makes a writer. Experience, certainly; but the experience must come of itself and not be sought, and very little of it goes a long way with a good imagination. Natural ability—well, you had that, in whatever quantity, at your birth, have it now, and my conviction is that it doesn't increase or decrease. The third thing is reading. That is very important, and it is something you *can* do. So my advice is to read widely for the next ten years, and not worry about writing.

1. Reproduced in *Voyages*, V (1973), 51.   2. *Ibid.*, 50.

To Allen Tate
ALS/NjP

August 27, 1930   *Falls Village, Connecticut*

My thanks for "Three Poems," which I had only to glance at to realize that I knew the contents very well. The Ode I cannot compare with its three earlier versions until I am back in New York, where I possess them all, but even with such changes as I thought I recognized it was as familiar to me as any classic. And so with Message from Abroad and The Cross, which you sent me in manuscript from Paris. I found that they too had carved a very solid, a marble place in my memory. Well, I have read the book through carefully now, several times, and I must tell you how much I admire you for your power to make lines that last like these. It is a beautiful book—quite adequate payment for all you got from the Guggenheims, I think.[1]

One circumstance that stimulates my appreciation is this—my poem, done now at last, is 4000 lines long, and by comparison very wordy.[2] I'd send it to you if I had a legible copy here, and if I had an envelope for it. But I suspect you would have to be even more polite than you have ever been before. Whereas I was not polite at all in the above. If anything it was understatement.

You may have heard from a bird in Wisconsin or Minnesota who wants to know all about your agrarian movement—if you remember it. In an article I had in *Harper's* this summer, called The Real Tragedy of the Farmer, I alluded to you and your manifesto without mentioning names.[3] There was at least one reader who wanted to know more about you. He wrote me, and I gave him your address. I hope you didn't mind. . . .

1. *Three Poems: "Ode to the Confederate Dead," Being the revised and final version of a poem previously published on several occasions; to which are added "Message from Abroad" and "The Cross,"* (New York, 1930).

2. *Jonathan Gentry.*

3. *Harper's Magazine*, CLXI (August, 1930), 365–70.

To John Gould Fletcher
ALS/ArU

September 1, 1930   *Falls Village, Connecticut*

I learned with a shock, upon looking at your letter just now, that it had gone six months unanswered. I can hardly understand that—or rather I can, remembering how busy the spring was, and realizing that I wrote very few letters this summer because I had my poem so constantly in mind. It is finished now—4000 lines—and I will send you a copy when and if it gets published. Albert Boni, who promised to bring it out, as usual hasn't taken the trouble even to acknowledge the manuscript. But when I go back to New York three weeks from now I hope to find it under way. He too writes very few letters, at least to his authors.[1]

The poem isn't what I expected it to be, and in most respects it is not as good. But I still think it has a certain interest and at any rate I shall be eager to know what you think of it. It treats more or less faithfully the idea I sketched to you the day we had lunch down town two years ago, but does it in three stories separated in time. Well, you can see. I would send you a typed copy if I had a good clear one, which I haven't.

The immediate occasion I had for writing was the dedication of Allen's "Three Poems." I was glad to see that, and in my opinion you can be proud. Allen's poetry still has its difficulty for me, but I am more and more impressed by a hard, marble quality in his lines—which, nevertheless, are far from cold. He had sent me the second and third poems from France last winter, and I realized when I read them in the book that they were quite familiar to me, as if they were classics I had once studied.[2] Yet I had merely read them in a letter from France. . . .

1. MVD's *Jonathan Gentry* was published by Boni in 1931.

2. In addition to "Ode to the Confederate Dead," *Three Poems* included "Message from Abroad" and "The Cross," originally titled "The Pit."

To Allen Tate
ALS/NjP

November 11, 1930   *New York City*

Tate did not respond to Van Doren's letter of September 10, which included the manuscript of Jonathan Gentry. *Puzzled by the sixty days of silence, Van Doren wrote again.*

I am in a predicament, having so far failed to hear from you about the poem. The predicament is as follows. If I do not write you, and it turns out that the poem was sent and lost, you will be wondering why you don't hear from me, acknowledging its return. If I do write, and it turns out that you have been sick, or busy, or taken up with guests (Ford, Cowley, aut al), or at a loss to know how to sit down and say that you found the poem lousy—Why, I should be very sorry to have written at all, since a letter under any of those circumstances would either embarrass you or give you the notion that I was pressing you to discharge an obligation. Which could not possibly be true.

You will see, then, that if you did send the poem and it never reached me you are to let me know as much, but that if you haven't sent it you are to disregard these presents, at least in so far as they refer to that.

Carl has told me the very good news about Caroline's novel.[1] Perkins spoke of it to him with the greatest enthusiasm; and Perkins, you know, is perhaps the best judge of fiction among publishers.[2] Dorothy and I are both delighted—will you congratulate Caroline for us, and ask her when we can expect to be able to walk into a store and buy a copy? Or two copies.

As for yourself, do you know, I wonder, how famous you are becoming? I am asked to lecture on your theory and practice of poetry at New York University (I refuse, not being competent); I am pumped for information about you by my students at Columbia; I am complimented upon being your friend; and I see many references to you in the greatest variety of printed places. I have had only a glance so far at your Southern symposium. How is that going? And will Ransom demolish Barr at Richmond on the 14th? I was invited to come and sit on the platform, but decided I was not that rich—also, I didn't like the idea of being torn in two, since I like Ransom and Barr equally well.[3] I will read the symposium soon. . . .

. . . Dorothy unhappily waits—*and waits*—for an opinion on her fourth novel from Doubleday.[4]

1. *Penhally* (New York, 1931).
2. Maxwell Perkins was editor at Scribner's.
3. For a full account of the John Crowe Ransom–Stringfellow Barr debate in Richmond, see Thomas Daniel Young, *Gentle-*

man in a Dustcoat: A Biography of John Crowe Ransom (Baton Rouge, 1976), 217–23.
4. *Those First Affections* was not accepted by Doubleday but was published by Houghton Mifflin.

To Allen Tate
TLS/NjP

December 4, 1930   *New York City*

Tate, after his long silence, was less than enthusiastic about Jonathan Gentry.

No apologies. I was pretty sure—and should have been surer—that you were plagued, harassed, driven, etc., etc. It seems I did what I didn't want to do—forced you to speak. Not that I wasn't crazy with curiosity about your opinion, and not that I am other than very much pleased with the one I got. Your words schematization and monotony, particularly when you instance Virgil, are most illuminating. I agree that a poem of this sort ought to be a poem of that sort, and I suspect that I shall try to make the next one, for there is a next one, after such a model. But I cannot alter this one now, being incapable of the heroic work you yourself can do so well—the work of revision. No, I shall let J.G. stand where he is, if he is anywhere at all, and be satisfied that you found parts of him beautiful. So, my thanks. And my apologies.

When you come to a breathing spell, perhaps after Christmas, write me and let me know what all these things are that you have been doing, and what the new biography is about. I have kept up with you in part. For instance, Dorothy and I were in Charlottesville for Thanksgiving, and heard much about the Ransom-Barr debate. We heard also that in Barr's opinion you are worth all the rest of your gang put together. In other words he forgives you. But I think he doesn't forgive Ransom his personalities that evening.[1] By all local accounts your contribution to the symposium is the best one.[2] I realize that I must see for myself. I have been too lazy to seek out the book and read it. When I do go in for being lazy, you know, I make a thorough job of it. . . .

1. Ransom accused Barr of using Southern tradition "as a gardenia to stick in his buttonhole when he goes traveling in New York" (Young, *Gentleman in a Dustcoat*, 220).

2. Tate contributed "Remarks on the Southern Religion" to *I'll Take My Stand: The South and The Agrarian Tradition* (New York, 1930).

To Allen Tate
TLS/NjP

February 14, 1931   *New York City*

Seeing Cowley between the acts of a play the other night (he was there for the *New Republic,* I for the *Nation,* that being my newest job), I pumped him for information about the squire of Clarksville, and learned among other things that y'all live in a brick mansion with one of those there central halls, and a dining room big enough to seat Stonewall Jackson's staff.[1] It sounded fine, as did the news that Nancy was fat and that you and Caroline were happy, or reasonably so. And that you might be up here for part of next winter. That last is surely the only way we shall see you while we are still young. You accuse me of not *wanting* to visit you. Such is not the case. It is all a matter of what we would use for money.

I have instructed Dorothy to inform me just as soon as Tate on Unemployment appeared in the *New Republic.*[2] So far she tells me it has not, and she sees the paper every week as I do not, quite. The fact that you recommend this prose to me makes me very much interested in it. My interest is in the following question: What more could it have in it than your prose already has? Not that I am trying to insinuate what one of my friends up from Washington the other day tried to insinuate to me— namely, that one's prose may be more worth discussing than one's poetry. I do not praise your prose at the expense of your poetry. Far from it. But I do praise your prose. Which reminds me to say that I should like very much to see copies, if you have them, of those four new poems.

I agree that it is just as well for you to interrupt politics occasionally with poetry. Not that I haven't read the symposium and agreed, as you suggest, that we agree about some of those matters. But I think I have at bottom an incurable skepticism as to the power of the American people to absorb ideas. Your program depends, does it not, on the acceptance by considerable numbers of certain ideas? My notion is that they won't even take the trouble to understand them. Much better that they should have more of your poetry to neglect than they already have.

What of Caroline's novel? Dorothy and I want to be told that it is finished and being printed. Let her remember that Carl's report of Perkins's report of it was very passionate. Dorothy has had poor luck with her latest, as perhaps I told you last time. Several publishers to whom she has shown it have made courteous references to the poor season and regretted that, etc. Too bad, for temporarily at least she is discouraged.

In about three weeks now you will have *Jonathan Gentry* on your hands again, but this time between covers and without any obligation whatever to read it. Boni wanted to illustrate it. I objected at first, but when I found that he was disappointed, and thought he could sell more copies this way, I gave in. Who am I to prevent a publisher from making another ten dollars on the poetry I am mighty lucky to get published at all? You don't need to look at the pictures, then, though I am not saying that they are bad. They are only, like all such things, irrelevant.

My essay on Dryden is being reprinted in England this spring, curiously enough. Recently I wrote nineteen poems twelve of which will go into a fourth collection of short pieces to be published in the fall.[3] I review plays for the Nation in Krutch's absence. I teach school. I lecture everywhere. I have just written a children's book for Macmillan's.[4] Hence my waiting five weeks to answer your letter.

1. The Tates were living at Benfolly near Clarksville, Tennessee.

2. Tate's "Relief for the Unemployed" was not accepted by the *New Republic*. "The Problem of the Unemployed: A Mod-

est Proposal" appeared in *American Review*, I (May, 1933), 129–49.

3. MVD did not publish a collection of poems in the fall of 1931.

4. *Dick and Tom* (New York, 1931).

To Allen Tate
TLS/NjP

March 19, 1931   *New York City*

Well, the suffering of six months is over. As long ago as that I decided to carry out my still older intention of dedicating J.G. to your unworthy self. The decision was made after many doubts had been put down—e.g., as to whether you could possibly like the poem well enough to remain unashamed of your after all involuntary connection with it. Then another decision had to be made—i.e., whether or not to send you the manuscript. That one made, the circumstance that you found the poem to be not quite the most perfect poem ever written rendered still another one necessary—to wit, whether or not to reconsider. But later letters from you did convince me that you would not feel altogether disgraced. So. I might add that I wondered whether I should warn you, or ask your permission. Oh, it was a hell of a time, as Dorothy could tell you, who more than once told me for God's sake to go ahead and do what I did after all want to do. So.

Of course, as you yourself say in so lordly a manner, you are unworthy of the honor. I am quite willing to let it go as an act of friendship. But let me tell you, now that I think our acquaintance over, what deed of yours determined this reckless one of mine. You probably do not remember that you were at our house on Barrow Street one evening in 1927; that you went home by way of the stairs, as indeed most persons did in that particular house; and that as you went you said over your shoulder, "By the way, I should like to review 7 P.M. in the Nation." Odd as it may seem to you, that was one of the moments in my life. Others to follow when I send you my autobiography.

To leave this somewhat embarrassing subject, let me say that I have at last read something of yours I can disagree with. Is Roy Campbell really so good?[1] I haven't read him—and won't read him now, I might find you right. And it is necessary that I find you cockeyed at least once.

1. Tate reviewed Campbell's *Adamastor*
in the *New Republic*, March 18, 1931,
p. 133.

To John Gould Fletcher
ALS/ArU

April 26, 1931   *New York City*

Your letter could have disappointed me only by permitting me to detect dishonesty in it. Since it was palpably honest, and since it had some good things to say about *Jonathan Gentry*, I was more than satisfied. I was, and am, grateful for a most penetrating review of a poem that I never had considered perfect. What you did was to lay your finger on weaknesses I had not seen—though suspected.[1] You have taught me a great deal—not, perhaps, how to achieve this style you mention (I fancy it can't be done overnight), but how to reflect about the next thing I attempt.

I am delighted that you are going ahead with your own piece. I'd like to hear about it if you have time to write, and if you don't mind discussing a work in process. You probably do—I do—so I shall expect only news of the most general and unliterary sort in your next letter.

That will certainly reach me before I see London, which may not be for years. My Columbia sabbatical I have at last decided to spend here in the country, where I have always wanted to see a winter through. So you should take your jack knife and scrape off the false inscription in your copy of *J.G.*, and wait indefinitely for me to come along and fill the space, which of course I will gladly do. . . .

1. Fletcher had reservations about the Robinsonian qualities of the poem but did feel the long poem succeeded in spots.

To Allen Tate
TLS/NjP

April 26, 1931   *New York City*

If a sentence toward the end of your last excellent letter spoke the truth, you have lost your last friend, for I have bought and read your biographies. I wasn't to be dismissed so easily, or rather I wasn't to be retained with so little to do. I never had intended to leave the biographies unread, but so far I had. This struck me as the time to reform. I reformed, and I hasten to tell you—the *Davis* was finished only this morning—how much I enjoyed the experience.[1] I am sure you are honest in condescending to these books, since you are honest in everything, but I am even surer that you are wrong. They tell their stories terribly well; they are full, not only of what must have been called (up here) paradoxes about the war, but of observations that only a very superior knowledge of life could have inspired; they were written, or at least they read, with the speed of an angry and ironic arrow; in a word, they are exciting and shining books. They have filled me incidentally with a vast depression because they have reminded me so forcibly of that war which I still consider the most cockeyed event in history. But I shall get over that and remember chiefly the brilliance which gave me this reminder. Now don't protest. You are the last man to know whether these things are true. They are, and they are important because they reveal that large fraction of you which was submerged—not wholly reveal, of course, but at any rate suggest and promise. . . .

One thing I didn't like so well in the *Jackson*. That was the boyhood stuff, and particularly the fancy that even in short pants Tom might have said to himself: "Let's cross over the river and rest in the shade of the trees." That had always seemed to me about the best of all dying speeches, and I hated to see it given a date well in advance of the appropriate death. I am expressing, of course, a biographical prejudice. You undoubtedly share it with me. Also, while I think of it, don't you say in the *Jackson* that $500,000,000 worth of cotton was not shipped at the beginning of the war because of negligence, and in the *Davis* that it was not shipped because it did not exist? These are details which I slip in to relieve you of the embarrassment my praise otherwise would cause you. . . .

It was handsome of you to read *Jonathan Gentry* again, and generous of you to have so many interesting ideas about it. The reviews have been so noncommital and for the most part so dull that I must still consider you, as I did with previous volumes, my best and indeed only critic. You are quite right, for instance, about the meters. Well, my next may be an attempt at the impossible. If I fail, though, I don't believe I'll blame the age. . . .

1. *Jefferson Davis, His Rise and Fall: A Biographical Narrative* (New York, 1929).

To Allen Tate
ALS/NjP

May 11, 1931   *New York City*

With your permission, still to be given, I'll keep "The Legacy," and keep it in this form.[1] You will probably rewrite it and rewrite it until it doesn't have precisely this same backward and forward glance that I like so much, and this sentiment. My advice is not to change a word. I know you won't take it, but I assure you that what lies on this page I have is very lovely, and some day it will be my proof of the completeness—therefore the purity—with which you identified yourself with your ancestors in the years 1929, 1930, 1931, et secq. Do you realize—of course you do—how good the word "strangely" is in the 6th line? And are you unwilling to publish the poem as it stands? If not, Henry Hazlitt will certainly want it for *The Nation*. I like to think of *The Nation* as still eligible for publishing you, though it may not deserve to be. As a matter of fact Dorothy has just come in and said that she has spoken to Hazlitt about the poem. So send it.

She also brings Caroline's nice letter, which bears the good news that you really will visit us, and the almost incomprehensible news that you now weigh 160 pounds. Good God! What will become of your intellect?

Probably thrive. I'll have a barn for you to move in Cornwall. You can just lead it to the place I want it.

Your autobiography is successful as it stands, though it is also tantalizing in many places—e.g., for me at any rate, the references to Southern Illinois, and the account of your father's indifference to his family.[2] My father is the same way—though I never felt any contempt there. But I don't begin to know as much about the rest of my family as you do about yours. I wish I did. Are you sure that the war is the sole cause of things as they now stand? Isn't the American family, North and South, always ceasing like this? Maybe not, but in your book, which can be so fascinating, I would make both the resemblance and the distinction very clear. . . .

1. The poem was not published under that title.

2. Tate's parents lived in Mount Vernon, Illinois, from 1889–94. Radcliffe Squires says that after 1907 the young Tate saw little of his father, who was involved in a scandal and had been asked to resign from a club. According to Squires, the father "resigned not only from the club but from society in general and seemed to behave almost as if he had lost his will" (Squires, *Allen Tate* [New York, 1971], 21).

To Allen Tate
TLS/NjP

May 23, 1931   *New York City*

Tate had sent Van Doren a copy of "Tatal Splinterview" (unpublished) and "Emblem II" from Clarksville, Tennessee.

Beer Gallon:

Tatal Splinterview was gland, and cranks for sticking a surden little lark linnet. Bard he never wart, but that dozen mattra tall. Will glue bubbulge it in the Nude Repubic—hair, hair? Why knock elsewhere? What udder whoor but Slur Endman Axel's would open?

Enough of this. I can't go on, except to say in plain syllables that I had a good time with your foolishness—and, joke on you, that I *will* comment on Emblem II by saying that though very good it is not perhaps quite as good in my eye as Emblem I.[1] Now damn my eyes if you will, and give them fifty extra lashes. But remember how much I liked Emblem I, and consider that I committed the error upon reading it of supposing that it was final. I can't help readin[g] EII as a sequel, which probably isn't fair. But what the hell? You asked me not to comment at all, and here I am doing it.

I was inaccurate about the barn. It was to be torn down, not moved, and as a matter of fact it is already down. Three men levelled in one day what a dozen old New Englanders must have been a month erecting. So you won't have anything at all to do, and there is no place, I regret to say, for your thieving and I suppose blaspheming tenant. But there will be plenty of sward for you and Caroline to lie around on, and plenty to talk about. . . .

1. "Emblems" appeared in the *New Re-public*, September 30, 1931, p. 182. Number III was added later, and all three ap- peared in Tate's *Poems: 1928–1931* (New York, 1932) and in later collected editions.

To Allen Tate
ALS/NjP

September 12, 1931   *Falls Village, Connecticut*

This is to say that I found New York exactly where it had always been, and containing, I was glad to discover, Dorothy, who took me out to dinner and asked me many questions about your way of life in Tennessee. A good way, I told her; and further reflection convinces me that it is the best way.

That is why it is necessary for you and Caroline to visit us up here. As seasoned homesteaders you can give us a notion of the possibilities in Cornwall. You are warned, therefore, that you will have to make your promise good. You too are committed. Incidentally, as I drive around this country I keep seeing things that you should be shown—partly, of course, to repay you for showing me so many things, but partly also because I shall be interested in the excursions involved.

I hope your line of communication with Lee, broken for three days by Federal interference, has now been reestablished, and that you have him already a professor—possibly, even, entombed. Go to, young man, and be done in this way with biography forever.

I have finished "Penhally," and with pleasure to the last word. For all I know I am so familiar with the terrain it treats, and so full of the true stories out of which it was made, that I am in no position to judge it calmly. But why in hell judge it calmly? It is a rich, exciting book, full of fine language and fine deeds, and that's all there is to it. Anybody would know that much, though he might not have seen the Meriwether land as I did. Old Nicholas is the best man in the novel, isn't he? I won't forget *him*, or Jeems, or Tom and Charles and Frank and Chance, not to speak of the many ladies—none of whom, however, quite comes up to the men in my opinion. Caroline probably won't agree. . . .

To Allen Tate
ALS/NjP

December 21, 1931   *New York City*

Mark Van Doren was preparing the anthology American Poets, 1630–1930 *for Little, Brown and Company.*

I have become, or am about to be known as having become, the kind of son of a bitch I hate most—i.e., the kind who anthologizes American poetry. I think I bragged to you this summer about how I had resisted all offers to pick the bones of our predecessors and contemporaries. Well, Little Brown come along now with an offer which I *can't resist,* since I owe money I can't otherwise pay, and since the book they want me to do is the only book I would do at all, namely one which has few poets in it and a good deal of poetry by each poet. That is to say, instead of the hundreds of poets to be found in Untermeyer, Kreymborg, Stedman, et al I shall have about fifty—which over three hundred years is not so terribly silly. At any rate I have found it fun to pick the fifty. Quite exhilarating, really, and every now and then not so easy.

Do you object to being one of them—the last one, I believe, in point of time? And if not, do you mind letting me know which ten or fifteen poems of yours I ought to put in (Oh, you will get rich)? And when is your new volume to appear? If not very soon, may I have some extra proof sheets? Or some manuscripts? What ho! . . .

By the way, are the old Southern poets any good? I mean Pinkney, Timrod, and Chivers? They are making a fuss about Chivers, and I find him a rather fascinating fool.[1] Do you? And what about those other two? *Really.*

1. Edward C. Pinkney (1802–1828), the Maryland poet, was author of *Look Out Upon the Stars, My Love* and *Poems.* Henry Timrod (1828–1867), the South Carolina poet, was known as the "Laureate of the Confederacy." Thomas Holley Chivers (1809–1858), the Georgia-born physician-poet, charged that Poe plagiarized from him, but Poe's supporters have insisted that Chivers plagiarized from Poe.

To Allen Tate
TLS/NjP

December 27, 1931   *New York City*

*The Anthology of American Poetry selections were the subject of much
discussion between Van Doren and Tate. Tate made suggestions about titles
of his own poems for possible inclusion in the anthology.*

I think it will be about as you say, except for *Causerie* which I may want
to leave out and except for one or two poems from *Mr. Pope* which I may
want to leave in—the fact that they have been liked being nothing against
them if I like them too, as you know I do. The title poem, certainly; and
what of *To a Romanticist?* Well, don't bother to answer that last question.
It is only asked in passing. The truth is that I am not making up my mind
all at once. I find it best to walk away from a poem and come back to it
many times before deciding—and then there is no deciding; there is
simply a conviction, born of satisfied expectations.

This may sound as if I were taking my job as anthologist seriously. It
means exactly the opposite. I am doing it with the least possible effort—
vide my asking you to choose your poems for me. The only reason I am
not doing that with anybody else is—besides the fact that I trust nobody's
judgment as much as I do yours—that it would be too much trouble.

I promise to see that Little, Brown approach Scribners as soon as possible. It won't be tomorrow, since the whole business of copyrights has to
be taken care of in one transaction. But it will be soon, and I hope you get
paid enough to suit you. That, too, as you know, rests with the publishers.

Mother and Son may have to go in, too. Zounds, this Tate is a poet!

Timrod will get in, I think, purely for his war poems. Pinkney maybe,
merely as a whiff of Cavalier. Lanier only for his moments.[1] And Chivers
as a curiosity—and a poet. But who is Thomas Malone?[2] Never heard of
him. Don't bother to answer that either. After all, you are not doing my
work. I'll look him up. Ransom, of course. And I'm blessed if I can get
half a dozen of Merrill Moore's sonnets out of my head since you read
them to me on Bank Street and since I read them myself in the Fugitives
book and in The Noise that Time Makes. If I meditate on them I find I
don't take them very seriously. Yet, as I say, they do keep occurring to me.
And I am afraid I shall not be able to resist them.

When the proof comes from Scribners and I have made the final fatal
choice I'll write you again and make sure just what order you want the
poems to appear in. Perhaps chronology will support theology here, but
if it doesn't, and you want the poems to represent the four stages you so
interestingly define, you must let me know.

You ask me what I am doing besides this. There was some talk again of that life of Milton, but it now seems to have fallen through. So nothing, except teaching and fathering my family and occasionally hacking. This will be the first December in eleven years that I haven't written a poem, unless I write one during the next four days, which is impossible since I have no ideas. Indeed I don't know when I shall have ideas for poems again. I have always felt this way, to be sure, but never so strongly as now. Probably I shall dismiss the whole business for a year or two and see if I don't turn up transformed and renovated. But that will be melancholy. I have never written poetry except in December (or January) and July (or June), and I hate to look forward to a July as unhappy as this month now passing.

You haven't told me anything further about the Lee, which I assumed you finished in the fall. Then what? Is Caroline writing another novel?

Dorothy and I saw Léonie Adams at a party last night.[3] Dorothy and Leonie, who were in high school and college together, talked about those old days. Léonie and Mark insulted each other very gently in their cups— or so she construed what seemed to me a conversation full of loving kindness.

1. Sidney Lanier (1842–81), American poet.

2. The Southern poet Walter Malone— the name seems to have been misremembered by MVD—is now chiefly remembered for his epic poem *Hernando De Soto* (1914).

3. Léonie Adams stayed with the Tates in Europe, 1928–29.

To Allen Tate
TLS/NjP

January 31, 1932   *New York City*

From Benfolly, his home near Clarksville, Tennessee, Tate had suggested an ordering of his poems to be included in the anthology.

Too bad about your flu. It is something I have never had, but for that very reason I respect it highly, and urge you to do likewise—e.g., stay in bed until your head stops swimming.

I was being silent on the anthology until I heard from Little, Brown about their negotiations with Scribners. Friday I went up to Boston with the manuscript and got what I take to be the final truth about you, namely that Scribners have refused to yield more than five poems by you. Now since the Ode must in their estimation be one of those five, I told Little, Brown to say that the five were to be:

Alice
The Paradigm
The Cross
Emblems
The Ode

I am sorry there can't be more than this from the new book, but I can see their point, which is also yours if you would only confess it. This leaves five from the first volume, and so but ten in all. I wish it were more, but I assume that you would not like me to pad the Tate section with a disproportionate amount of early Tate. If, by the way, you have any great objection to the whole selection as it now stands, will you let me know? Naturally I hope you haven't.

Page proofs came from Scribners a few hours before I left for Boston and I glued them into place. So you need not fear that I have an antiquated text—i.e., one six weeks old.

I did put myself in at the last moment, leaving the selection, you being farther away than was convenient, to Dorothy and Carl, not to speak of myself. I should have loved to retain you as inquisitor, but after you see the book you can tell the three of us where we erred. Singular, isn't it, how hard it is to see that one of one's poems may be better than any other? I like all mine equally well. Which doesn't reveal how high I put them. Only how wide. They spread easily.

The principal reason for my going to Boston, by the way, was a lecture which I gave in the afternoon, the subject being my own poetry. That was new for me, and in anticipation it was terrifying; but it proved in act to be most pleasant. And I actually learned something, I think, about what I have been doing. Indeed I have the uncomfortable belief that certain things, realized by myself now for the first time, cannot be repeated for the simple reason that they *are* realized. However classical I may think I am in my theories about art, I find that I do still believe in the value of one's not fully knowing what one is doing—even, the value of supposing that one is doing something else. Well, when I get going again, if I ever do, I might try this out. That is, I might take one of the themes which in my lecture I claimed to have succeeded with, or at any rate to have accomplished certain results with, and see if I could do so again in fairly cold blood. As I say, my religion is that such a thing ought to be possible. But I wonder if it is. . . .

To Allen Tate
TLS/NjP

February 12, 1932   *New York City*

Little, Brown write me that Scribners have at last allowed six poems from the new book, which leaves in *The Wolves,* that having been first on the list of poems which I had urged Little, Brown to try to get in addition to the famous ten. But what's this about its having taken off from one of mine? You probably mean the one about spiders watching men, but I should never have known it if you and Caroline hadn't mentioned it last summer. There is about as much resemblance between the two as there is between Clarksville and Cornwall.

I am returning all the manuscripts which you furnished me while I was making up the anthology. They are old versions, and pasted up for this purpose alone I imagine, and it is almost certain that you don't need them back, but I hesitated to throw them away. For all I know you have a building full of old versions, and these belong there. My own collection of Tate primitives is not complete or I would add them to it. As it is I have enjoyed seeing them around. And let me say once more that I am very proud to have you in the anthology in a representation of which you do not disapprove—to have you in at all, of course, but after that to your own satisfaction.

You may be amused to hear that Hazlitt sent the Landor poem by Dorothy to me for gloss and explication.[1] I sent back a simple statement suited to Henry's head, and hope it worked. It was not that he hesitated to accept the poem, he said, but that he feared someone would ask him what it meant. Boiled down, he didn't know who Helen was.

Query: What would he do with either of the two poems you sent me last?[2] The owl and the anabasis? Well, he would probably ask me about them; I would make up a plausible yarn; I would tell him they were good; and years later, meeting them in your collected poems, he would know it for himself. They are so good that I wonder whether you had better not take to eating the germs of flu as a regular thing. I have been known to doubt the efficacy of wine as inspiration, but I do not see how I can doubt a bug. . . .

1. "Unnatural Love" appeared in the *Nation,* March 16, 1932, p. 314. Henry Hazlitt, literary editor of the *Nation,* was apparently satisfied with MVD's explication.

2. "The Learned Owl" and "The Anabasis."

To Allen Tate
TLS/NjP

February 23, 1932   *New York City*

This is simply to report, though late, that I received your final (?) versions and sent them on, arranged in the order already imposed by the table of contents, to Little Brown, who will by now have substituted them for the hopelessly archaic versions of your page proof. I must hold on, I see, to my copy of the first edition of *Poems,* for it is certain that this volume will be recalled within a few days after its publication and burned. Ah, but not my copy. God, what are bankvaults for?

The order you suggested in your last letter would have been my order had the letter come in time, but as I say the table of contents was already in Boston being set up, and I thought I had better not change it. My order, in case you don't remember, is the one I set forth in my last letter to you. I do hope you don't mind my keeping it.

No, I don't agree that the end of *Obituary* as it now stands (February 23, 1932, 11:39 p.m.) is better than the original end, if the one I know is the original one, which it probably isn't. It is probably end number 382. I don't say it is worse, either. But I do say that after I have got very well acquainted with a poem, after it has been in a book for four years, and when I like it there extremely well, its author has no right to change it on me, especially by substituting for a long, strong last line two (or is it three) shorter ones. Not that it is any of my business, and not that Horace's nine years are up yet. Nor that I mind having a hitherto unprinted version in an anthology of mine. But that I am a tory in these really important matters, however much I may once have appeared to be in league with Oswald Garrison William Wendell Lloyd ap Lloyd Villard.

No more flu, I beg you. How do we know that for such a satanic gentleman the third time is not a charm?

To Mortimer Adler
TLS/P

April 15, 1932   *New York City*

*   *   *

Kip has read my novel and decided to present it to Essandess under an assumed name so that they will not accuse him of pushing his friends—or, if you like, because he doesn't know whether it is any good or not.[1]

But each page of the manuscript was marked MVD, as is my custom. So I had to make a new title page bearing a name that would fit these initials. It was fun naming myself—Montgomery Vernon Dale, Montmorency Valentine Deodati, Michael Vincent Doyle, Mortimer Verome Dadler, and the like. Kip's suggestion was the vilest of all—Miles Vorst DeLeon. I finally chose M.V. Doyle.

So now I await the great decision. Meanwhile I can bask in the memory of your passionate curiosity about this work, which equalled—I shall not say surpassed—the almost paranoiac way you have of always insisting on talking about my poetry.

You may be even more interested in the fact that before I leave libraries for Cornwall I am to do another anthology—this time the Oxford Book of American Prose, for which I have agreed to accept a flat fee of two grand when the manuscript is handed in, namely on or before June 1st, the degree of beforeness depending, as you can imagine, on the degree of my financial behindness toward the middle of May.

Get rid of that flu. I don't like it.

1. Clifton Fadiman was reading the manuscript of *The Transients*. "Essandess" refers to Simon and Schuster, the publishing firm.

To Allen Tate
TLS/NjP

May 3, 1932   *New York City*

Caroline Gordon received a Guggenheim in 1932 and the Tates returned to Europe.

First of all let me tell you what you already know, namely that we hope you do sail from New York and that you do have some days free to spend with us in Cornwall. We are really counting on you this time. So pay us mind. And understand that you are to let us know whenever the time arrives. Any time will be a good time for us, and for that matter the notification need not be more than a few days or hours in advance.

Secondly let me confess to you that I am no good as an adverse critic where any writer is concerned whom I have decided I like, particularly if he is my good friend. This is in answer to your request that I pounce on something of yours. I can't, not because I am complacent or cowardly (I hope), but because when I get interested in a mind, and attached to it, everything it does interests me, and I do not think of its products in terms of good and bad. You know well enough that I have liked some of your poems better than others—therefore some of them less than others. With that you must be satisfied. I have heard this complaint before. Apparently it is a real defect in me. And I wish I could convince someone that I am not talking nonsense when I give my reason. You for instance are not convinced.

Consequently I am embarrassed about praising your introduction to "White Buildings," which I reread last week before writing a *Nation* editorial on Crane's suicide.[1] Whatever you may think of it now, I assure you that it is a classic. So was your piece on Donne in the *NR*,[2] and so—but I shall not offend you with any further praise. Only, I shall suggest once more that you collect your critical articles some day.

The book about which you are so mysterious—is it your genealogy, altered perhaps to be any Virginia-Tennessee-Kentucky genealogy? Do not answer the question unless it is a proper guess, since you have a right to be secretive. I remain curious, however, and decidedly attracted.

Since finishing the Little, Brown anthology I have done another one, a prose one, for the Oxford Press—nothing less, indeed, than The Oxford Book of American Prose—and have written a novel.[3] If the novel ever appears I'll send you and Caroline a copy. If it doesn't, I'll tell you about it when you come to Cornwall. It was great fun—82,000 words in four weeks. I rather fancy that way of writing fiction, at least for myself. I couldn't have done anything at all if I had had more time. Fadiman likes it, and has recommended it to Simon and Schuster, who haven't spoken yet. I'll let you know.

All this means that I have had a busy spring, that I have needed to make a good deal of money for next year, and that I am now tired. But not of receiving or writing letters. Or of seeing people I like on the green grass of Cornwall.

1. MVD's unsigned editorial on Hart Crane appeared in the *Nation*, May 11, 1932, p. 531.

2. "A Note on Donne," *New Republic,* April 16, 1932, pp. 212–13.
3. *The Transients.*

To Bernard De Voto
TLS/CSt

October 23, 1932   *Falls Village, Connecticut*

In a review of De Voto's Mark Twain's America, Van Doren wrote: "Mr. De Voto would have written a better book had he known the kind he was writing—if he had known that in his book, too, thought was required." He believed that De Voto met Van Wyck Brooks's theory with another theory: "Mr. De Voto thinks he is meeting a theory with facts, but as is usual in such situations he only gets tangled in a profusion of data."[1] De Voto, on October

17, 1932, wrote Van Doren an angry letter, insisting that the review had misrepresented his book.

You may be surprised to hear that I was far from being a partisan of Brooks when I began reading your book—which, by the way, I did read throughout, and with more respect, I now realize, than my brief review (brief by order) indicated. I have always held Brooks's theory in a sort of contempt, and have had much the same attitude that you seem to have toward the whole whining school.

Yet as soon as I was in the middle of your Foreword I found myself for some reason on the defensive. You had *my* back up. You were saying something about literary theory which I felt to be misguided, and you were dismissing too briefly, I thought, a critic who after all possesses some important merits. I got to thinking those merits over. I got to thinking about the whole matter of Fact vs. Theory in literary or any other discussion. And so I was off.

You misrepresent me when you say I accuse you of being wrong in your facts. I made no such accusation; I am aware, of course, that you are infinitely better acquainted with the period than Brooks is, or than I am. I only accused you, for the pleasant purposes of irony, of using *your* facts to support *your* theory. You see I am more of a literary skeptic than you are. I cannot accept the statement that Mark Twain was something in general as a fact; though I can accept as facts any number of particular statements about him. Nor can I believe that any period of history can be finally said to be such and so, regardless of how much knowledge of it the speaker may have. For general statements belong to the realm of theory, and a theory is supported not by facts but by arguments. It is merely illustrated by facts.

That last sentence will seem to you nonsense, but to me it is plain sense. No theory was ever disproved by a fact in my opinion. Nor do I believe that particular truths ever yield a general one; they only yield the general statement which the student was already disposed by temperament to believe and make. Brooks examined certain data and extracted from them what he thought was the truth about Mark Twain. So did you. The fact that you examined more data does not matter in an argument about theories.

You say your method is "to assemble the facts that relate to Mark Twain's books and then to state the conclusions they indicate." You call this "the inductive method." But I don't think there is any such method. I don't think that facts indicate conclusions. Facts are inert things which we can do anything with that we like. They can mean anything. Of course they must not be misrepresented or perverted in themselves. They must be left inert. But I am convinced that if left perfectly inert they will also be perfectly meaningless—i.e., susceptible of any meaning we want to give them. Their meaning is something that we give them. I am sure of that, as I am sure that if we had to wait until we had enough facts about any given thing to establish the truth about it we should wait till doomsday.

Meanwhile we get something which is perhaps more interesting—in the present case "The Ordeal of Mark Twain" and "Mark Twain's America." I submit that the first of these two books tells more about its author than it does about its subject. And I submit the same thing about the second. I might submit, too, that my review of your book tells more about me than it does about you. That is the basis of your objection to it, I think, and I don't know that I can blame you for being irritated. But you were also irritating. You began disputatiously. And I do not see how you can be surprised at disputatious reviews. You might, indeed, be pleased.

If I misrepresented you I am sorry. I had no desire to do so, and certainly no motive for doing so. I am aware that this letter can hardly seem a satisfactory answer to yours. But in the nature of things no letter could be that, and so I close with assurances both of regret and of esteem.

P.S. The *Nation* occasionally prints letters about reviews, and I think it might print one from you. Why not try them? If I did misrepresent you there ought to be a public statement to that effect; you ought to be allowed to say that you believe it—to a larger audience than one.

1. MVD, Review of Bernard DeVoto's
Mark Twain's America, in *Nation*, October
19, 1932, p. 370.

To Mortimer Adler
TLS/P

October 23, 1932   *Falls Village, Connecticut*

You should have been here this evening. I had to answer a letter I got from a guy last week objecting to a review of his book which I had written—I confess it—under your inspiration. The guy is Bernard DeVoto, and his book is "Mark Twain's America." The book professes to be an answer to Van Wyck Brooks's "The Ordeal of Mark Twain," which DeVoto says is only "theory" about M.T. His book on the other hand is the "facts." He is a heap big scholar who "assembles all the facts relating to Mark Twain and then states the conclusions they indicate." Well, I said in the *Nation* that his stuff was theory too without his knowing it—and not very good theory for that reason. I said: "The only thing that can be opposed to a theory consciously held is another theory consciously held." Right? Anyway, here comes a three-page letter from the guy giving me hell and calling my sentence nonsense. I almost sent for you to write my reply. You could have done it beautifully, whereas I did it more or less in the dark. But whatever cogency I achieved, Sir, I owed to you—especially when I was replying to his claim that he had employed "the inductive method." Now don't tell me you have deserted me and gone inductive. Or that you now believe that facts are capable of "indicating conclusions." I would shiver with loneliness in that event. I would not know where to turn. . . .

To Allen Tate
TLS/NjP

November 8, 1932   *Falls Village, Connecticut*

*   *   *

We are beginning—have indeed begun—what promises to be a very satisfactory year up here.[1] So far both Dorothy and I have been completely occupied with jobs around the place, so that the well known intellectual life has languished. But this very circumstance is delightful. I get a great kick out of working outdoors every day until it is too dark to see anything any more, and Dorothy for the first time in ten years is finding out what it is like to be the domestic kind of wife all day long. She says she likes it. So do the boys undoubtedly like what they do and learn and wear. They go to school every morning in this room I am writing in, Dorothy being the teacher; the rest of the day they go about in overalls and look like little roughnecks. . . .

   1. MVD had a sabbatical for the 1932–33 academic year.

To Bernard De Voto
TLS/CSt

November 20, 1932   *Falls Village, Connecticut*

De Voto, often tenacious in his literary debates, was far from convinced by Van Doren's first response. Van Doren, however, was not willing to prolong the disagreement.

I guess we agree pretty well, considering our autobiographies. You see I come from Illinois. My grandparents were pioneers. And I never liked Brooks when he talked about pioneers. It was not until I began reading your book that I ever thought of defending him. To defend him was, I admit, perverse—a thing which I hope I seldom am in reviews. But it also was satisfying to a certain portion of myself which has been under the influence recently of some very good philosophical friends—men of the intellectualist persuasion. They have taught me how much theory there is, even where theory is not easy to see.

For instance—although I don't want to seem to be reaching for the last word—there is not only the fact that you investigated Brooks's theory, and, as you say, exposed its absurdity in 12-point Caslon for our amusement (which I gladly acknowledge). There is also the fact, isn't there, that you and this age had begun to tire of Brooks and his tribe generally? Isn't that implied in your words, "The yeasty liberalism of those days"? Isn't another age invoked when you use words in that way? And mightn't such an age have its point of view as Brooks had his? Furthermore, mightn't this age be a bit more sure that it was objective than its successor might be? In other words, action and reaction are mysterious things, and I am not sure how much the discovery of facts has to do with them. I am not being dogmatic. I am only saying I am not sure. You were too sure, I thought, in your book. That was what I was trying to say. And only that.

I trust that this debate of ours can end some time in conversation. Meanwhile let me assure you that I have enjoyed both of your very good letters.

Before the War
1933–1940

During 1933–1940, the Van Dorens continued to live on Bleecker Street in New York and on the farm near Falls Village, Connecticut. These were years of great productivity for Mark Van Doren: *A Winter Diary, Now the Sky,* and *The Last Look* (all poetry) were published, as well as his *Collected Poems* in 1939, which was to be honored with the Pulitzer Prize the following year. His book on Shakespeare, a distillation of his justly famous course at Columbia, was written in the summer of 1938 and published the following year.

As he made plans for his second Columbia sabbatical, he applied for a Guggenheim Fellowship in order to have a full year to complete a long narrative poem, *The Mayfield Deer,* based on a story by Dr. Hiram Rutherford (1815–1900) who had lived in Oakland, Illinois, not far from Van Doren's boyhood homes. The Guggenheim award was not made, but the Van Dorens spent the entire year in Falls Village on half salary from Columbia.

These were years of Van Doren's great popularity among Columbia students. His courses were large, and students interested in writing poetry found him especially sympathetic. John Berryman, Thomas Merton, and Robert Lax were all students of his at this time and were to become lifelong friends.

To Allen Tate
ALS/NjP

January 19, 1933   *Falls Village, Connecticut*

From Paris, Tate had sent copies of the three poems discussed in this letter.

Your three poems with their (as usual) Westward reference—how thou art tethered, even in thy hate, Oh Allen Tate!—came bringing pleasure. But the pleasure increased as they were read again, and now this evening it increases once more. So I write to praise the last line-and-a-half of *The Meaning of Life* and all of *Picnic at Cassis*.[1]

I am not being invidious. The foregoing parts of *The Meaning of Life* are necessary to the part I praise, and they are of course good. But in them you affect prose to no especial advantage—abandoning the rigid line you once held out for—and are therefore merely clear and interesting. You can be so much more, as for instance you are in *Picnic at Cassis,* all of which is rich and excessive and powerful—one of your best poems so far, I think. *Aeneas at Washington* is a more explicit treatment of a similar theme.[2] While I like it, I keep returning to the quatrains of the *Picnic*. You wield a wicked quatrain. Perhaps it is your form.

Now by God maybe I have paid you for threatening to sack fifteen of my sonnets.

The only question is, which fifteen? I can't wait to hear.

The winter goes swiftly on—too swiftly, and with too little snow to suit the boys, who nevertheless are very happy. So are Dorothy and I, for whom work again will be literal hell. Even at that I am doing a little up here—a few reviews, and now a few short poems. If I feel like it I shall write two longer ones in the spring and summer, a ghost story and a *Winter Diary.* . . .

1. "The Meaning of Life" was published first in *New Verse,* no. 2 (March, 1933), 9–10. "Picnic at Cassis" was published as "The Mediterranean," *Yale Review,* XXII (1933), 474–75.

2. "Aeneas at Washington" was published first in *Hound and Horn,* VI (1933), 445–46.

To Allen Tate
ALS/NjP

February 19, 1933   *Falls Village, Connecticut*

First let me protest against your announcing that "this damned book" is to be dedicated to me. To me by all means, yes; but is it therefore damned? I am delighted, of course, and more curious than ever as to its kind and contents—for it has been "this book" so long, and little more, that I have only the vaguest conception of it. A hint here, a hint there; but I am not sure that the hints have been consistent with one another.[1] In short my curiosity is ravaging me. So hurry along with it, and God be with you till you finish.

You did a magnificent job on the sonnets, and paid me a compliment that I seemed suddenly not quite to deserve. I wish I could discuss your comments one by one. But there is neither time nor paper for that; you will be satisfied, perhaps, to know that I am studying every one of them with care and prayer—acknowledging your wisdom most of the time, admiring your penetration always, and only now and then arguing that you are wrong as hell. Just how the printed book will look—just how many of your marks it will bear—I can't say at the moment, for I am taking my time. But things will be different because of your letter, be sure of that, now and in the future. I mean, you have instructed me. For which my profoundest thanks.

Of course I am not at all confident that this or any other book of mine will ever be published. I have had enough reverses this year to discourage anyone less vain or stubborn. Just now it does look as if John Day *might* bring out the sonnets and the other poems I have been writing over four years. But I am the firmest sort of pessimist, and don't believe anything.

If you are coming home for the summer, and are going to be in New York, I'll be damned if I see why you can't pay us the visit you have been such a piker about for years and years. In fact I shall see that you do. So be warned.

Shadow and Shade is one of your best poems. Don't change it too much, and certainly don't change the first three stanzas, which catapult into poetry a new and bold and beautiful image. Nor, now that I look at it once more, should you change the rest. You see I don't belong to the school of change, or at least in this case I don't.

If I were not so glad to have your criticism of the sonnets I should be sorry that I interrupted your labors to get it. As things stand I merely am grateful—and do not let the brevity of my acknowledgment make you think otherwise.

Send me *Picnic at Cassis* when you have it in another form. And anything else you write—including, if possible, the damned book. . . .

1. This would seem to be a reference to Tate's unpublished novel, first called "The Ancestors" then "Ancestors of Exile." Tate did dedicate his *Selected Poems* (1937) to MVD.

To Allen Tate
TLS/NjP

June 6, 1933   *Falls Village, Connecticut*

I made still another lecture tour after I wrote you. But I am settled for the summer now, and only last night I was encouraged to ponder about you in connection with a hopeless job I was trying to do.

Namely, arrange a volume of poems for the John Day Company, which alone among the publishing houses of New York expresses a willingness to bring it out.[1] Scribner's would have none of it, and so on down the line. For that matter I am not Simon sure about John Day; yet I have reason to hope.

The job I referred to is the job of arranging the poems—which were written over five years—and of deciding which ones to omit. If I had you here, as of course I never shall, I would lock you in a barn and let you out only when you cried through the cracks that the book was ready to mail. For I have confidence in your judgment. Last night, reading once more your marginalia on the sonnets, I was freshly struck by your penetration and rightness. I have made as many of the alterations as I had the wit to make, and I have deleted some—not all—of the sonnets you socked. You will not be satisfied with the result, wholly; but you will be able to discern here and there an improvement mostly of your own making.

What of Merry Mont and les Tate? What of your book or books? Write me for God's sake. And when you do, tell me that you have conveyed my most affectionate greetings to those inhabitants of the Mont whom I met summer before last on a day that I remember with exceeding clearness.

Two letters from Fletcher in Little Rock make it appear that he has done himself a great deal of good by coming home. I have had nothing so cheerful from him since I first knew him—this being partly because of his delight at my having selected only from his later poems for the American anthology. I ignored the chromatic symphonies, etc. The copy of the anthology I sent to France for you was never delivered, the postoffice tells me, because you had left before it arrived. . . .

1. The negotiations with John Day fell through.

To Allen Tate
TLS/NjP

June 29, 1933   *Falls Village, Connecticut*

A word in haste (more or less) to assure you that no ms is being mailed. You are a noble fellow, and I would give a good deal to hear your opinion of this or that masterpiece manqué; but there was only one completely legible ms, and it is with John Day—who, cautious creatures that they are, admit that they almost certainly want to publish it, but insist that they must have weeks and weeks in which to decide when. You would think the world's economic recovery depended upon this issue. I suppose they are in constant cable communication with J. M. Keynes about the matter.

Speaking of John Day, who I believe published Leonie Adams's second book, what have you got to say about her marriage to Bill Troy? I am meeting them at a tea in this neighborhood next week, and if you like I'll report their demeanor to you. All I can say at present is that each of them has married a mad soul—have you ever set eyes on Staring Bill? Not that I don't wish them good luck, and plenty of money for liquor.

The Ancestors I didn't understand at all until I read the title, which for some reason escaped my eye the first few readings.[1] Then it was not only clear but good—one of the best poems you have written since you went down there among the bones. It comes, I reckon, from your being so much engaged with genealogy these days—so *that* is the book!—as well as from your chronic companionship with the past. I assure you that the penultimate line is not true. Me, I never think of my ancestors. But that does not matter. It is your poem, and a mighty good one. Terrible, as you say, and unpatriotic. But what is more important, a poem. So leave it in, and coals be on your head. (Which reminds me to say that I finally omitted six of the sixteen sonnets you stepped on, and fixed up most of the minor ailments you merely touched with a skilful finger.)

Scott Buchanan was here recently and told us of a week in Charlottesville with Eliot as his guest.[2] Eliot came to lecture and was to have been put up at the country club, but followed Scott right home from the train and never willingly left the house except to lecture. He was evidently charming. I wish I could have seen him.

It is almost unbearably hot, even in this study near an ice pond. So I'll let you be—thanking you once more for your offer to read my poems, and urging you as always to write me as often as you can.

Did you mean, by the way, that Nancy had summer complaint? If so, I hope she is better. Give her a kiss for me and tell her of the *Winter Diary* I am writing. The thought of it may do her good, even to the point of lowering temperatures. If she expresses keen interest and curiosity, tell her then that I am doing it in heroic couplets and being decidedly Augustan for a change. . . .

1. "The Ancestors" was originally published in the *New Republic,* November 1, 1933, p. 331.

2. Scott Buchanan was then a member of the University of Virginia faculty.

To John Gould Fletcher
ALS/ArU

August 4, 1933   *Falls Village, Connecticut*

Henry Hazlitt, literary editor of the Nation, *had asked Fletcher for poems but after several months had returned them.*

Hazlitt is first of all a sloven—and perhaps last of all, so you needn't let him make you too downhearted. He kept some sonnets of mine four months this winter without reading them; returned them to my agent (I have an agent during my exile) with a curt note by his secretary; was jumped on for this; asked for them back; and printed eight! What are you going to do with an editor like that? Or—I grant you—like anybody, for they all are mad.

After being given to understand by John Day that they would publish my new book I suddenly heard the other day that they were rejecting it because after four readings they had decided it had nothing to say. Well, my answer was to go right on with still another book I am doing—"A Winter Diary," being an account of our year up here which I am writing for ourselves, alone, in heroic couplets, by God, and let the contemporary boys go hang. I am enjoying it so much that I find I don't care about anything else. You ask whether poetry will come back. I am sure it will— though I don't say when. There were plenty of poets in England in the seventeenth century who found themselves in an even worse fix than ours. But poetry went on, and I am confident that it always will. To say that our generation has killed it is to flatter the generation beyond its deserts. . . .

To Allen Tate
TLS/NjP

December 19, 1933   *New York City*

One reason I hadn't written was that you owed me a couple of letters. Another and better reason was that I was engaged the whole fall with an article on Walt Whitman for the *Dictionary of American Biography*. This was a tough job. One couldn't be too personal, and yet without being reasonably personal one couldn't say anything of value. Also there were hundreds of books to read, most of them worthless. And Whitman to come to some conclusion about. I have just finished the article and sent it off, and am very glad. If you want to know what my estimate of W. is at the moment, I will tell you. Pretty high. He surprised me.

I wanted to write you many times during the fall and ask you about that book of yours on your ancestors. I have seen announcements of it, and have even been asked to review it. But I haven't seen it or found anyone else who has. Have you held it up for some reason? Let me know, for I am really very eager.

The news of the fall and early winter is simply that all the Van Dorens have been homesick for Cornwall. None of us knew how sick New York would make him, I think; at least I didn't, though I was aware of not wanting to leave Cornwall in October. It took a good month to get over the actual physical distress. Since then we have been coasting along, anaesthetized, waiting for May. We have lived quietly on the whole, among other reasons because we are poor, and have seen relatively few people. Therefore I haven't much gossip for you, nor will you care that I haven't.

I should have got you another copy of the American anthology by some device. I am ashamed that you had to wait until it could be a Christmas present. But of course I am glad that you have it and like it. You mustn't praise me for my selections from you—remember, they were picked by an expert. As for the other selections, they may be what you say they are, and indeed I hope they are, yet the book seems to have made no impression—perhaps because the selections were *seriously* made.

Your Christmas poems seem to me at the moment, with none of your others by, among the very best poems you have written.[1] They are wise and old, with a kind of superhuman humor that I find myself liking in more ways than I would like mere wit. Some of the earlier poems you wrote in this autocontemplative vein—I take it that you have been in that vein chiefly since you settled in Clarksville—were brilliant but a little hard. I mean, I suppose, that the hardness in them was occasionally, to borrow a word from Eliot, irrelevant. Here it belongs, and since it belongs it loses its asperity, being perfectly understood. If you don't mind my saying so, these poems are the most perfect expressions of yourself you have ever achieved. You will believe, I am sure, that I am not subscribing to any of the cant about self-expression. You know how I am using the word "self." In other words, I like the poems every way, and in the same way—if you will pardon me again—that I like their author. Send me some more on New Year's Day, St. Valentine's Day, and the Ides of March.

The ten I send you I wrote last winter in Cornwall, being interested at the moment in doing the most abstract and at the same time the most musical thing of which I was capable.[2] I like them, I confess, and want you to. But you will tell me if they should not be liked, and I promise not to abide by your telling—though secretly I suspect I will. A few of them have been published in magazines. Does that rule them out? I wanted you to see them anyway, and so copied them out. This is a tribute which you will underestimate, since neither you nor anyone else will ever know how much I hate to retype poems. If magazine publication disqualifies them for your mysterious purpose, let me know and by that time I may have more. I am not even any too certain which of these have appeared anywhere. I use an agent now, having sickened of editors and publishers.

My father died in October. I went out with two of my brothers and found the other two there—the five of us together for the first time in eleven years. My father's death has affected me in many ways which seem to me strange; so strange, indeed, that I would never think of trying to put it into written words. If I see you reasonably soon I should enjoy talking about it. Enough to say now, perhaps, that the entire world has been changed by the event, and that this is true in spite of the fact that I had seen my father very little in recent years, and had not been conscious of thinking about him very often, though I was devoted to him. I suspect that all of it is something I want very much to write a poem about. How to proceed, however, I do not care to decide. . . .[3]

1. "Sonnets at Christmas (1933)," published later as "Sonnets at Christmas," first appeared in the *New Republic*, December 26, 1934, pp. 185–6.

2. MVD sent ten poems to Tate.
3. MVD wrote about his father in "Here Then He Lay."

To John Gould Fletcher
ALS/ArU

April 19, 1934   *New York City*

So you are a teacher.[1] I hope you like it, and I hope you don't find that it hurts your writing. After 14 years of it myself I am inclined to doubt the old notion that it kills you. Of course I don't *know*. I may have died without realizing it, and who ever knows what he would have been had he done otherwise? My only advice to you, if you keep it up, is to vary your material frequently, so that you will have new things to read and talk about—or rather, *some* new among the old.

I should enjoy reading Long's new book, and I am interested in the "publishing soviet" you allude to, but I couldn't review Long and be consistent with a practice of about five year's standing—namely, of declining to review poetry.[2] This may be shirking my responsibility, but I don't know that I either can or should keep poetry alive if it doesn't know how to live by itself. Not that I think criticism irrelevant or futile, and not, really, that I expect poetry to perish. The truth is that I got tired of doing it and have enjoyed not doing it, and plan never to do it again. Maybe it is vanity—a conviction that I am one to be reviewed, not to review. Anyhow, I got bored by "keeping up" with every new name and movement—and, another sign of advancing age, began to realize that I didn't care for every kind of poetry being written (well) today. I don't read much any more. When I can I write. If this is treason you may hang me. At least I still enjoy your poetry—and so does one of my students, judging by a very favorable section of a paper on modern American poets he recently devoted to you. Without coaching from me he decided, too, that your best book, among many good ones, was "The Black Rock."

I have about given up hope of ever being published again. Boni having come as near folding up as it is possible to come without disappearing, I have been unable to find another publisher willing to take his place. Temporarily it has stopped bothering me, and it has never stopped my writing. In time it may—and in time I may beg permission to join you in a campaign for rehabilitation. But not at the moment. . . .

1. Fletcher was teaching in a junior college in Little Rock, Arkansas.

2. Haniel Long had privately published *Atlantitudes* (Santa Fé, N.M., 1933). Co-operative publishing is the "publishing soviet" being spoken of. Fletcher had had some contact with the group Writers Editions in Santa Fé, New Mexico.

To Allen Tate
TLS/NjP

May 10, 1934   *New York City*

*   *   *

I am not doing much at the moment outside of articles and reviews, which as you know I consider nothing. This summer I hope to write either a long poem or a novel. I haven't decided which, and probably shall not be able to until I get a letter from you telling me. I say I consider articles and reviews nothing. I mean mine. Yours are different. For instance, the other day I ran across your letter to *Poetry* about Hart Crane and read it again. Now there is a piece of writing.[1]

I enclose a poem I wrote about my father in December.[2] No comment is expected; I send it merely in order that you may have some notion of how I regarded him. It comes far from saying what could and should have been said.

1. "Hart Crane and the American   2. "Here Then He Lay."
Mind," *Poetry*, XL (1932), 210–16.

To Carl Van Doren
ALS/NjP
July 1, 1934   *Falls Village, Connecticut*

＊　＊　＊

Friday was a good day too, since it brought a letter saying that Macmillan's will publish all my unpublished poems—the *Diary*, the Sonnets, and the short ones—in one big volume. I am so happy that I am perfectly calm.

To Allen Tate
TLS/NjP
February 17, 1935   *New York City*

I wrote Ransom that I couldn't come to Nashville next year.[1] It would have been pleasant for many reasons, chief among them being that you and Caroline would have been within reach. But there were many complications; I am, in effect, immovable. That is a poor thing for one to be, I admit, but at the moment I can't see how to be otherwise.

Incidentally I made it clear to Ransom what my chief reason for regret was, and added a few words which I hoped would lodge in his mind, and in that of the university, the thought that you are the prophet to be considered. Save, of course, that it is your own country. I wish they had the gumption to bring you flying from Memphis. Is it possible that they will?

I must confess that I didn't get much satisfaction out of your reply to my question about a Northern job. For instance, when I brought your name up in a conference we were having at Columbia Friday afternoon, and after I had been pleased to hear that some of the professors wanted to send for you immediately, I realized that I didn't know and couldn't say whether you would entertain the thought. At bottom, I suspect, I harbor a guilty feeling, as if it would be somehow treason to you to drag you so far away from home. But maybe that is nonsense. At any rate, you might let me know what your general sentiments are about teaching at Columbia. The job in question, incidentally, is merely an instructorship which would pay $2400 (I think) and which would mean ten hours of teaching a week, six of them in freshman courses—not composition, since we don't teach freshman composition, but a sort of introduction to literature. This is not an "offer," you understand. It is only a request for a statement as to your probable or possible desire, so that I would know what I was talking about if I brought the matter up again, as naturally I should like to. Columbia is for me at any rate an easy place to teach, and the students are not at all bad. Well, if this interests you, let me know.

Eda Lou is an idiot, but Genevieve Taggard,[2] who reviewed me in the *Herald-Tribune* this morning, is doubly one. Very depressing, I assure you.

1. MVD had been invited to Vanderbilt to fill in for a professor on leave.
2. Eda Lou Walton reviewed Tate's *Poems: 1928–1931* in the *Nation*, May 4, 1932, p. 519. Genevieve Taggard gave *A Winter Diary* a mixed review in the New York *Herald-Tribune Books*, February 17, 1935, p. 4.

To Allen Tate
TLS/NjP

March 22, 1935   *New York City*

Tate had been appointed lecturer in English at Southwestern University in Memphis. He had taken the place of Robert Penn Warren, who had gone to Louisiana State University to help found the Southern Review.

A very noble letter, Sir, which I lack the brains to answer in kind. Not that there is anything to answer, for I think you have said everything, and stated the difference between us so accurately that it almost ceases to be a difference. What more natural, if we are both poets, than that our circles should only slightly intersect? I thank God they intersect at all; and wish I could write something intelligible about *your* poetry. I was to lecture about it at Hunter College this spring, but the series (Léonie was to appear also) fell through for lack of funds. I was going to see if I could say anything that way, and then, if I could, discover or create an occasion to speak in print. Of course the greatest difference between us is that you start with an inner complication. I'm not sure that I start with anything except a desire to write a poem. I told you in my last that I put thoughts and feelings in. But I do not start with a consciousness of them. They come in only too profusely as I proceed.

I forgot to tell you before that I agree with you about The Eyes.[1] It took that moral turn without my wanting it to, and though I tried to bring it back to pure ghostliness I found I couldn't; it was quite as if the wand were being turned in my hand—by the ghost himself, perhaps, if ghosts can be so perverse. Now you wouldn't have printed it under the circumstances; or wouldn't have tried to finish it. I finish everything, though I don't print everything. Maybe I can learn from you how not to stick my mistakes out to the end.

I suppose you know that The Mediterranean is becoming a more and more famous poem. For instance, I have here Ford's new book, dedicated to you and Caroline and built in a loose way around the poem—which, by the way, seems singularly beautiful in all that context.[2] I mean by singularly, newly; and I suspect that any context would do it. In other words, it is a poem capable of growing after it has left the author's head. In still other words, it is good.

Fletcher brings it into his notice of you in the *Westminster Magazine,* which he recently sent to me.[3] I wrote him then, perhaps absurdly, that the evidence of these notices, plus the evidence of his Incantations, plus the evidence of several really decent letters from him of late, had got me to thinking hopefully of him, and thinking that he had after all come back to America with something to say. Now your letter casts me down. He is probably hopeless. Not that my spirits stand or fall by whether he is or not. But I was grateful for what seemed to be an opportunity to write him a pleasant letter. You simply remind me of the old truth, that he is not to be lived with. Don't, by the way, regret your paragraph concerning him. It should have been no news to me, and in fact at this distance it is amusing.

I am sure there is a book in your articles and reviews, and it is a good sign to me that you think so. Send it to Perkins as you say, without correspondence; of course he will publish it.[4] And I for one shall be glad to have it, the reason in my case being partly that I have never been able to keep up with your criticism. I have heard of more than I have read, distinctly to my loss. . . .

1. Probably a reference to the poem "The Last Look" in MVD's *The Last Look and Other Poems.*

2. Ford Madox Ford dedicated *Provence: From Minstrels to the Machine* (Philadelphia, 1935) to the Tates.

3. "The Modern Southern Poets," *Westminster Magazine,* XXIII (1935), 229–51.

4. Maxwell Perkins was an editor at Charles Scribner's Sons. Scribner's published Tate's *Reactionary Essays on Poetry and Ideas* in 1936.

To Mortimer Adler
TLS/P

April 13, 1935   *New York City*

Didn't I tell you, or rather didn't you believe me when I told you?[1] Of course the trustees didn't pass the promotions until April 1, but this catalogue you saw was even then ready to come out, and did indeed come out the next day. I take pleasure in your congratulations, Sir, but the pleasure I take in the thing itself is somewhat diminished by Raymond's failure to be advanced—particularly since mine seems to have been the result of his literally heroic efforts for me, with McBain and others.[2] There is the additional irony that he wanted it worse than I did, and was more confident he would get it. The gentle lightnings seem to have struck rather haphazardly on the whole—Neff was advanced with me, for instance, and I. Edman is by the same decree full professor.

The fundamental satisfaction I feel is over the apparent decision of the department to accept me on my own terms—not as a scholar, not as a politician, not as a useful person in any sense, but simply as a teacher and a poet. This gives me a real feeling of security and freedom on the Heights; it is nice, I mean, not to wonder what they are expecting from me. They are expecting nothing beyond what I like and want to do. They have made this plain, mind you. . . .

1. MVD had been promoted to ass   2. Raymond Weaver was MVD's col-
ate professor of English.   league at Columbia.

To John Berryman
ALS/MnU

July 2, 1935   *Falls Village, Connecticut*

John Berryman entered Columbia in 1932 and was greatly influenced by Van Doren. For a perceptive account of Berryman's college years, see John Haffenden's The Life of John Berryman *(Boston, 1982). Berryman said of Van Doren: "If during my stay at Columbia I had met only Mark Van Doren and his work, it would have been worth the trouble. It was the force of his example, for instance, that made me a poet."*[1]

This won't be a magnificent letter, even were I capable. For I haven't recovered yet from the trip, which was fun but strenuous—500 miles one day, for instance, and 400 another.

I can tell you, though, not to mind what *Poetry* says. Go on and strain. Naturalness will come later. It would be shocking for you to be natural now, as it would be for you to know everything about death and women. This is the time to strain—i.e., to pull at yourself until you assume the shape which is to be yours uniquely and permanently. Only God knows what that is. I don't want to know, even if Delphic Harriet does.[2]

The poems you sent I am returning because of the priceless words you will find on some of the margins. Those words don't mean that I didn't like the lot as a whole very much. I did, even when I underlined certain phrases as questionable. As usual, pay as little attention or as much as seems reasonable.

My regards to Halliday and Aylward.[3] But you and Aylward are advised not to take my lectures. I'm sure they won't be worth it, and I don't say that to be contradicted. . . .

1. John Haffenden, *The Life of John Berryman* (Boston, 1982), 72.

2. *Poetry* had rejected a group of Berryman's poems, commenting, "We recognize the quality here, but I think you have strained too hard for your effects" (Haffenden, *The Life of John Berryman*, 73). Harriet Monroe was editor of *Poetry*.

3. Halliday and Aylward were undergraduates at Columbia. Stephen Aylward was to enter and then leave a Catholic religious order. Milton Halliday became an editor of *American Heritage*.

To Allen Tate
ALS/NjP

October 3, 1935   *New York City*

I have sent Warren the poems—plenty of them, I hope—and now you may put in your oar, if you are still so minded.[1]

Among the mail I found at Columbia was an announcement from the Alcestis Press which prompts me to ask—indelicately—whether the copy of "The Mediterranean" you are sending is a free one. At their prices I hope it is—indeed, I insist that it be. A free one, I mean of course, for you.

The Mediterranean is a noble poem and one of your best (you sent me a MS., remember, from France), but it is wholly characteristic of you and hence not different in kind from many other good poems you have written.[2] Don't pay such people no mind is what I say. Not that I have the right to give brave advice, since I can be blasted as easily as anyone, and most easily by some well-meaning ass who slanders with kindness. . . .

My agent (I have one because I can't bear to have direct relations with these publishing bastards) is looking for a more perceptive house, and promises me she won't let me know anything until the novel is accepted— or until she has decided it will never be.

Meanwhile I teach, as you do, and bother myself with scarcely anything else, it being something of a relief for me to hear the chain snap and the ball drag—for a while at least.

1. The poems were sent to Robert Penn Warren, one of the editors of the *Southern Review*.

2. The poem was then titled "Picnic at Cassis."

To Robert Frost
ALS/NhD

October 5, 1935   *New York City*

I am sending you my last book, "A Winter Diary and Other Poems," and the back numbers will follow after a decent interval.

If I had not been given to understand on Wednesday that you wanted a quiet lunch I would certainly have come along sooner, for there is nobody I would rather see than you, and there is still something I want to tell you about your poems. You asked me if they stood up. I say, the best of all. The article I spoke of, by the way, seems not to have appeared.[1] When it does I'll send you a copy.

I hear you are lecturing in New York soon, on Thursdays. I don't know how busy you will be, or how many people will be after you, and I am anxious not to add anything to the complications of the city. But you know you are welcome here for any amount of time you could spend with Dorothy and me, and we both urge you to let us know if and when you can come, for dinner or anything, as often as you like.

1. Probably a reference to MVD's "The Permanence of Robert Frost," which appeared in *American Scholar*, V (1936), 190–98. This essay was included in Richard Thornton's *Recognition of Robert Frost* (New York, 1937).

To Allen Tate
ALS/NjP

November 18, 1935   *New York City*

Let me tell you in haste that Warren, much to my surprise, has (a) accepted about 15 poems (b) said he was going to ask Howard Baker for the critical note.[1] I don't know much or anything about Baker, but that's not the point; you were to have done it. I haven't said anything to Warren because I didn't know what you had said to him, or whether there had been an understanding. If there was none, I suppose nothing can happen now. But in that case I remember the 80 bucks and mourn.

1. The *Southern Review*, I (1935–36), 584–600, published MVD's "Winter Tryst," "Sin of Omission," "The Bundle," "Two of You," "Private Worship," "Is This the Man," "Millenium," "Old Landscape," "The Last Look," "Neighbor Girl," and "Animal-Worship." Howard Baker in "A Note on the Poetry of Mark Van Doren,"

Southern Review, I (1935–36), 601–608, said that MVD's "most important poems . . . are psychological lyrics which trace out some portions of the obscure inner fabric of human beings, and which, in a way, are artistic counterparts to the formulations of certain modern psychologists."

To Allen Tate
ALS/NjP

November 26, 1935   *New York City*

Again in haste (life isn't worth it, this pace) let me tell you that I have written Warren saying in effect that although I had expected you to be the critic I realized how far his plans for Baker had gone and that I had no desire to interfere with them, or at any rate no intention. You see, Baker must actually have finished his note by this time—they are rushing to make the December issue—and to change anything now might be to change everything. Having been an editor, I take last-minute changes seriously. Meanwhile I appreciate your good words about Baker, and trust that ultimately you don't much mind.

Good luck with the Alcestis MS.—but don't alter anything beyond recognition.[1] I would say, don't alter anything, but I know how little effect that would have.

By no means throw away your introduction to the critical volume. I tell you, man, it is hunky-dory—or, if you prefer, okey-dokey. It is almost true that if I don't find it in the book I will refuse to read the book. Does that jar you? I hope so. . . .

1. Tate's *The Mediterranean and Other Poems* was published in New York by the Alcestis Press in 1936.

To Howard Baker
ALS/P

December 28, 1935   *New York City*

I am not a psychologist, and my intentions were always simpler than you say.[1] But I have waited fifteen years for such criticism as this. Nothing like it has happened to me before, and I am so grateful that you will scarcely find me articulate.

My intentions, of course, are irrelevant. I recognize the accuracy of your description of what is there to see. You *are* talking about the poems, and what you say is immensely interesting, as well as convincing. Furthermore, by your dissection of the longer poems you have confirmed me in what has hitherto been a vague suspicion—namely, that after I have completed the series of lyrics represented by these you discuss my business, perhaps for the rest of my days, should be and will be to write a long poem—a real one, which will stand up. Now don't be horrified. I know the hazards. And I shall not mind failing. But I have written enough short poems—more would be simply more—and a big project is worth while even if it never becomes more than a project. It will be something to think about, to read for, and to center life about.

That sounds rather dramatic, and for all I know I will commit defections. But it is a program, and I thank you for it.

1. See Baker's "A Note on the Poetry of Mark Van Doren," *Southern Review,* I (1935–36), 601–608.

To Allen Tate
TLS/NjP

January 10, 1936   *New York City*

You know perfectly well I never called you a classicist. I don't use the word—I haven't the slightest idea what it means. Evidently Jim and I wrote you the same evening—and on that evening, I believe, you were writing us, or at any rate me.[1]

Strange, but one of the things I sat down to discuss with you the other day was Flint's review of you.[2] I hadn't seen the book, but that didn't matter; I was going to say that while he was interesting he was only about half right. Now you put your finger on the half that is wrong, so I don't need to. But I hasten to agree that it is nice to be written about. I almost never have been, outside of your reviews; indeed I can say never, outside of them. And it suddenly is clear to me that the accuracy of the critic on a certain level is of no importance. For instance, I am no psychologist, and my intentions were almost never what Baker said they were. Yet as description he was often good, and as analysis when he wasn't stepping beyond the bounds of *literary* analysis. Did Flint, by the way, ever hear of the genealogical work you projected and got part of the way with? If not, he's a good guesser; but I suspect him of knowing. And I say with him that I want some day to see such a book.

I don't know Baker's poetry, and confess myself unable to decide where to look for it. Could you steer me?

Why don't you send your proofs on Property?[3] I know even less about it, but I can tell you about your rhetoric perhaps. I use the word in its noblest, its medieval, sense.

Now I spend my days in looking forward to your poems and your book of criticism.[4] If it has become inconvenient for you to give me a copy of the poems for any reason, don't hesitate to say so. Of course you know I have only one reason in mind. Then I'll cheerfully subscribe for my own copy. Meanwhile Berryman, the young man I spoke of in my last letter, is "studying" you, and he will want to study the new work as soon as he can get it away from me. He came to me today with the most serious look on his face—as if there were a tripod in the room—and said: "Mr. Van Doren, you know Tate is one of the very best poets we have!"

"Sure," I said.

1. James Rorty had earlier brought Robinson Jeffers' poetry to MVD's attention.

2. F. Cudworth Flint reviewed Tate's *The Mediterranean and Other Poems* in *Southern Review*, I (1935–36), 660–70.

3. Tate's "Notes on Liberty and Property," *American Review*, VI (1936),

596–611 was reprinted in Herbert Agar and Allen Tate (eds.), *Who Owns America?* (Boston, 1936).

4. *The Mediterranean and Other Poems* (New York, 1936) and *Reactionary Essays on Poetry and Ideas* (New York, 1936).

To Carl Van Doren
TLS/NjP

February 2, 1936   *New York City*

*   *   *

I have just finished the hardest job I ever do—assembling and arranging a volume of poems. The *Southern Review* (run, I fear, with some of Huey's money[1]) printed eleven pieces in the Winter issue with an accompanying article on their author by Howard Baker of California. This is the first article about me and not a bad one; but the pernt is that the Alcestis Press, on the promise of these eleven, asked for a volume to go in their series of very high hat honeys at $7.50 a copy, limited to 165 copies, etc., with no strings on trade publication after six months. Well, I was cute enough to have Nannine Joseph[2] ask Macmillan what they thought of this, and they said: No! Six months! Too long a time! We may want to publish this book next January. They probably will back out before it is done, but at any rate I am sending them the MS. tomorrow. These are the last poems I intend to write for years, and perhaps the last short ones. I have an idea that I want to spend several years, perhaps the rest of my effective days, getting ready to write a good long one. But we'll see about that.

Have you heard about the citizen who was stopped in Washington as he went about muttering: "The President's a son of a bitch"? He said to the policeman who stopped him: "Oh, you misunderstand me. I mean President Calles of Mexico." "You can't fool me," said the policeman. "There's only one country got a son of a bitch for a president."[3]

1. Huey Long was governor of Louisiana, 1928–31.

2. Nannine Joseph was MVD's agent.

3. MVD, however, was an admirer of President Franklin D. Roosevelt.

To Allen Tate
TLS/NjP

February 13, 1936   *New York City*

Now that Dorothy and Caroline have discussed the New York week I can say from the sidelines how glad I am that both of you are staying here, and how sorry I am that Nancy isn't. If you want to consider bringing her at all, remember that she would be welcome at Cornwall during the week in question. I could come down to meet you and take her up with me, and you could come up when you got through telling the people about poetry. The weather is almost certain to be good for her, and the boys—well, I won't promise that they will be polite to her, but I can assure her that they want her there. As for yourself and Caroline, plan to spend either the week before or the week after the lectures with us in the country, or both. Simply let us know when you decide, and remember that you cannot stay too long. Not possibly. And let me explain that my own desire to see Nancy is not merely the desire to see a or your child. I like her personally, very much. She was one of my best hostesses at Clarksville those years ago. All in all, young man with the black family past, it is eleven years since we sat at Times Square and discussed Wordsworth, you having hobbled down from Patterson on frostbitten toes. Not ten.

The Rorty situation is one of those hellish ones of which we shall have more and more as the classes war.[1] I broke out here the other evening and told him he didn't understand a tenth of the things he said, and Dorothy from her corner thought he was going to come at me with his shillaly. The fact that he called me a few evenings later and asked me to come over so that his wife could hear me say those things again, she having relished his version of the battle, was not especially encouraging. He thinks he understands, but he doesn't. Not that I understand much about all this myself. It is very confusing and depressing, and I sympathize both with you and with your president—all the more because Jim means so Irish well. I hope there is no permanent embarrassment, and that the university loses no endowment; but look out, for this will happen again, with or without Rorty. I like him too, and told him so; I merely wanted him to stick in his conversation to what he knew had meaning. Incidentally, I didn't go over to repeat my performance for Winifred.

The Alcestis Press (run, it appears, by one of my old students who has changed his name from Leippert to Latimer) has asked me to publish some poems with them. But upon investigation I find that Macmillan doesn't want to postpone their volume that long—I mean the volume of which the *Southern Review* poems would be a part. And between the two I prefer the trade publication, though I should like it if both were possible. Macmillan will probably bring the collection out (called since your letter *Millennium*) in January next. And that, you will be glad to hear, is my last collection of short poems. I have written enough. If they are no good, more wouldn't be better, and if they are some good there isn't need for more. No, I have my eye on a long poem now, to be finished perhaps ten years from now, or at the most twenty, and to be distinguished by its profundity, its usefulness to this age, and its consummate art. What say?

Dorothy says baloney; says I'll never be able to stop writing short ones. We'll see. We'll see, that is, whether after *Millennium* Mr. Allen Tate ever again has an opportunity to slur my fecundity publicly. He has always averred that I wrote too much. Let my ambition be then to make him cry out because I write too little. I can hear him.

Some day Fletcher will take away the wife of a man who really wants her, and then where will his body be found?

Monk's book on the sublime, which I have been reading for Warren, seems to me very good, and I am only waiting for a hunch as to how to discuss it for the *Review*.[2] Tell him for me, if you think he would be interested, that I welcome him into that small band of Ph.D.'s who know or care what literature is about; who actually like it, by God.

What would you think—at your leisure—of a Selected or Collected Poems by M.V.D., to be published perhaps in 1940? And if Collected, should *Jonathan Gentry* be between the same covers with the short ones? Macmillan tentatively, oh so tentatively, propose two books, one *J.G.* and the other *Poems*. In any case, of course, I wouldn't reprint everything. There would be plenty of death.

But table the question until August. We can allude to it then. Meanwhile my thanks for some very kind remarks concerning *Millennium* and *Animal-Worship*.

1. In the spring of the preceding year, Tate had taken Rorty to a community called Marked Tree, near Memphis, for Rorty to study landowner-tenant relations. Rorty argued with a preacher about tenant relationships, and later a group from Marked Tree visited the president of Southwestern, where Tate was teaching, threatening to release a statement branding Tate as a communist. Tate then threatened to sue for libel, and apparently no accusation was ever released. Tate, though, was concerned that the unfounded charge of his being a communist would be detrimental to the local fund-raising drive being conducted for Southwestern.

2. For the review of Samuel H. Monk's *The Sublime: A Study of Critical Theories in XVIII-Century England,* see *Southern Review,* I (1935–36), 904–905.

To John Berryman
ALS/MnU

March 12, 1936   *New York City*

Confined to his bed by an ear abscess, Berryman sent Van Doren a lyric beginning, "On a winter night."

Now I tall dat a dood pome. Abscess makes the art grow grander.[1] But I read in the papers that you live in New Jersey. How come? How go?

Didn't I tell you to stay home? But Hamlet and I are both sorry about your ear, and won't preach. Simply remember—abscess thee from criticity until everything, absolutely everything, is all right again.

1. John Haffenden provides this important information about Berryman's illness: "Early in 1936 he began suffering from strain and fatigue which was further complicated by a dangerous ear infection. He was in such pain that he underwent an emergency operation to open an abscess, and the doctor advised Mrs. Berryman to withdraw her son from college at once, 'as the boy was on the edge of complete breakdown'" (*The Life of John Berryman,* 75). Mrs. Berryman did not follow that advice because Berryman was hoping to be appointed to the Kellett Fellowship to Cambridge.

To John Gould Fletcher
ALS/ArU

March 24, 1936   *New York City*

. . . I shall not mix business with the pleasure of this letter, whose purpose was, is, and shall be to congratulate you upon your marriage, and to felicitate your bride.

The news was a complete surprise to me, and very good news indeed.

You never wrote me a completely cheerful letter before. But you did this time, and I cannot say too forcibly how happy I am that you are happy.[1]

1. Fletcher had recently married Charlie May Simon.

To Allen Tate
TLS/NjP

April 23, 1936   *New York City*

A better review is undoubtedly R. P. Blackmur's, which I haven't seen yet but which will appear in the *Columbia Review* next week.[1] I'll send you a copy. It seems that Blackmur has been persuaded to come down from Boston to be guest of honor at a Columbia poetry reading, and that when he was asked what book if any he would like to review for the occasion he wired promptly: Tate's Reactionary Essays. Berryman, your admirer, says it is a fine job, and I have little doubt that it is. Meanwhile I bask in your approval of my really very simple-minded analysis. (The praise as such was profound.)

All I know about Latimer is this. He never asked me for holographs, but he came here recently to talk about a book for the Alcestis Press—which may or may not come off, since my agent told me today that she had heard nothing from him for weeks. I scarcely remembered him as a student, though I did remember disliking and distrusting him for some obscure reason. I asked him pointblank why he had changed his name and he said it was because he wanted his mother's rather than his father's—also, there was Latimer money if he denied his origin. He seems to have little enough money now, and I suspect that that is why he has disappeared, if he has. The chances are that I shall not publish with him.

But the worst thing he has done has been to delay *Mediterranean*. I asked him about that too—six weeks ago—and he put it off on the rascally printer. I'm sure he is fertile at excuses, and generally pretty slick; though he does seem devoted to poetry. Not that I like people who go around being devoted to poetry. I never trust them, any more than Shakespeare did—witness Faulconbridge, Hotspur, Hamlet, Jaques, fine poets who loathed, or affected to loathe, the very thing they will always live by. That's the attitude if you want an attitude.

I'll inquire about Latimer and let you know what I hear. But I warn you that my inquiries to date have dug up little positive knowledge. I do hope that *Mediterranean* is only postponed, and I honestly believe it is. But how long?

1. Blackmur's review of Tate's *Reactionary Essays* was reprinted in Blackmur's   *Language as Gesture* (New York, 1952), 341–47.

To Allen Tate
TLS/NjP

May 7, 1936   *New York City*

Mark Van Doren had received a note from Nannine Joseph, his agent, informing him that Alcestis Press was unable to do his book until the following January. Van Doren sent her note to Tate.

You will see from this that Miss Joseph (my agent) has finally heard from Alcestis. But she tells me over the phone that the letter was signed by Willard Maas, not Latimer; so there is still no news of Latimer. She says, however, that Maas speaks of their program as in process of going forward, and I take this to mean that your book will come out. As for mine, no. The delay would shift the Macmillan date ahead six months, and God knows what they would do with that leeway, considering that they have been known to change their minds in six minutes. I gave Blackmur the top of your message the other evening, and he was pleased. A nice person, very Bostonian, with the smallest mouth I have ever seen, a mere whistle vent, matched perfectly by a mustache seven-sixteenths of an inch in diameter, and circular. Probably explains the special quality of his seriousness.

To Allen Tate
ALS/NjP

July 15, 1936   *Falls Village, Connecticut*

Since I wrote you last "The Mediterranean" has come and Dorothy has brought from New York the copy of the *S.R.* containing Flint's review of "Reactionary Essays." [1] So I am up on you unless you have published another volume since the 4th of July.

   A second reading of the poems has made one thing clear about them and you. Tate lives in Eternity. He calls it Tennessee and even affects the local speech, but the landscape is his very own—immense and motionless, and contorted with grimaces (originally volcanic) at the antics of that fellow Time. Time has built Troy, washed Aeneas to Lavinia's land, elected Jackson, laid out Confederate cemeteries, and brought Progress to the South; it has paused here and there to set love affairs going, to put small boys up to tricks which they will remember as men, and to make Edmund Wilson write "Axel's Castle"; oh, it has performed a million acts, and Tate's book is about several of them. But his gaze is never upon the act itself. It is on its temporal environment—an environment vastly conceived and ruthlessly understood. What scoriac diet has this man been given by the Gods, what granite carved his eyes? Cudworth Flint puts a good question to Tate about religion and time, and I think I know how Tate will answer it as a critic. As a poet he has already answered it. Religions are environed too—ringed round with stretches of before and after, and there is absolutely nothing to be done about it.

You may not have gathered from the above paragraph that I was praising your poems for their temporal magnitude. I was, and could praise them for many other things—for their wit, their stony music, and their frequently fine effect of casualness when important things are being said. But I will particularize along those lines when you are here and can escape to the corn patch if you please. Pausing only to record that on July 15 the best ones in my opinion are the 1st (a wonderful poem, truly), the 2nd, the 3rd, the 4th, the 6th, the 7th (certainly), the 8th, the 9th, the 10th, and the 14th. You will see from this list that the *causeries* strike me least forcibly. Well, we shall see if they haven't stolen into another position by August. Even today, of course, they stand high. . . .

1. F. Cudworth Flint reviewed Tate's *Reactionary Essays* in "Contemporary Criticism," *Southern Review*, II (1936–37), 208–224.

To John Gould Fletcher
ALS/ArU

August 6, 1936   *Falls Village, Connecticut*

*   *   *

Allen is coming next week and will bring the *Southern Review* prize poems. I don't know at all that we can agree on anything, but at any rate this is the way to do it, as votes by mail are almost as absurd as prize contests themselves. As for your not being represented, I am sorry—and suspect that you exaggerate when you imply that Allen is glad. He is giving some lectures at Columbia this week, and when I see him (and Caroline) it will be for the first time in five years.

I am delighted to hear that you got so far along with your memoirs. I have often thought of them since our lunch in New York and am still convinced that they will be important and interesting. I hope you remembered to be personal.

It was a great pleasure to meet your wife, and to see you so happy in her presence. I am sure she has worked some magic on you which was long overdue. Please give her my warmest regards. . . .

To John Berryman
TLS/MnU

August 12, 1936   *Falls Village, Connecticut*

Tate and Van Doren were judges for the Southern Review *Poetry Prize. Berryman submitted "Ritual at Arlington."*

Reflect a moment and you will see that Tate and I cannot open the large envelope which came from you this morning. Not only would it tell us which one your poem is; it would mean that you had had the advantage over the others of revision. Reflect further and realise that the more you do about all this the less chance your poem has. As things are now, as soon as we are sure that we have your poem in our hands psychology and honor will begin operating against you. For God's sake, forget it. That is my advice, as it is Tate's.

He enjoyed seeing you in New York, and says he will telephone you tomorrow about The Mediterranean. But he joins me in urging you to control yourself about this matter of the prize so that nature can take its course.

To John Berryman
TLS/MnU

August 18, 1936   *Falls Village, Connecticut*

When are you sailing? Under the pressure of many guests—three of whom, the Buchanans, are coming back today for lunch on their way to New Hampshire—and under the tension of waiting with Tate for the Southern Review poems—which have not arrived even now, though he had to go yesterday—I must confess that I lost sight for a time of the ship and the tall, excellent young man on it, waving farewell to his land and city. Above all now I feel I must make sure that this letter, rather than the one last week, is the one you will remember. That was written under pressure too—to catch a certain mail—and since you have not answered it I am afraid I can assume it meant too much. It did mean what it said, but no more; and what it said was of no permanent importance. You must realize that I understood your enthusiasm very clearly, and intended no more than to protect both you and us from a self-consciousness which after all is the curse of any contest. When I consider how little I believe in contests I wonder why I ever got drawn into this one. Oh well, forget it. And be sure that I will read your poem with the most affectionate care, and with all the criticism of which I am capable, when I know which it is. I'll write you about it, too; either to New York or to Cambridge. It has my curiosity up, you know; perhaps too much so in the present situation. Meanwhile, I sit waiting for the big package from Baton Rouge.

When are you sailing? Let me know. If soon, or right away, this will be the parting shot of love from Dorothy, the boys, and myself; and the final message from me bearing upon the importance of your enjoying yourself in England. If not soon, then there will be another delivering a similar salvo but coming precisely in season. At any rate, this says that you are a good guy and a good poet; that Tate thinks so too (and that he is never wrong); and that Columbia College is going to be barren bricks this winter.

To John Berryman
TLS/MnU

September 8, 1936   *Falls Village, Connecticut*

Montreal is no place to write a man, and anyway you are on your way home now.[1] So this to 115th Street, and may your vacation have done all sorts of blessed things to one who a few weeks ago jumped when he opened a letter and read the word honor. How about it, didn't you see the quotation marks? They were faint I admit, but they were there. And where were you? Up a nerve tree, picking tantrums. No, this isn't fair. But to hell with it, and on to the poem.

Which I am not going to write you a critical article about, because a good one would take many pages and you wouldn't want anything less than a good one, even supposing I could write it. I would I were in Blackmur now, wherever he may be; I would I were in Blackmur now, or else he were in me. You will be sorry of course, as I am, that Tate and I couldn't read Ritual at Arlington together. You see how we couldn't, don't you? And so far there has been no time for him to write me about it, since all our correspondence has been about how to make our prize lists converge on a winner. You may or may not enjoy hearing that Ritual averaged on our two lists the fifth place among forty-five poems; and it may do you good to know that in our present bleariness it could well be higher still. The point is that both of us must have liked it greatly. Believe that I did. It is a noble poem; much your maturest thing to date; and concerned with something vastly more important than Arlington itself. Something, I should say, called Death; and the best set of parallels (your word) along which to sight at the thing called Life. A noble poem, I repeat, for which I admire you enormously.

All of the revisions that I can recognize are good save one. Or is it a revision—there at the bottom of page 1? "As if a light he hadn't known was on"—now I ask you, does that lie down with the fierce latinity before and after? "On" is too colloquial, I think, for its really august context. Your progress throughout is by way of a series of statements made with magnificent indirection, in symbols of permanent bronze. This "as if" line interrupts the progress, and like so many lines of its kind could come out. I am not picking. I am only saying how high the poem holds itself in every other place.

Some day it might not hurt to consider your latinity. I like it; am familiar with it; know you by it; but do not care to imagine its ever becoming a manner with you. Don't believe me at once or ever, perhaps. Simply consider; and perhaps try now and then the bonier music of monosyllables.

I am not saying goodbye, for I expect to see you on Morningside Heights about the 25th. You say the 20th, but you must mean November. I am speaking for Dorothy now. If I am wrong, drop me a line to say so and I will come through with steamerbaskets of farewell, with tugboatblasts of God (no reservations) be with you. So say we all, your young boy friends included.

I forgot to say that if you want to send Tate the Mediterranean his address is Care of Andrew Lytle, Monteagle, Tennessee.

1. Berryman vacationed in Canada before sailing for England.

To John Gould Fletcher
ALS/ArU

September 27, 1936   *New York City*

I am back here at last . . . and am proceeding to drop *The Legend* into the mail.[1] But before it leaves let me say that I found among many other things here your *Epic of Arkansas,* and have just finished reading it.

I envy you the opportunity to appear before such an audience and in such a form.[2] If more poets had this kind of opportunity today we should have a new kind of poetry—or perhaps many new kinds. But at any rate we should have a living art. Your poem is very much alive as a whole, and I enjoyed it. At times it was rough going as verse, but I dare say you had more than the verse in mind. You had the idea and the movement. These are real, especially in the parts dealing with De Soto, Jefferson, the Civil War, and Reconstruction. I am not sure that you gain throughout by varying your measure. I am beginning to believe—in the face of *Jonathan Gentry*—that the effort should be made to sustain a single measure, even at the risk of monotony. This, however, is debatable; and the burst of lyricism with which you close the Civil War would be your best argument against me. Incidentally, I am curious about the reception of the poem among the people for whom it was written.

I am not settled here yet, and scarcely know which necessary chore to do first. It is always melancholy moving back from the country. You and your wife are lucky in having another month at Peterborough. Best luck to the memoirs (how long is the beard?) and as always my best regards to the magician.

1. An editor had lost Fletcher's "The Legend of the Western Dawn," and MVD sent back his typed copy.

2. Fletcher's poem appeared in the Little Rock *Arkansas Gazette,* June 15, 1936, pp. 1–25.

To John Berryman
TLS/MnU

October 20, 1936   *New York City*

For a man who hates letter-writing you have done nobly. I am not sure that I hate it. Indeed I think I like it. But only after I am settled to the task, as now, and begin to see somebody at the other end who makes it after all not a task. Try to see me as something less than that, and fire away whenever you are ready; I shall always be very happy to hear from you. Charlie, by the way, values your letters if only for their stamps—you know, the new ones of King Simpson.[1] He cuts them off and takes them to a girl at school whose father is not so favored from England. But let me add that Charlie and Johnny both like your letters for themselves; appreciate your greetings at the close; and never tire of asking how big you are now. So, what with Dorothy interested too, we are a good audience.

I hope you like London better the next time. There are plenty of places in it where you never think of traffic, and on the whole it is my favorite city next to New York. It is very beautiful, I think, as well as fascinating in its perverse, clammy, stinking, foggy way. Remember, however, that I lived there for months, and that it takes time to fall in love with it. When or if you do, let me know what you think its smell is. It is compounded of many simples, and you must make a list of them for me. I suggest tobacco, damp dust, and the bones of dead poets; but there are many more.

Next to London I liked the fens best—the whole of that flat country where you are now. Ely, for instance, whose cathedral is the best of all, and entirely incredible. I stayed there one night, in an inn across from the cathedral, and walked out east in the early morning so that on the way back I could see the monster rising improbably out of nothing.

Not that Ely was better than Cambridge; you know how I liked *it*. I take great pleasure in thinking of you there, a citizen of the present moment as well as of that past which was the only thing I as a tourist could know anything about. I envy you the chance to know the place in terms of its movies and its bookstores, and its good living guys. Your poem after seeing "The Prisoner of Shark Island" is an excellent sign, Sir. And incidentally a good poem. What a picture! I wonder if you have seen Chiappe yet.[2] He said he would look you up. I enjoyed a brief talk with him at the end of September, and he told me he had enjoyed one with you. As for Rylands, I am delighted.[3] I reviewed his Shakespeare when it came out here in 1928 (Payson and Clarke), and have always wanted to hear more from him. Didn't you notice me in my Shakespeare class using "Words and Poetry"? I did.

As for my own poetry, which naturally he doesn't know, I got a body blow this summer. Macmillans rejected the manuscript I prepared for them with every confidence that they meant what they said when they said they would publish it. A reader's report had been unfavorable, and so the machinery turned me out. Who the reader was is of course a question; from my experience of such things he or she *could* have been a pestilent nobody; but on the other hand he could have been somebody; and in any case, as I have suggested, the blow landed over some fairly vital organ, possibly the spleen. The volume contained those *Southern Review* poems and a good many others, and I'll swear—but no more of this. There are other publishers, and in God's good time—but I say no more of this. Simply adding that the news came about the time I wrote you the unfortunate letter from Cornwall. Not that I was taking anything out on you, but that I had had to recognize all over again the importance of that least dramatic of virtues, patience, and took too short a cut against what seemed to me your impatience. No more of *that,* certainly.

I hope the *Review* does print "Ritual."[4] I have heard nothing from the source, though once I did get a roundabout rumor that a number of the best poems would be published; and of course yours was high among the best. I haven't even been sent the fall issue containing the prize pieces;

except that I glanced into a copy at Columbia and saw that their author was Randall Jarrell, no more and no less. I don't certify the spelling. The *Nation* prize has been won by Wallace Stevens, but I haven't seen the poem. Dorothy says it is good.

Columbia is a pretty poor place without you. Another generation will grow up, I suppose, and be mowed down by Neff;[5] but at the moment I don't see them growing. And even then I don't expect soon to see another Berryman—so early ripe, and yet with so many a generous year ahead of him in which he will become still riper. One who knows and is the best, and whose magnanimity prevents him from liking or being anything less.

You ask me what I am writing. Well, no poetry for the present. But this summer I rewrote a novel—one I had written last summer and ended wrong. Strangely or not strangely, the end was as I had planned it; my error was in failing to recognize that the beginning and the middle as I wrote them demanded something different. I refused to admit this for a year, then gave in and spent a very interesting month at the difficult business of revision. I learned a great deal from it. Now whether anyone will ever learn anything from the novel remains to be seen. For that matter I still don't know whether it will be published.

Send me letters, and certainly poems, whenever you can. The four of us in this house remain, as I say, your faithful and affectionate audience. And you may like to hear that Weaver sends his love from Hamilton Hall.

1. King Edward VIII's affair with Mrs. Simpson was being widely discussed.

2. Andrew Chiappe, whom Berryman had known at Columbia, was also studying at Cambridge.

3. George Rylands was Berryman's supervisor at Cambridge.

4. The poem was never published.

5. In "Crisis" (*Love & Fame* [New York, 1970]), Berryman gave this account of his troubles with Emery Neff, who had given him a "C" in a course:

They held unhappy meetings for two days.

To change the mark of a colleague in his absence?

Finally, a command decision:

they'd give me a second exam, invented by themselves,

& judge it, & if my paper justified,

they'd elevate the highly irrational mark.

I took it—it was fair, hard—& I killed it.

I never knew what I got, but the course-grade

cranked upward to a B. I graduated.

To Allen Tate
TLS/NjP

November 13, 1936   *New York City*

Tate came to believe there was no future for him at Southwestern in Memphis and resigned in 1936. After lecturing in the Columbia summer school, Tate returned to Benfolly to work on The Fathers.

You certainly may, provided it isn't a device to bury me in the same grave with your muse.[1] Not that I believe in her demise, any more than you were willing last summer to believe in that of mine. I shall consider that the honor you pay me is the honor of erecting my name on an important milestone, after which there will be others. Indeed I see a row of them stretching well on through this century. Of course this first one will be my favorite for reasons of vanity; but I shall visit the others, and I know I shall stand at the final collective stone with my hat off, even in the chill winds of that distant day.

Caroline will call this another exchange of empty compliments, but in fact it isn't, for the truth is that I am tremendously pleased and flattered. The simple truth.

The preface is snippy, all right—al*most* snippy to your friends.[2] But I gather that they have argued with you about these revisions, and so deserve this clipped kindness. I was sent in haste to my library of your works—to see what was the matter with the jaguar (I don't see), and to find out why you didn't like the fifth blood sonnet. I suppose it's the football game, and particularly the tackle. I can agree with you there, I think, in spite of much virtue in the remaining parts. As for the Zeno line, I assume that you didn't like the repetition of "rage" from the line above. You are probably right; though I would point out that "muted" (excellent in itself) adds to the number of epithets in that vicinity. As for Gertrude, it wouldn't hurt a bit to leave her out in view of her extreme unimportance, at least as a Social Thinker. The preface in general is delightfully to the point. Use it by all means.

I have not written partly because I assumed that you had left Monteagle and partly because I have had a bad cold for three weeks; something like the flu, but not enough like it to keep me in bed where I ought to be. My discouragements are not of the same sort as yours, since I haven't tried writing. They are simply that the poems are still untaken and that the novel I rewrote after you and Caroline left is ditto. As for the poems, I indulged myself with a long hot letter to Macmillans, but only indulged myself; for the answer, while equally long, was as cold as a witch's tit (did you hear this simile as a boy? I did). Fletcher was here the other evening with his wife, and we cursed out Macmillans in chorus. I like Mrs. Fletcher very much; and as for John, he is almost perilously changed. I don't think I could endure such thoroughgoing alterations myself. He constantly, I mean, deferred to Dorothy; agreed with everything she said; and once or twice went so far as to apologize for interrupting her. . . .

1. Tate wished to, and did, dedicate his *Selected Poems* (New York, 1937) to MVD.

2. In the preface to his *Selected Poems*, Tate wrote that Yvor Winters had "insisted

that the passage about the jaguar [in "Ode to the Confederate Dead"] is very bad; it may well be; I hoped at one time that he might rewrite it. I shall never touch the poem again."

To John Berryman
TLS/MnU

November 28, 1936   *New York City*

To think you should have worried Warren this way. I wrote him saying he shouldn't take your silence too hard—that you were doubtless drawing up some big guns and would shoot in his direction before too long.[1] Keep his letter anyhow as evidence that you count.

Your mother was good enough last week to type and send me the poems she had had from you. Some of them I had seen, some I had not. I find them most eloquent of you, and as poems good. Your mother had some scruple about showing them to me in their perhaps unfinished state, but if they are unfinished you must not mind. I like your work in process too, and in fact these seem to me finished. Particularly the ones on change, "Now in another land" and "Here is a day." The letter from Yeats is grand. Your mother read it to me before your letter came, and I agreed that you should be delighted.

You don't seem to realize how many things are happening to you. You have heard from Yeats, you have listened to Eliot and argued with him,[2] you are in another country, and you have read a remarkable number of new books—many more, judging merely by the list you sent, than you suppose. I don't mention, of course, a million imponderables. You simply aren't lonely at all. And now that you are in Paris—Good Lord, man, you are where at this time of life you ought to be. I heard Hawkes telling an alumni committee the other night about the Kellett fellows. It seems they all go through definite stages. One of being lonely and bewildered. Two, after several months, of being busy and enthusiastic. Three, in the second year, of being serenely mature. And four, at the very end, of being happy to come home again. Click? I mean so far? Not that I would want Hawkes telling me how I should feel about anything at any time.

The Richmond meeting Warren refers to in his second paragraph is a meeting of the Modern Language Association. Tate, Brooks, Warren, and I are to do a symposium on "The New or Intellectualist Poetry."[3] Vile phrases, and I don't know that I have much to say; but it will be fun meeting Warren again, and of course Tate. Brooks I never saw.

That paper is only one of many jobs I have ahead of me and behind me. It has been a busy fall. For instance, I have just finished 2000 words on the rival *Hamlets*—Gielgud's and Howard's—and of course there are always the movies. Speaking of which, if you have a chance anywhere to see a Russian one called "Son of Mongolia," by all means do so. But what takes the most time is my graduate course—those long poems, you know. I am working very hard at that, and only wish I had a student or two like Berryman to disagree with me occasionally. I get the impression that anything I say to these graduate students is all right with them; which makes it hard to talk.

I'm sure I have got all your letters—four in all since the one I answered—but I won't guarantee to be answering every point in them with this. You are simply to know that I read all you write with the greatest interest. As for Arsehole Alley, I accept the gloss. I don't know who wrote the lines in "Poems of Affairs of State"—yes, they are good. And as for the echo from Milton's Ode, all I had in mind was stanza 20 of the Ode. Anything there, do you think? Possibly not—in 1936.

Don't think too much about this mask you need for your life, unless your art is to be that mask. Don't think too much about your life. The curse of modern poetry is that its writers—its best ones too—are exclusively interested in themselves. The only discipline you need is a systematic interest in something outside yourself, and in point of fact you already have several such interests, chief of which is poetry—not yours alone, but It. I don't worry about you a bit. Think about your life, of course, for the sake of living; the more of that the better; but not for the sake of writing. Think about the writing, which is longer than any life—see Hippocrates. Plays, yes, by all means if you can write them; but try your best to make them about other people, other things. I don't need to be telling you all this. You may even have forgotten what in hell I am talking about.

You are very generous in your anger against Macmillans; and don't overestimate my patience, either. I am doing nothing because there is nothing to do, but every third day or so I boil. Well, we'll call up that agent and see what has happened.

Reading this over I realize that I was fatuous about your loneliness. Of course you are lonely. You won't be indefinitely, but while you are you are, and I imagine you'd better keep on admitting it, and I'd better stop trying to deny it for you. I am sorry, too—don't make any mistake about that. I only hope you aren't sorry you ever went to Cambridge. Oh yes, I forgot to mention a fifth point in the Dean's analysis. They always find English girls they want to marry. But that also comes in the second year. She's waiting for you right now, somewhere there in the fens. Ely, mely, mily, mo, catch her, catch her by the toe.

We are spending Christmas in Cornwall, whence wordless messages

will wing to you from all of us. Stand by to receive them. And meanwhile
Charlie sends you this drawing of Giant Berryman—who, I take it, will
cross the Channel with but a single stride.

[P. S.] My regards to Gordon Fraser, please. I wrote him about his edition
of my *Dryden,* but never knew if he got the letter.

1. Robert Penn Warren was one of the
editors of the *Southern Review,* which first
published Berryman in the summer
of 1938.

2. John Haffenden in *The Life of John
Berryman* quotes Berryman's views on Eliot

and Yeats in the chapter "Distinction and
First Fiancée, 1936–39."

3. Cleanth Brooks was professor of English at Louisiana State University and an
editor of *Southern Review,* as was Robert
Penn Warren.

To Allen Tate
TLS/NjP

February 11, 1937   *New York City*

First of all, notify Caroline that she is nuts about her novel.[1] She writes
Dorothy that she didn't finish it, but I cannot see that anything has been
left undone. I admire it immensely, and what is more I read it with the
greatest absorption to the end—which I found very painful, for I did not
want Rives to be killed. And I consider that Caroline absorbed her "research", since the effect of the novel is to give us the war as well as the
stories of George and Rives. I found myself particularly interested in the
gunboats at Fort Donelson, where you took me in 1931; but I did not
forget the fable at that point, and I don't think any reader will. I hope she
gets rich right away so that all three of you can come and see us again this
summer. Neither you nor I have been appointed to lecture at Columbia, it
seems; so some such miracle will have to happen. Perhaps "The Fathers"
will be another one. I hear you have the disease, even to rising in the
middle of the night to put down a speech or an idea. Well, well. I wouldn't
worry about the omniscient narrator. It all depends on the quality of the
things he knows; and I depend on you for the quality.

Frankly you don't inspire me to stretch my thoughts very far on the
subject of Pope. I'll have to believe first that the enterprise is going forward as if without me—then I could hop on. I haven't a spark of initiating
zeal; though I would consider something like this if I were convinced I
had to: Pope's problem as the successor to Dryden, who had announced
and partially achieved an Age of Augustus—with all the wars over, and
nothing but a perfect and permanent poetry to write and set in the center
of civilization as its chief gem. Human nature now known, and the rules

of art within reach. This meant not merely that Pope had to refine on Dryden at every point—the Homer on the Virgil, The Rape of the Lock on MacFlecknoe, the Satires on the Satires, etc.—but that he had to take every position and hold it against even hypothetical rivals; hence his malice and suspicion, and his attack in The Dunciad against literally everybody. Swift is the counterpart in prose—jealous of any theory, scientific or otherwise, which threatened the wisdom he thought good enough for all time to come. But another age was already planted; another class was heaving up in Defoe and Richardson; and so the ground was being broken for whoever comes in our next chapter. The essay would be chiefly an analysis of Pope's "refinements"—which, in fact, have never been improved on, and which can be said to have been absolutely successful within the limits of his vision. Anything in that? Yes, you should do Donne; and I hope you say something about "A Lecture upon the Shadow," which I particularly want to see discussed somewhere.

I have gone over your Contents very carefully, reading first the poems you left out and then reading the book as it will stand.[2] I wish as evidence of this that I could quarrel over a few titles; but your hand has descended with an uncanny rightness, and for the most part I cannot quarrel. It is a pity to lose certain lines out of "Mr. Pope"—for instance the 10th line of Light—and in spite of everything I wish you could save The Progress of Oenia, not merely for III and IV but for many other brilliant things in it. I think I know what you feel about it; but what about giving it another chance in your merciless thoughts? Otherwise you have had an accurate ear for that hard and irreducible arrow-music which is the distinction of your poetry. I heard it plainly throughout the revised volume, and admired it more than ever. These poems would not be so familiar to me if they did not deserve to. They have established themselves in the air of our time, where they ring with their own quality of sound; and I predict that they will keep on ringing. The order of the poems is occasionally arbitrary, perhaps, but I have no suggestions there. The Ode should of course come first, and Ignis Fatuus last. Epistle to Edmund Wilson I take to be page 36 of "Mr. Pope". And I look forward to your revision of A Pauper. Sir, I salute the selection; and trust that the dedication has not been recalled or revised.

I have taken you at your word and sent you a copy of J.G. with the changes pencilled in. They ought to be clear. Omissions are signified by brackets in the left margin—look for one in III which runs to six and a half pages—and the rest is substitution. There might have been an advantage in typing a clean copy for you so that you wouldn't be tempted in passing to consider the things left out; but this way you have your choice, and after all you are reading as an expert who can be counted on to keep his head. If you tell me I have cut too much out of III I shall be pretty stubborn in rebuttal; evidently I was trying to write a novel in verse there, but it is clear to me now that it is not a good novel. It should be either longer or shorter—and if shorter, less like a novel at all. With that in mind I have rooted out several irrelevant themes; and if the result is a part weaker than the first two—well, it was weaker anyway, and the logic of the whole poem calls for a dwindled end. However, let me leave the poem to you.

It is coming under separate cover, but I enclose a list of the poems I have considered cutting out of the putative Selection.[3] I don't know that you have "Spring Thunder et al", and you may not have the other books with you. I could supply sheets of "Now the Sky" if a crisis demanded them, and could even mail you one of the two copies of "Spring Thunder" I have with the understanding that it would come home again. But perhaps nothing of all that is necessary. What I do know is that it is a devil of a job to select. Certain poems are clearly bad—cute, perhaps, or else simply false—but others are at least not bad in their setting or as of their time. I think I have been harsher in this list than I would be in a volume; though if you insist that I should be still harsher I shall pay attention to what you say.

The point is that you should take your time about the whole matter. Do not let it press you, and wait on any given day until you are sure you have nothing further to give the novel; or Caroline, or Vili,[4] or the stove in the hall, or Nancy. If and whenever you want to let fly with critical remarks I shall be profoundly grateful for them; but if you never do I shall not telegraph you.

[P.S.] On second thought I have put a few queries after titles in the list, indicating my private doubts. I do not assume that these will coincide with any doubts you may have.

Also, I have not touched "A Winter Diary et al." But you may.

1. Caroline Gordon's *None Shall Look Back* (New York, 1937) had just been published.

2. Tate's *Selected Poems* was published later that year.

3. MVD was preparing an edition of his *Selected Poems*. The long list of poems he was considering omitting has been deleted.

4. Vili was the Tates' dog.

To Richard H. Thornton
TLS/NjP

April 1, 1937   *New York City*

Thornton, president of H. Holt and Company, acting on advice of Robert Frost, wished to become Van Doren's publisher.

When I said this morning that the novel was less important to me than the poetry I didn't mean it wasn't important.[1] I believe in it very strongly, and if the question is still open when I see you I may want to argue with you a bit. It is of course an entirely separate matter from the poetry, which I am delighted to have you publish, with or without the novel. I must confess that I can't see how anyone can know that the novel is without commercial possibilities. Everyone who has read it among my acquaintance seems honestly to believe that it is exciting and original; and I should suppose that those qualities were more promising than many others. . . .

1. MVD had difficulty finding a publisher for *Windless Cabins,* and it did not appear until 1940.

To Allen Tate
TLS/NjP

April 2, 1937   *New York City*

I have studied your notes and laid them away in my mangled copy of J.G. until I am free to put them into effect. For most of them I will put into effect. You were quite right in assuming that no explanation or argument was necessary; I usually understood your reasons, and could see them clearly once they had been hinted. You probably appreciate the predicament I was in, having passed the point where I could know how any passage would count with the reader. But don't think I appealed to you as *any* reader. You were *the* reader; and I can't tell you how grateful I am to you now for these further evidences that you are the best of friends and critics. Very few persons would be as generous as you have been, either in this case or in the case of the sonnets—let's see, four years ago, or is it five, when you were in France. I wish I could have done you an equivalent service with your list of poems. The truth is, however, that you had done it for yourself. The more I studied the poems and the list the more I agreed; and at last could say little more than that. You may be amused to hear that my original impulse to cut J.G. came from Louis Untermeyer's remark in his last anthology about my "facility." I have never thought I was so cursed; poetry is not easy for me by a hell of a long shot; but I did look at J.G. with a pretty cold eye after that crack, and I found these lukewarm spots. I shall have the most trouble, of course, with the passage or two where you think I should rewrite rather than cut. I shall probably end by leaving the lines as is. Once more, Allen, thank you.

Don't give the other volumes another thought until you are running smoothly at Benfolly—where it will be a pleasure to think of you on the porch by the river or in the dining room over fried chicken. Or in that square drawing room which I remember perfectly. Or do I? Is it exactly square? You're right, we'll all have to visit you some day; though we shan't have the money to do it this summer.

That my activity with J.G. and the other volumes is not academic any more will be proved by the following tale, which I scarcely believe myself. Five weeks ago I had a note from Richard H. Thornton, president of Henry Holt & Co., inviting me to lunch. I went, and actually heard him proposing to become the publisher of my poetry. He was interested in a collected edition, but when I told him of the new volume (the one Macmillan turned down last summer) he said: Well, we can bring that out this summer and then the Collected Poems next year. I found no catch in it anywhere, and the contracts are now being signed. By no catch I mean that I made him say he didn't care whether the books sold well or not. It seems he is interested in the poetry—or rather, Frost is, for the suggestion came first from Frost, may God make his last days easy. So I have found a place to rest my bones, as I believe you have at Scribners; and rejoice with you. And so your remarks on my list of poems will not fall on hopeless ears. Remember, however, that there is no hurry; and that when you do make them you are to cast a side glance at any pieces in "A Winter Diary" which you thought or think impossible. After that I hope never to be a nuisance to you again.

So you recognized Dorothy under the name Caroline Smith. I said you would. She wrote the review at the last minute, having been seized by Joe Krutch after he found the review he had ordered to be hopelessly bad.[1] She would have liked more time and space, of course; but she is glad you were pleased with it, and hopes Caroline Gordon will be. When you consider that I am to review the novel for the S.R. you will see the reason for the pseudonym; there was Carl too, remember. Not that the pseudonym was invented for this crisis. Dorothy has been doing a sort of column for Joe ever since she left the paper, and it was thought at the beginning that she should hide a bit. . . .

1. The review of *None Shall Look Back* appeared in the *Nation*, March 20, 1937, p. 332.

To John Berryman
TLS/MnU

April 3, 1937   *New York City*

I have been waiting to answer your *two* letters for a reason having solely to do with myself and my fortunes. Let me confess that right off, and incidentally explain what I mean. Five weeks ago I got a letter from Thornton, president of Henry Holt and Company, asking me to lunch. I went, and through the smoke and cocktail fumes heard him suggesting that he become the publisher of my poetry. I had ceased to expect that this would happen, and I didn't really believe there wasn't a catch in it. I pressed him for his reason; he said he liked the poetry. I pressed him a little farther and he admitted that the idea had come originally from Frost, whom he also publishes, and who about a year ago began to propagate my cause. Then I made it clear how unlikely it is that my books will ever sell well; and he countered OK. So I seemed to be set. And I would have written you at once except that I wanted to be sure—the contract signed, etc. Or contracts, for there is to be a volume this fall (the one Macmillans turned down) and then a Collected Poems next year. But five weeks went by without further news. Thursday I telephoned him and was reassured. He is a southern gentleman who takes his charming time. So now I *am* sure, and am telling you. You will forgive, I am sure, this occupation with myself at the beginning of a letter. Not only because you are generous but because you understand how important this sort of thing can be to one. To you, for instance. If I prayed[,] it would be to the effect that you should not have to wait so long for some such thing to happen to you. You won't, I think; for I reflect upon the vast distance you are ahead of what I was at twenty-two and in some respects still am. Don't worry, when I say Collected Poems, lest I include all. There will be many cuts; Tate, by the way, is helping me make them, and helping me also to decide on some changes I have decided to make in Jonathan Gentry. I am shortening the third part. He is writing a novel, or he calls it that. It started out as an autobiography, or rather as a genealogy of his ancestors, several years ago. He picked it up again this winter, and yesterday I heard from him that 43,000 words of fiction had flowed. I am delighted, for any kind of stoppage bothers him dreadfully. He is one of the best of persons, as I think I have told you before. He is publishing a Collected Poems of his own this fall, with Scribners, and he went through the motions of submitting the contents to me for approval. I could make few suggestions, for he had done exactly the right thing in almost every case.

But to you. I was grateful for the carbon, since without it I would have learned less about you at Cambridge, talking on Yeats and growing so rapidly every minute that the air, I fancy, is full of gentle, popping sounds as the green tissues swell, lengthen, and turn to a daylight gold. That is an elaborate way of saying that I approve of your progress and believe that you are advancing in wisdom steadily. I wish I could have heard the session on Yeats; and which two stanzas of Crashaw is it, or are they, that can keep you going for ages? He has never been able to do anything for me. I am not at all sorry that you see Chiappe in a softer light.[1] It is proper that you be full of rages against a world of obviously empty persons and fake programs; the measure of a young man is the number of things he hates rightly; but there should be one or two creatures whom he can enjoy at his side, even love. To whom he can say anything, and with whom he can agree that the universe is mostly holes. Joe Krutch was this man for me. Our girls, later our wives, thought us conceited in those days; and we were conceited; and still are; but in those days it was all for the best in a strangely imperfect cosmos. I am not saying, of course, that you do or should love Andrew of the unagued cheek; only that your relenting to-ward him suggests to me that the better thing has happened or com-menced to happen. To put it briefly, don't live alone. Don't think it is you against all creation. It is all creation against you and your friends. And may there be several of them. Not here, not Halliday or MVD, but there, where letters don't have to be thought of.[2] And—glancing back at what I have written—I don't for God's sake mean Chiappe. To hell with him. Why does he keep rolling back into this paragraph? I mean Y and X, and maybe L (short for puella).

Returning to myself, Holt's have been considering the novel too, and sound rather cold-footed about it. This time I am going to break through my most immodest reserves and give them a song and dance, saying in effect that I am a great author whom they'd better hold on to while they have him. Even if this doesn't work I'll enjoy it. For you should know that I have come out from my hiding places. I read my poetry in six cities of America this winter, ending up at Atlantic City last week where I took my family with me for weekend sport. It was great fun, the reading, if only because it seemed to be going against my nature. Actually it went well. Atlantic City went well most of the time, though once Dorothy and I lost the boys and meanwhile they had lost each other—this in the boardwalk throng of a Palm Sunday.

You will be amazed to hear that in my opinion at least Milton Crane has moved to the front among Columbia students.[3] The front is not where it used to be by a long shot, but that is where he is. Still practically inaudible, yet sounder and decenter than the rest.

Last week I got a twenty-two-page-single-space letter from Aylward, who had written me once before from the monastery but not at such length.[4] I can't describe his letters in print, for they are truly wonderful: eloquent, perverse, fantastic, brilliant, and quite human. The move was not a bad one, I am convinced; and I am convinced chiefly by the candor with which he criticizes the holy tunnels through which he creeps. The letters, mind you, are documents. You may want to see them some day. You really may.

The boys still think of you as enormous, and we all think of you as one of our best friends on any continent or island. Don't ever feel obliged to write, but when you do write have plenty of confidence that we shall read every word with affectionate eagerness. The Shakespeare book, I forgot to say, I am also discussing with Thornton next week. But I had rather discuss with you my new long poem, which should be written by 1950. Not much before.

1. Andrew Chiappe, also at Cambridge, later became a member of the Columbia English faculty.

2. Milton Halliday had been one of Berryman's closest friends at Columbia.

3. Milton Crane received B.A. and M.A. degrees from Columbia.

4. Stephen Aylward was also a friend of Thomas Merton's.

To Allen Tate
ALS/NjP

May 18, 1937   *New York City*

*　　*　　*

I've been looking over your notes again on *Jonathan Gentry,* and appreciating them freshly. You say once that you found several Robinsonian lines but were afraid to cite them. If you marked them and have a record of them, however, I want them. I am dead against them, and can scarcely believe my eyes when I come across them—at this late date. This, mind you, only in case you can say where they are without trouble.

To Allen Tate
TLS/NjP

July 7, 1937   *Falls Village, Connecticut*

*　　*　　*

I have heard from Donald Davidson too that the Ransom evening went off well in its own terms, if not in the terms of Vanderbilt.[1] Is Mims really such a blockhead?[2] Not that I doubt it, after your priceless image of the whorehouse. You may be edified by the tale of my telegram, which I telephoned to Waterbury. The operator there understood every word in it except "poet." "Thole" was nothing compared to that, though I can believe that "thole" never got there whole. But "poet" was a dark word, a word scarcely born yet, for this wench of Waterbury. She came back with "fort," "port," "fourth," "part", and doubtless in her own mind "fart." You see where we stand with the world. Seriously, however, I can estimate how much you will miss John Ransom; and I can form an idea as to the labor which the whole thing was for you. You are one of the few who would have done it.

My comments on your MS are not to be mentioned in company with yours on mine, whether for number or for worth. I simply cannot tell you how valuable yours are, or how generous a being they imply. I have gone over them twice, adopted many of them without question, and reserved the rest for study later on in the summer. You don't need to be told, I imagine, that those which I eventually reject will have been as useful as those I accept; they will have raised questions I could not have raised, however I manage in the end to answer them. The point is, as Dorothy says, that I got what I asked for: clear and positive advice. A rarer commodity in my experience, perhaps, than in yours. I gather that you have traded wisdom of this sort with many of your friends for years. But most of my friends—all indeed save one—are incapable of such commerce. I have missed it. . . .

1. Donald Davidson, a friend of Tate's, had been a member of the Fugitives. He was well versed in Vanderbilt matters.

2. John Crowe Ransom had an offer from Kenyon College, and Edwin Mims, chairman of English at Vanderbilt, and other administrators, made inadequate and half-hearted attempts to retain Ransom, one of Vanderbilt's most distinguished professors. Tate was deeply involved in attempts to keep Ransom from leaving the university. At the June dinner for Ransom, the poet announced his resignation. For an extended account of this controversy, see Thomas Daniel Young, *Gentleman in a Dustcoat* (Baton Rouge, 1976).

To John Berryman
ALS/MnU

September 19, 1937   *Falls Village, Connecticut*

This is not the letter you asked for. We are moving back to New York and I must wait until then to cover a couple of pages with fine print. Now I merely warn you that a copy of my new book of poems is coming from the publisher, who may ask you for an opinion. If he does, don't bother. He asked me last spring for a list of better spirits, and of course your name went on it; and of course I was innocent enough not to anticipate, what I now know, that he was interested in replies and publicity. Naturally enough—but also naturally the book is for you, as a present from me, and you are simply to unwrap it and read as much of it as you may.

The Ransom thing was a demonstration, arranged by Tate & others, of Ransom's significance as a poet—for the benefit of Vanderbilt University, which seemed to be letting him go to Kenyon College. The demonstration (telegrams, speeches, letters) was impressive, but Vanderbilt sent no representatives and Ransom is now at Kenyon. The moral, as Tate says, is that universities care no more about the literary distinction of their professors than whores do about chastity. A thought for you, John.

This summer I have spent almost entirely on my "Selected Poems"—a terrible grind the effect of which will be visible to few. And I am tired of contemplating myself for four months. I wish, for instance, I could see you.

Your month in Heidelberg sounded good. Dorothy and the boys send their love, and the boys thank you for the stamps.

To John Berryman
TLS/MnU

October 1, 1937   *New York City*

You're right, I haven't written. And I'll repeat my excuse for a summer's silence—you will admit I wrote you last winter. The excuse is the mirror, the Selected Poems, and all that. The experience absorbed and even I think drugged me, so that I wrote few letters and read almost nothing, and never thought at all. Not exactly pleasant—I feel quite free from myself now—but as I saw it necessary; I shall never be sorry that I made the book as good as I could make it. I rewrote Jonathan Gentry, retouched many lines elsewhere, modified the punctuation everywhere, and among a hundred poems which I reread till I was dizzy I found about fifty to discard. Even then it will be a long book, perhaps too long for Berryman. But remember, Berryman, that much of what it reprints is out of print and in my opinion worthy of recovery. It isn't as if all my volumes were lying around everywhere and as if this were to be merely another, a sample, to put beside them.

But I expected to be talking long before this (the drug still works, you see) about your Meditation, which your mother was so good as to mail me last week.[1] I wonder if you like it. I do, enormously, and consider it your best so far, leastwise at this length. The first reading was not enough. I read it again the next day, and today I read it twice on the subway, once going uptown and once coming down. And I have just now looked at it again. My experience with it is this. Neutral at first, and almost voiceless, it has deepened in sound and color with every trial, and I am positive that it will go on doing so; in fact, even as I think of it now,

disregarding the tap of keys, I hear it growing steadily in its own illumi-
nated darkness, coming out at me, so to speak (unless the comparison is
offensive), as music or voices can mount to clarity inside a radio that has
just been turned on. The poem is very rich, and of course it was never
neutral had I but known it. I like the phrasing throughout—apparently
effortless, as graceful as ripe thought, and abounding in felicities (I
paused here to quote some of them, but found the whole thing continu-
ous, a phrase of nine stanzas); and I especially like the firmness with
which in each stanza you write the final line. It is not a Yeats poem, either,
as you may suspect it of being. I find it veritable Berryman, and I know it
is good. More meditations to you.

I envy you all that Shakespeare. Last year we had Maurice Evans's
Richard II, and that was wonderful as you must know, but we have
nothing like what you saw in September. I am impressed too by your
reading. Why, you have almost done enough. Since you insist I may begin
my Shakespeare next summer, provided I have the courage. It takes courage for some reason, and of course we both know the reason. A letter
from Wilson Knight that I have just been answering makes it clear, incidentally, why he can be so wild and foolish (your words): he utterly lacks
humor. In his mad way, yes, he is right, and I do not deny madness to any
critic, indeed I demand it; yet I miss in his case the other side of the moon,
which for all we know is feathered with soft uncertainties and sleeps com-
fortably in its own arms, not raging after Onlyness and The Vision.

Would you mind writing me something about that young lady you are
in love with?[2] All you tell me is that you are in love, and while I am delighted that this is so I find I have much curiosity—respectful and dis-
creet—about who, what, and where she is. Say nothing if you prefer not
to, but otherwise I can take a lot of it, since I am really interested.

The news about Columbia is that Krutch has come in this fall as Professor and is very happy about it. So are Weaver and I, for Krutch is something rare to have around: my oldest friend, as perhaps you know, and
one of the most interesting persons in the world. So are all the rest too,
although they don't know what they've got and never will.

The boys and Dorothy were pleased this morning because you had remembered them; of course they remember your Greatness, and what
is more important they remember your niceness and your goodness.
"They" here means the boys; Dorothy remembers still more. The fact is
that you stand high with us, and that I for one am counting on the sight
of you again before too many revolutions alter the world. Also, I don't
agree that you did little last year. You did much; your letters prove it.
Write more.

1. "Meditation" appeared in James Laughlin (ed.), *Five Young American Poets* (Norfolk, Conn., 1940).

2. In John Haffenden's biography of Berryman, the young lady Berryman was in love with appears under the pseudonym "Beatrice." Her name appears in these letters, but I will substitute "Beatrice" throughout to protect her identity.

To Allen Tate
ALS/NjP

October 10, 1937   *New York City*

A word to say that I have called up Holt and seen to it that a copy went to you at once.[1] I am both sorry and ashamed because things turned out this way—I'll never trust even a benevolent publisher again. You can in reality wait, I know, but there is nobody I'd rather have been prompt with.

As for your book, all you need to remember is that Mediterranean, to discuss nothing beyond page 3 is one of the finest poems in the world, and that you will write more. But I suppose I know how you feel, and I am not sorry in the circumstances that you have got going on the novel again. Good—and forget [Ford Madox] Ford, who has no right to step out of the Nineties and lecture a man like you. My God, the novels—yours, Caroline's new one (which I sit up for), and Dorothy's, which she is now resuming after almost three months away from it. It may be just as well that I didn't start (and of course finish) another one this summer. I probably won't now, ever.

We can't visit you at Christmas because we are taking the boys and must spend every available day with my mother in Urbana. There aren't many days at best. You know, of course, how much we would enjoy coming—and seeing your twelve-year-old daughter.

1. Holt had recently published MVD's *The Last Look and Other Poems.*

To Allen Tate
TLS/NjP

November 9, 1937   *New York City*

*   *   *

All that you say is of course beautiful in my ears, and would be even if I heard it addressed to someone else, since it is noble praise: a rare commodity.[1] As to Young Woman and Like Son, I shall not protest, except to assure you that I was aware in writing them of no special sort of success. What you say of them is true of good poems, and I am glad to have such proof that you think these good; but I have no inkling as to why or by what accident they came out well. My interest, as always, was in the subject matter. In one case I was writing to a young friend of mine in Illinois, a girl of about 24 who had written me about how she had sat that evening in the open window as a soft November wind blew against her—had sat there, she said, and decided certain things, among them the name of the boy she wanted to marry. My poem was the answer, and my desire was merely to assure her that the important things are not so decided. In the second case I started from Charlie's telling me one night as I was turning off his light that he was in the habit of watching the people in the windows opposite this house. I wrote that poem, of course, for myself; and I was not surprised that he didn't understand it when he saw it, or guess that it had been written at his suggestion. My point in neither case is that the occasion has importance or interest, but that in all cases I must have occasions, and think only of them as I write. I have, for instance, never thought of myself as writing "a poem." Neither on the other hand have I ever thought of myself as "expressing" my "experience." You ask if I have had any reviews. Only one of consequence, by Peter Monro Jack in the *Times*, and it made me quite sick with its talk about my "experiences," of which, like you, I have had none *qua poeta*. He rebuked me for not having had more, or at any rate for not having made them clear to Mr. Jack. A joke on him was that The Last Look, which he supposed was based on a very deep and personal one, took off from three words spoken by Chard Smith in my hearing. He said he had been to see Robinson (dying) and as he entered the room there was nothing visible but "those great eyes." This was all, except to be sure that I did remember my father's eyes the last time I saw him alive. Well, the matter is irrelevant to my next project, which is no more short poems but a long one, to be started, I hope, on my sabbatical in 1939.

I must look up Zabel on you; I don't see the NR regularly.[2] Meanwhile you should know that in my graduate class the other day, a class of perhaps seventy-five people who are studying with me Homer, Virgil, Milton, Dante, Lucretius, Spenser, Ariosto, Byron, Wordsworth, and Chaucer for what they can tell us (really me) about the art of writing a long poem, I read your Mediterranean as the best modern statement of the Virgilian journey. I read it also as a great poem—twice—and I could tell that the best of them agreed with me, heartily even if (in a lecture room) silently.

Dorothy is writing Caroline about "The Garden of Adonis," but I shall address this paragraph to her as from one who is mainly an amateur at fiction. I liked "The Garden," and read it one night long after I should have stopped, but I didn't like it as well as "None Shall Look Back." It needed, I think, to be longer; perhaps three or four times as long. It was rich in themes which in most cases were not developed to the length proper to them, and proper to Caroline's clear gifts. There was nothing bad in the book, but the good things were nipped off. This is equally true for me whether the book is a story or a study; I read it, needless to say, as a story, and among other things vastly enjoyed the conversation—the best, I am sure, that anyone writes nowadays. I should simply have liked to hear more. Wrong? Probably. . . .

1. MVD had sent Tate a group of recently written poems, which Tate then praised.

2. Morton D. Zabel had reviewed Tate's *Selected Poems* in the *New Republic*, October 20, 1937, pp. 315–16.

To John Berryman
ALS/MnU

December 12, 1937   *New York City*

This is mainly a Merry Christmas—and of course a Happy New Year, with plays finished galore, and several of them produced.

It is also to congratulate you on the Oldham (swell) and on your Harness essay, your mother's copy of which I have just read.[1] I found it mature and continuously interesting; henceforth I will not say certain things I have said, ever again. And on the news that the *Southern Review* is probably publishing you in July—good—and on the fact that you have a very charming and I am sure gifted young brother. And then that lady—[2]

In short, my fine fellow, the world should look good to you. It does to me, through you.

1. Berryman was elected, after rigorous examinations, Charles Oldham Shakespeare Scholar. Berryman's essay was not awarded the Harness Prize.

2. "Beatrice."

To Allen Tate
TLS/NjP

December 18, 1937   *New York City*

*   *   *

The end of February, which you gave as the time of your lecture in Cambridge, is too far away. Yet it will come, and we are already looking for you and Caroline. Don't let her back out, and as for yourself, remember that we expect you to do more than pass through New York twice. We have plenty of room for you to stay as long as you can. As for a lecture subject, I don't suppose you want to develop any of several hints you dropped in Reactionary Essays. It is rich in them, however, and here are some (I have been rereading the book today, in preparation for one of my Chicago papers; though I would have remembered them anyway):

"Bad" history
Poetry by resistance (pp. 74, 78)
The literary situation
The styles of Shakespeare (I am going to write a book with this title, and I
    want to know more about it)

Outside of RE there are these further subjects:

Sensibility (the word is overused in criticism, and needs examining with
    respect to the hole it covers)
Metaphor (V. Richards in The Philosophy of Rhetoric; he is interesting,
    but there is more to it)
Emotion in poetry as the expression of the poet's love for his poem
Wyatt
Shakespeare's prose
Fiction
Lucretius
The bird images in Dante's tale of Paolo and Francesca (cranes, starlings,
    doves)
Exaggeration in poetry and in humor (analogue?) . . .

Eda Lou I saw, yes. Unspeakable.[1] Zabel was not at all bad—not even highfalutin, which I believe was your word.[2] You have done better than I, for I have had no such review. Ransom's in the *Herald-Tribune* may have been true—I wouldn't argue—but I am embarrassed by what I thought its condescension, as if he were lecturing a ten-year-old; and by what I take to be an utter humorlessness.[3] Don't quote me. Just hold on to Zabel. . . .

Dorothy and the boys are going with me to Chicago. We stay three days (I read two papers) and then go on down to visit my mother for three more. Looking back I see I have struck the wrong note about Ransom. It is not at all that I think he should have praised me all around, or even a little bit, but that I shan't know what to say about the review when I see him at Chicago, where I believe he is going. I have decided to say nothing; yet that may be embarrassing too. Well, I am being much too serious about this, especially as my high opinion of him is not in the least affected. . . .

1. Eda Lou Walton, reviewing Tate's *Selected Poems* in the New York *Times*, December 5, 1937, p. 5, said that Tate's obscurity was due to his "lack of poetic ability" and his "lack of any deep passion or intuitive grasp of life."

2. Morton D. Zabel in his review of Tate's *Selected Poems* in the *New Republic*, October 20, 1937, pp. 315–16, spoke of Tate's "high seriousness" and "acute critical intelligence."

3. John Crowe Ransom's review of MVD's *The Last Look* in the New York *Herald-Tribune Books*, November 21, 1937, p. 20, was long and generally unfavorable.

To John Berryman
TLS/MnU

January 8, 1938   *New York City*

Your fine letter arrived pleasantly in time for Christmas. My own note to you, scratched off in too much haste, may have been late. I have been a poor guy all fall—but I have read you to good effect, and I'm sure I haven't missed any letters, so don't worry about lost ones. There is, as it happens, one more theme for congratulation: the SR group. Their winter number announces it as coming, and I know no better reason for the spring than that it will bring five lilacs out of the dead land, or is it five Sweeneys. Till then I have only your Dublin poem to chew on.[1] It is good nutriment and condiment, though the fourth from the last line tends to break a tooth. I am not certain that "the eighteenth century" can be said in a poem; or rather I am, but perhaps not this one. At any rate, there and there only the poem rubs bare. Oh yes, I have your monkey verses too. Now that was a Christmas card.

Your remarks about The Last Look etc. were very valuable. I had spent the summer removing dashes, hyphens, and Ohs from the big MS., but I went in again and got some more out. You are perfectly right. Some of the compounds I can't remove, however, and I hope you will accept them. To date I have suppressed upwards of forty poems from the collection. Does that sound like enough? I want as much as you to be rigorous; my only difficulty is that the advices I get vary so oddly. For instance, your list of approved pieces from the LL agrees with Tate's in only two particulars; and the other day he sent me a second list which overlapped his first one only fifty percent. And there is the fact that you are the only person who has ever mentioned Spectral Boy. Tate's counsel is to make this book big, and to let him later on pick the 100 best for a small one. But even this book won't have anything in it I am sure is bad. Now are you satisfied?[2]

You ask if I have any suggestions about living, and I answer in strict confidence that Columbia may soon offer you something to do. I don't know what, or for how much; and of course I don't know positively that they will do it. But Steeves is well inclined; Weaver, Krutch, and Van Doren of course are; Dick is on leave; and Neff[3]—well, that's probably all right, though the matter hasn't been discussed in meeting yet, and who knows what Neff will say? Of course you may have no interest in this at all. But I have no further suggestions at the moment which would have cash meaning. Don't peep that I have peeped, even perhaps to your mother; and as soon as I know more I will tell you. Or you may hear from Steeves first. At least there is this, and my private opinion is that it is pretty certain. But remember that it is a private opinion. There could be worse lives.

Halliday called me the other day about something and promised to come and see me soon. I hope he will. Now I must go to the New Republic office and help confer honors on twelve movies of last year. Dorothy and the boys send their love.

1. "On A Portrait in Dublin," later published in James Laughlin (ed.), *New Directions in Prose & Poetry* (Norfolk, Conn., 1939).

2. MVD was at work selecting his *Collected Poems* and sought advice from several of his friends about revisions and omissions.

3. Harrison Ross Steeves, chairman of the Columbia English department, joined MVD, Weaver, and Krutch in wanting Berryman to join the faculty. Emery Neff had given Berryman a "C" during his last semester as an undergraduate. Without Neff's knowledge, Berryman was given another examination and the grade was changed to a "B."

To Allen Tate
TLS/NjP

January 8, 1938   *New York City*

Your good letter arrived in plenty of time for Christmas, the day after which we started for Chicago and Urbana. I never saw John after all, unless I made him out in the audience at my last speech.[1] I had to hurry from that meeting to the train for Urbana, and so couldn't verify my dim sight of a man in a grey suit high up to the right. I missed seeing him, even if there wouldn't have been much to say about his review. I have just now written him about that; and now that I have had a couple more weeks to think of it, I am sorry I teased you to write me about it. For one thing, its summaries of the poems were such as few writers ever hear—scrupulous, missing nothing—and for another thing, his general ideas are his own and good, and would call for a long conversation the conclusion of which would be that they are still his own. My first paper at the MLA, on metaphysical poetry, ran to the effect that criticism of it has been too solemn and has neglected to point out that it had humor as well as wit. That is where any argument between John and me would start, but it is just as well that it should wait, or for that matter never take place. I agree with all you say about him, and of course am interested in the strokes you add. I hope he likes Kenyon. And I don't mean I am sorry you wrote.

In Chicago I had dinner one evening with Borgese, author of "Goliath."[2] He knows the Divine Comedy by heart, and when I mentioned your favorite lines he rattled them off reflectively.[3] And when I quoted your superlative he mused, after staring at the ceiling: "Well, why not?" Yes, it is a fine passage, taken after what comes before, and it could very well be your text at Cambridge. I hope indeed it will be, and make no further suggestions. You would have been welcome to Shakespeare, of course; my book may not be written for many years, if ever. I can never be convinced that Shakespeare needs books.

So your address after Feb. 1 will be Greensboro, N.C., and both of you will be Full Professors. A house full, I'd say. But good, and I should think very reassuring on the budget side. Ben Kendrick was never a teacher of mine—a colleague, rather, in my first days at Columbia—but I remember him as most likable and sensible. You couldn't have a better boss, just as I am sure your students couldn't have better teachers. Take it easy—insist on a lot of time to yourselves—and I am sure it will do very well. We want to hear all about it when you and Caroline are here. Don't let any duties keep you from coming.

I don't know De Voto except as a writer, in which capacity he is a solid brass ass. I once had a controversy with him over my review of his book on Mark Twain. He had said he was writing without a theory about Mark Twain, and I had said of course he was not, since nobody can write two consecutive words without a theory, but that since he didn't know it the theory and the writing were both bad. The article is in character. The vulgarest of all errors is to say: Now we have the truth. As if all history were but preparation for Clifford Dowdey, and of course B. De Voto.[4] To hell with B.D.V.—he can't even initial his underwear straight.

1. John Crowe Ransom had published a largely unfavorable review of MVD's *The Last Look* in the New York *Herald-Tribune Books*, November 21, 1937, p. 20.

2. Giuseppe Antonio Borgese (1882–1952) published *Goliath: The March of Fascism* in 1937.

3. Tate's interest in Dante is discussed

perceptively in Radcliffe Squires's *Allen Tate*.

4. Bernard DeVoto in the *Saturday Review*, December 18, 1937, p. 16, praised Clifford Dowdey's first novel, *Bugles Blow No More*, and expressed reservations about Caroline Gordon's *None Shall Look Back*.

To Allen Tate
TLS/NjP

February 27, 1938   *New York City*

I seem to remember a rumor about phonograph records of poems by their authors. Possibly it came through Greet, as most such things do.[1] I'll ask him, and then if necessary I'll ask farther. Columbia (Greet) has been "taking" poems for several years—Eliot, Frost, Sandburg, Fletcher, Masters et al—but not for commercial purposes. Merely as record of how the poets intended their poems to be heard, on the theory that it would be nice to know how Milton would have recited Lycidas. If the thing is to become commercial I wonder if you can stop at the best poetry. Won't every kind have to be tried, as every kind *now* is published? The best may owe its opportunity to the worst, and of course there is the old question which is the best. There are, come to think of it, records of Edith Sitwell delivering some of her things to music. But that is freakish, and it will be important to avoid preciousness on any level. There is also the curious fact that some poets cannot read themselves at all (Robinson never did), and that others do it less well than strangers would. You will note that I have reservations, and that I do not appear to be enthusiastic. For some reason I'm not enthusiastic—mainly, I suspect, because once when Greet asked me to do it for his collection I summoned only the deadest of voices, one I scarcely recognized when it was played back to me, and missed the emphasis here and there. I can read sometimes effectively when I have an audience; an audience of Greet and his machine was not enough, or shall I say too much. Yet this obstacle could be overcome by practice, as it has been in broadcasting, and I promise at any rate to see Greet as you suggest. The thing would succeed in enough cases to justify it, and if there is a public—well, I admit that that is what we want.

May I keep this copy of the *VQR* you sent me, and stand it among your works? If it is your only copy I'll send it back, but in that case I'll certainly provide myself with another. For I have never learned more from an article—about the Ode, about its author, about the South, about the

North, about the world since Cowley, about poetry. It is a superb thing, and never more so than when it is taking care of the reader who would say, as perhaps Davis himself did, that this was a strange thing for Tate or anybody else to be doing. I know of nothing like it, or more worth doing. I mean it too when I say that I learned much about the Ode I hadn't known before. I thought I knew the Ode all the way through, but I had missed the full force of the crab. Not of the jaguar (Winters is of course wrong about the jaguar), but of its ancestor among the images.[2] And the anatomy of the rhymes and rhythms—you have provided something there of the greatest value, indeed of unique value. Why didn't you mention this article when you were here? I hadn't heard about it. I should have enjoyed pushing you into other portions of the poem. The connection is slight, but my Webster gives "orient" as an adjective, meaning he simply says bright, lustrous, as of superior pearls, or rising, as of the sun. . . .

1. William Cabell Greet, professor of English at Barnard College, made many recordings of writers reading their own works.

2. In "Narcissus as Narcissus," *Virginia Quarterly Review*, XIV (Winter, 1938), 108–122, Tate said about the jaguar, "In the entire poem there are only two explicit symbols for the locked-in ego: the crab is the first and less explicit symbol, a mere hint, a planting of the idea that will become overt in its second instance—the jag-uar towards the end." In his review of Tate's *Poems 1928–1931*, in *Hound and Horn*, V (1932), 675–79, Yvor Winters wrote of the jaguar in "Ode to the Confederate Dead": "To have a curse stone the eyes is a strain on the mind's eye, and to transform the curse into a jaguar and then to make the jaguar perform in a manner so impossibly unfeline is worse. . . . Even Mr Eliot's sleek Brazilian jaguar, verging on doggerel as he does, has more poetic identity."

To John Berryman
TLS/MnU

March 22, 1938   *New York City*

I waited a month to write you not through neglect but through attention. I mean, I have been attending to the question of a place for you in Columbia College, and this has meant waiting. And I still don't know enough. But it is more than time to write and tell you what I do know. It is not encouraging. Steeves is more doubtful than he was, and refuses to commit himself. The budget is bad, there may be no vacancies at all next year, and at best the only thing available may be a half-time job reading freshman papers for English C. I suppose I should be sorry I wrote what I did when things seemed so much more promising. I shall continue, however, to tell all.

The following paragraph is confidential—you must not remember that I have written it. Neff got to Steeves, I gather, and under cover of a great solicitude for you suggested that it might be best for you to start teaching in a college where you had no "friends." This is vulgar nonsense to me, but Steeves has been impressed, and I believe will continue to be. Such truth as there is in the principle has nothing to do with you *or me;* the more friendship the better among scholars, gentlemen, and poets, say I. Yet there it is, and so I ask whether you want me to start anything going at another place, say Queens College, a new branch of the City College on Long Island. Or anywhere else. Of course you may have devices and connections. If so, you should employ them all without delay. But if there is anything I can be doing at this range, let me have it, also without delay. Teaching is not the best of all occupations, and you may decide to get along without it, at least for awhile. The Columbia situation is unspeakably stupid. Not, by the way, that it is merely a matter of you and me; Steeves and Neff, I suspect, would say that it was rather a matter of you and Columbia. But in any view it is abysmal. Write to Steeves if you like, suppressing the above; though he told me a letter from you was unnecessary. I hope you have written the Dean. As for Neff, he should not know that you know this, since in a possible future it might need to have been forgotten altogether, and even forgiven.

Your poems are a much more comfortable subject. Your mother tells me that another one is waiting for me at Columbia, but these are enough to inspire the prophecy that if they are among your SR group the name of JB will be a good name beginning—is it April or July? The Translation is the right title, I think, for a very fine poem, one of your best so far; the beaver is a most potent creature in his two lines, and the whole says libraries. The Apparition and The Trial are likewise at your top: the first for every line (I started to name several, e.g. the 6th, 11th, 15th, and 21st, but decided they could not be detached), and the second for "Historian"—and of course for your old word raven again, which reminds me of Blackmur. Epitaph is slighter but still powerful; the Shakespeare prayer I find nothing in at all—the first line is sentimental, and what "knowledge" are you talking about? That which M. Arnold said was positively outtopping, don't you know, or what? The rest of the poem doesn't say, and so I don't know. Not, probably, that you were prepared to swear by the epigram.

To Scott Buchanan
TLS/MH

March 23, 1938   *New York City*

Mark Van Doren first met Scott Buchanan in the late twenties in the Nation
*office. Buchanan and Stringfellow Barr were prime movers in originating the
Great Books curriculum at St. John's College. Buchanan was one of Van
Doren's closest friends.*

Want to do me and possibly St. John's a favor? If so, read the enclosed
letter and poems which came to me a month ago from John Berryman in
England, and after you have heard certain other things I have to tell you
about him, consider whether he wouldn't be a valuable addition to your
staff next year, provided you are to be indulging in additions.

I am sure I have mentioned him to you once or twice. He is the best
student I have ever had (yes, better than Kip);[1] his appetite for knowledge
and wisdom is enormous; and he is undoubtedly a fine poet. The poems I
enclose came with the letter, and are representative; but another group of
five is to appear in I think the spring issue of the Southern Review. . . .
His special passion is Shakespeare, whom he studied with me and has
been studying at Cambridge (along with Yeats and everybody else) for
two years. He competed for the Oldham Prize and won it just before
Christmas—an annual Cambridge prize given for the best three-day written examination in Shakespeare. He probably hasn't much knowledge of
the classics, though I may underestimate him there; but no matter, for he
would take to them like a duck and it is time that he should. He is a pleasant and generous young man of perhaps twenty-four, capable of the most
noble enthusiasm and devotion. He is already, I may say, devoted to you;
and my sons are devoted to him ever since a day he spent with us before
he sailed two summers ago. He has great intelligence and the most sensitive critical equipment I have ever seen in a student, and writes excellent
prose. He went to Cambridge as Kellett Fellow from Columbia.

I must explain why his hopes as to Columbia have been dashed, and
why therefore I am writing you. Six weeks ago I suggested him to Steeves,
the head of our department in the College, and Steeves seemed to say yes.
But then Emery Neff got to Steeves—Emery Neff, whose course in Vic-
torian Literature Berryman simply couldn't swallow in his senior year.
Neff probably hates him, but under cover of a great solicitude he recommended that Berryman start teaching in some other place "where he had
no friends," meaning I suppose chiefly me. Steeves fell for this vulgar
nonsense, with the result that I wrote Berryman last night to say that

nothing was in sight. Then just after I had mailed the letter I thought of St. John's. I spoke of the whole matter to Mortimer today, and he thought Berryman might be precisely the sort of young man you needed. The more I think of it the surer I am, and I rather like the idea of pushing the best candidate Columbia has had in years towards the best college there is—a good joke on Columbia, and I should think a good thing for Berryman, not to say a good thing for you. Nor do I think of St. John's as a place where B. would, as Neff says, merely "start."

Such suggestions may be fantastic to you at the moment, but I make this one for what it is worth. And I would appreciate it if you could give the documents a fairly quick reading and dictate a note indicating the degree of your interest. For B. will be heart-broken when he gets my letter, and it would be pleasant to follow it soon with better news—not that you had decided on him necessarily, but that you had given him a thought, and had perhaps expressed the desire to hear from him directly. Meanwhile he might be digesting such of your literature as was available. I have distributed all of mine. . . .[2]

1. Clifton Fadiman.

2. Berryman was in an agitated state after his return from Europe, and in August he was informed that he would not receive an appointment to St. John's. He was then under even greater strain, and John Haffenden in *The Life of John Berryman*, 104, suggests that the poet then "had a form of nervous breakdown."

To John Berryman
TLS/MnU

March 25, 1938   *New York City*

An hour after I mailed my melancholy letter of last week I thought: But there is St. John's, that is better than Columbia anyway, that is the place for St. John Berryman. I wrote to Scott Buchanan, its dean, enclosing for documents your last letter to me and the poems that had come with it. I told Scott, what he knew already, that here was a poet for him as well as a scholar and a good man, and asked him to let me know whether there was any point in urging that a correspondence take place between you two. This telegram is the answer, and I take it to mean that if you are interested in him and St. John's you should immediately write him about yourself, adding whatever you like to what your letter to me set forth. He is clearly interested in you. You know of course that he is one of the best readers of poetry alive. And St. John's is in my opinion the perfect place for you to continue your education under the disguise of being a tutor or something of the sort.

St. John's is the third oldest college in the United States (late seventeenth century), and sits very prettily across the street from the Naval Academy at Annapolis, four hours from New York. Its history does not matter in view of the fact that it has started a new life this year with Stringfellow Barr as president and Scott as dean, and (more recently) with Hutchins of Chicago as chairman of the board of trustees. All this means that St. John's has become overnight the one conspicuous place in America where a true liberal-arts program of studies is possible. The student body will for four years engage in a reading program which they share with a staff of fellows, tutors, and lecturers, and which embraces in their original unity the disciplines of literature, philosophy, science, and mathematics. Everybody learns Greek, Latin, French, and German; reads Euclid and Newton as well as Homer, Dante, and Shakespeare; and emerges in theory—also, I predict, in practice—educated. You as tutor or fellow (I don't know which) would have to learn the languages and read everything while you taught it, though you would have time to write your poetry too, and they would particularly want you to do that, for they need a poet among so many philosophers. I have been giving a series of lectures there this spring, on Homer, the Greek tragic poets, and Aristotle's *Poetics;* but it is strenuous for me, what with all my business here. I had a chance, however, to see the program in act, and was much impressed. There is nothing like it in the country, and nothing so good. The three big freshman courses at Columbia, in literature, science, and the social sciences, are after all not related to one another; there they are one course, and the benefits for insight are tremendous. I need not remind you of the advantages there would be in having Scott to talk to all year; he has no parallel.

I urge you to look into this, and when I do so I have your poetry in mind—nothing else. I think it might make all the difference between your becoming a good poet and your becoming a great one: a wise one, I mean, with something like the knowledge I kidded you for attributing to Skakespeare. Shakespeare had it, of course, in part because of his intellectual environment, which this discipline will restore in so far as it can be restored. He had oceans of genius in addition, but that is something one does not go anywhere and get. You have your own genius; and here is the environment. The emphasis of course is upon the classics, upon the tradition: the best emphasis in my opinion for a living poet, who can thereby become alive. Also, you will constantly be reading the best books: a superb opportunity for a critic of contemporary literature, most of whose colleagues in the game know nothing and fall for tripe. The best poet we now have, for instance, your Yeats, has in him if I mistake not some phony mysticism. Don't get riled; I may be wrong; but at least you will be able to decide for yourself at St. John's whether I am. The program, I may add, comes down to our day, and the interest of the college is in this day's mind, ultimately. And you would find down there a group of men who knew all about the contemporary scene. More, that is to say, than anywhere else—e.g., at Columbia where Contemporary Civilization is taught by persons who know no other.

What do you think? But don't tell me. Tell Buchanan, who will want to know whether you look upon such a project with enthusiasm, how old you are, whether you are willing to learn Greek the first year with the students (I seem to remember that you have no Greek; if I am wrong, so much the better), and exactly how you would want to spend your time.

The Return is swell, but this is a business letter and is already long enough.[1]

P.S. I'll have to confess to a sneaking pleasure in the thought of the joke on Columbia this would be. I believe too that St. John's would pay as well as Columbia, though I know nothing definite about salary. That's something for you to ask about—ask Buchanan, I mean, to make clear. Meanwhile I hope he is sending you the literature I told him to send—one or two articles by him, and the list of the books they read.

1. "The Return" was published in *Five Young American Poets* (Norfolk, Conn., 1940).

To Allen Tate
TLS/NjP

May 8, 1938   *New York City*

I waited to write you until I had seen Scott and learned from him the whole truth about your conversation at Chapel Hill. After I had reported your praise of his lecture, which pleased him, and heard him say how much he had enjoyed an hour's talk with you, I asked what all was said. "Well," admitted Scott, "I told him that several passages in your lectures here ran off like—" "Blank verse?" "Yes. But I made him promise not to tell you." "Then why are you telling me?" There was no answer to that, so he went on to say that there had been some discussion of my poems, and particularly of a small selected volume which ought to exist, either before or after the collected. I sighed and agreed, but declared that I was not the one to pick it—that if the public had not done so, perhaps there was none there; or if there was, I did not know its character or its limits. You are so familiar with this ground that I don't need to cover it again. I was flattered, however, because two such men had discussed me; and I acknowledge that some day the small book should be made, say when I am palsied, and you and Scott still have the strength to make it. Meanwhile the materials are being restored to print—that is my interest in the big volume—and I'll now go on to another subject.

Eliot's fear for your play is simply his way of saying that it might be terribly effective. Of course there is always a problem there: a play can be too terrible to please. But on the other hand there is Prince Arthur in *King John,* not to speak of Mamilius in *The Winter's Tale;* and recently *The Children's Hour* was a year's hit. My own notion is that the play as it stands crosses no line, or at any rate no such scruple as Eliot's entered my head as you read. I am partial to horror, but isn't Eliot? Have you considered the explanation that he has no children of his own? Such people often can't take it, or imagine how easily children can.[1]

Why don't you send me the poem that convinced you that you oughtn't to write others for a while?[2] Somehow I am suspicious; though if I agreed I would say so. And of course there is the question whether this one, even if disappointing to you, proves anything about the ones to come. Its function may have been to disappoint you—as an artist, which you are—and make you try again. Not that I am whooping it up for composition. As for the short ones you say I still should write, I have no idea what they should be, and do have some dim idea after two years as to what the long one should be; so I shall be starting it next, I hope in 1939. It won't hurt to wait on further short ones, since I have so many, and especially since the impulse is absent. I'm glad the mythology pieces interested you, and invite you to see the whole series in the *C.P.* Twenty-one in all. . . .

1. Tate and Anne Goodwin Winslow collaborated on an acting version of James's *The Turn of the Screw.* Tate sent the play to T. S. Eliot, who according to Radcliffe Squires in *Allen Tate,* 134, "felt that the imposition of evil on children would be unbearable."

2. "Love Song." Tate did not publish the poem, but Radcliffe Squires in *Allen Tate,* 149, published one quatrain from it:

O Love, have no fear
Where damned souls leer
In nice optimism
Salvation of schism.

To John Berryman
ALS/MnU

May 8, 1938   *New York City*

This is a note upon my return from giving a last lecture at St. John's to say that Buchanan liked your letter very much—took me over to his office to show it to me—and explained that certain financial worries have kept him from answering it. The College has been in danger of closing, you know. But some money has been found and they are going on—and I gathered that S. B. would write you soon, though I can't promise exactly when. Nor can I say what he will say, or whether there will be an outright offer to begin with. He still counts on seeing you, either in N.Y. or at Annapolis, as soon as you are home—this not because he doubts you, but because he wants to be sure that you understand the situation as it will affect you. He is a conscientious man.

So try to bear up until you hear from him, and if he sounds cautious or tentative don't be too much worried.

Meanwhile I hasten to agree that Yeats is a great poet—I never denied it, did I?

This is all for tonight, as Columbia's last week begins tomorrow and I have papers.

To John Berryman
ALS/MnU

June 28, 1938   *Falls Village, Connecticut*

I had your note from Cambridge too, but you seemed to be in some doubt when you would sail and so I waited to hear from you here. Welcome back, even if it is hard. I can remember how hard it was for me to accept the United States. New York was hideous, and—well, doubtless we aren't talking about the same thing at all, but at any rate we can agree upon the difficulty of this first summer. Courage, however. You have plenty of it—at least you should be glad of that.

I'd say to come up this week-end, but this small house is to have 15 people in it—Buchanans, Adlers, and Tates, with the young thrown in. The following week-end we are to have family. But any later time that you can, please come. Or, as you say, in the middle of any week if you can be driven. There is of course the New Haven Railroad, and if you don't show up in reasonable time I'll send you tickets—hush—gladly.

I can't promise on week-day mornings, from Monday to Saturday inclusive, not to be working. For I am at last writing my book on Shakespeare—have done 62 pages, and find it both hard and exciting. I'll talk to you about that when you come. Or maybe I won't if it has me down.

I very much hope you can see Scott in New York; but of course you should look Annapolis over if it can be managed. I'll learn from him Friday if he saw you on the way. I should think not, with all the baggage he will have. But perhaps, and if so, good.

My best regards to your family, and all our best to you.

To John Berryman
ALS/MnU

July 13, 1938   *Falls Village, Connecticut*

Unless I hear from you I'll expect you on the train that leaves Grand Central at 12:45 (Daylight Saving Time) Saturday. Get a ticket to *West Cornwall*—I am writing this in haste, 8 miles from the station, so I can't enclose one, but I'll make the presentation later. The railroad is the N.Y.N.H.&H, and the station is West Cornwall *Connecticut.* Don't take a New York Central train to West Cornwall, New York.

Kip Fadiman will be here, and perhaps can drive you back. I am making it the same week-end as his because the boys will be gone the next one, and they want to see you. As do we all. . . .

To John Berryman
TLS/MnU

August 10, 1938   *Falls Village, Connecticut*

The Sh. book takes literally all my time and mind, so don't look for much here besides answers to your questions. But I enclose one of the pictures taken at the Tates that day, and showing your beard. To me, at least in this picture, it looks artificial. Phelps Putnam, who has been visiting Cornwall frequently since you left, says it looks as if you had put it on just for the picture. All this is one more way of saying that I think you would do about a million times better without it. For instance, you would like New York better. And it is important that you should. It is fatal to hate the environment, especially when the environment will never know you hated it. And for all you know New York doesn't like the beard. But maybe it isn't there any more, and anyhow I shouldn't be bothering you about it.

Krutch of course would be in Colorado. But he will be back early in September—at Redding, Conn.—and I'd have a letter waiting there for him, asking him if he will help you to Orson.[1] I don't know Orson, or Orson me. Krutch knows about you, and won't mind doing what he can. As a matter of fact, I don't remember whether *he* knows Whoreson, as the man is called. The idea itself strikes me as good—and I am delighted to see you are having ideas.

Also, writing poems. Plumage comes out very well I think, though I am not sure that I see the function of the flatness in ll. 8 and 16.[2] I recognize that it is intentional, but temporarily at any rate it bothers me. Ceremony

and Vision is difficult, or was, and I will discuss it with Allen before saying more than that I find in it your best virtues—clear, carved form and a
fertility in pungent, gentle, unforced, and very human phrases.[3] In other
words, I like C&V, and am only waiting for Tate's remarks so that I can
deliver the two sets together. He and Caroline are coming for supper, and
we are going afterwards to a house where he can play his fiddle.

Putnam is a heart-breaker: big, blear-eyed, drunken, sentimental, inar-
ticulate, and desperate for companionship and praise. He has a wife but
she is in my quick opinion a fool, and though he has an income he needs
occupation. You are right in wanting occupation, which of course you will
have before too long. Which reminds me—read Scott's article in the SR.[4]
It is grand, and ought not to seem dull to any one. If necessary, study
Thomas to understand it—and Scott.

Tate prefers C&V to Plumage, as I do, and considers the SR group still
better, as with more reservations I do. We are home late from the music,
and I won't go into an essay.

Tomorrow morning I tackle Macbeth, after which there will be only 9
more chapters. Not that I am tired, or more than I should be from hard
work which is also happiness.

1. Berryman, unemployed, was thinking
of trying to work for Orson Welles.
2. Berryman's "Plumage" was not
published.
3. "Ceremony and Vision" was first
published in James Laughlin (ed.), *Five*
Young American Poets (Norfolk, Conn.,
1940).
4. Scott Buchanan, "The Metaphysics of
the Higher Learning," *Southern Review*, IV
(1938), 1–14.

To Allen Tate
TLS/NjP

October 6, 1938   *New York City*

*   *   *

After you left Cornwall I went over the Shakespeare three times, made
many minor improvements, and got it ready to bring with me on my first
trip to New York, the day after the hurricane. The publisher now has it,
likes it, and proposes to bring it out next September—not in the Spring,
because that would be too close to the *Poems*. Fancy mine delaying
Shakespeare's. I am a little restless at the thought, but I am told it is a
good one, and of course in a few weeks I shall have lost my impatience.
Carl likes the book very much he says, and so does Raymond Weaver to

whom it is dedicated. I have been tempted to be sorry that I didn't let you see it all this summer, but on the whole I am not, for the improvements I made later on were real, and in general I dislike showing anything before I think it finished. You must understand that I would have liked nobody's opinion better than yours. But you'll have to read the book—there's no getting around it—and there is plenty of time for that. You may be interested in the fact that both Weaver and Carl voted for the chapter on *As You Like It* as the best. . . .

. . . I haven't seen Berryman since I got back, and for some reason keep forgetting to do so. The beard still stands between us, as does the vewy.[1] . . .

1. Berryman's affected English pronunciation.

To John Berryman
ALS/MnU

October 20, 1938   *New York City*

I suppose I'd have been horrified if anything had come of the Orson interview.[1] I agree, in other words, that the thing to do is write—and meanwhile be ready to take anything real that comes along in the way of a job. As for Cowley, blast him.[2] And as for [Beatrice], I am delighted—partly for the selfish reason that I shall see her for myself.

The two poems you sent today I take less seriously than the Bird one I never acknowledged from Cornwall.[3] These are all right, but that was good—as were your remarks on E. A. R.[4] and M. V. D.

Let me repeat, I admire your present courage. And I expect it to continue.

1. Orson Welles.
2. Malcolm Cowley, one of the editors of the *New Republic*, had rejected some of Berryman's poems.

3. The two poems were "Conversation" and "Father and Son."
4. Edwin Arlington Robinson.

To John Berryman
ALS/MnU

February 3, 1939   *New York City*

I thought the Yeats ¶ very fine, and hope you did not mind some cuts Freda Kirchwey said she had to make in it—purely for space, since at the last minute space waits for no man.[1] She liked your piece as it came—that is something to remember.

I like *Winter Landscape*,[2] except that "tired" is weak in the 5th line (doesn't know whether to be 1 or 2 syllables), and "irrecoverably" in the 15th loses by unnecessary emphasis—perhaps the idea in it should be implied by other words, not stated. But the whole is rich and good. Do watch out, however, for the effect of accentlessness which you get almost too easily—of tonelessness, and the voice running slowly down. Keep up your tone, and be no enemy to firmness.

As for my health, I am still nursing it—going out only when necessary, and doing absolutely no extra thing. Payment, they tell me, for a year of overwork. But in another week or so I'll be as before—say two weeks, to be on the safe side. And then we can discuss the Yeats project.[3] Don't let this alarm you. I am not seriously ill. Merely that the sinus condition disappears slowly, and rest is good on general principles.

My best to B.[4]

1. Berryman wrote the untitled notice of the death of W. B. Yeats in the *Nation,* February 4, 1939, p. 135. He observed: "Yeats was the greatest poet of our time; he takes his place 'with Landor and with Donne,' as long ago he hoped he would."

2. Written on January 9, 1939.
3. Berryman planned to edit a volume of essays devoted to Yeats. Van Doren, Tate, and many other scholars had expressed interest, but the project was not completed.
4. "Beatrice" was in the United States.

To William Sloane
ALS/NjP

February 8, 1939   *New York City*

Sloan was MVD's editor at Henry Holt and Company.

Your telegram today (I am sure it was yours), added to the letters I hear you sent with the copies I autographed, and to the ads in the *Times* and the *Saturday Review,* has set a record so far as I know for editorial courtesy, and this note is to say how deeply I feel such kindness. It is new to me, if not to Henry Holt and Company—long may the latter flourish. My hope for the *Poems,* now that they have been made into so beautiful a book, and now that they are in such hands as yours, is that they justify their existence in their publisher's eyes. Nothing could please me more than to have them do so. . . .

To John Gould Fletcher
ALS/ArU

February 14, 1939   *New York City*

Writing from Santa Fé, Fletcher had praised many parts of Van Doren's
Collected Poems.

Your generous letter gave me the greatest pleasure, and not the least generous thing about it was your advice as to a measure for the long poem. I
have been much troubled about that, very much on the fence—a rail
fence, with splinters—and your word coming when it did has probably
decided me. I appreciate your remembering the problem, and your trou-
bling to revive it at a time when your novel must be absorbing you. I am
greatly curious about the novel. . . .

But to return to the subject of your generosity, I do hope *Poetry* lets you
review me. Harriet was always very condescending to me, but Dillon may
be different, and in any case it would be a pleasure to read you on myself,
regardless of why you wrote or what conclusions you reached—I mean
by the last that I am assuming no conclusions, not at all that your conclusions would be a matter of indifference to me.[1]

I am glad you still find *Gentry* interesting. But don't be too hard on
your own book. Its appearance was pleasing to at least one eye, even if
there should have been more of it and if—of course—there should have
been more and better reviews. I wouldn't assume too soon that the book
had failed to reach a certain number—it needn't be large—of good
readers. . . .

I didn't see *Time* on poetry,[2] but the article sounds wonderful and I'll
look it up. Laura Riding's *Collected Poems* was sent to me and I thought
it pretty terrible. . . .

1. Fletcher did not review MVD's *Collected Poems* for *Poetry;* instead, S. I.
Hayakawa did an unfavorable review in the
June, 1939, issue, pp. 157–60. George Dillon, who had been a member of the Advi-
sory Committee of *Poetry,* succeeded
Harriet Monroe as editor of that journal.

2. The Books section of *Time,* De-
cember 26, 1938, pp. 41–44, published
brief reviews of Laura Riding, Robinson
Jeffers, William Carlos Williams, Rainer
Maria Rilke, Frederic Prokosch, Joseph
Auslander, Kay Boyle, Merrill Moore,
Genevieve Taggard, Donald Davidson, and
Kenneth Fearing.

To Allen Tate
TLS/NjP

February 19, 1939   *New York City*

*   *   *

[L]ast week I had a relapse of some sinus trouble which has had me down for six weeks. . . . This is the first real illness of my life, and Hedwig says it is payment for years of overwork.[1] . . . I had always supposed that work one enjoyed was not dangerous, but of course there are limits to this as to any truth. There is also a bit of psychology somewhere in all this woodpile, too. Finishing proofs on the *Poems* and the *Shakespeare* all at once, and thus winding up twenty years in a day, was something like coming to a precipice and looking over. But I could easily talk you out of breath with my crisis. . . .

Your letter of course gave me enormous pleasure, and you are the kind of man of whom I can say that I think it gave you pleasure too. I refuse none of your praise, and I hereby promise to do anything I can to explain the Mythology. As I told Scott a week ago Friday, the only trouble with those gods is that they are heathen; that is, they have no center, and there might have been two hundred rather than twenty-one. This deficiency I am at present trying to correct, in the interest of my new long poem, by reading medieval philosophy—not specifically to become Christian, for I suspect the heathen streak is ineradicable, but to learn the secret if I may of what is after all the most comprehensive and unified account of reality ever given, and the most valuable description of the universe. I sound solemn, but you will discount me. . . .

You were nowhere more generous than in your recognition of the revisions, which of course only one or two other eyes will ever see. But don't think they were too easy, and don't go on telling me that I have written all this poetry "quietly" and "indifferently." Dorothy could tell you of fits and vertigoes, and the preparation of this volume was almost enough to alienate her from my side, what with my running to her every day with questions she had already answered and couldn't feign interest in answering again. . . .

Your way of referring to the many poems you don't like as well as the thirty you do should be set up as a model for Winters to study.[2] A letter from him the other day lectured me for deliberately making most of the poems bad—for sabotaging my art—out of a heretical devotion to the principles of Emerson and Frost. The principles (if any) I repudiate, but the funniest thing about Winters is that he should so conduct himself in the presence of what is after all a common occurrence: namely, that some of a man's poems seem better than others. He went on humorlessly to "admit" that he liked those he did like very much indeed, and as a matter of fact I don't want to speak ungraciously of him. But you know him of old. It was my first letter from Yvor. . . .

You are wrong about *The Fathers*. It is one of your important books, as Schwartz's article on you makes clear if nothing else does.[3] Have you seen a copy of that? Both of us, it appears, have been taken by Schwartz's poetry. I got it from John Ransom to review, and had no sooner read it than I wanted to see the author—a new thing for me.[4] I managed it through a young man at Columbia, and found him (Schwartz) all that I knew he would be and more.[5] There has been something of a correspondence, including recently a copy of his *Tate* for me to read. You may not agree with all of it and I am not sure that I do, but you will find much of it speeding to your center I think, and I for one admire it greatly. The compliment it conveys is one he has become embarrassed about because of the timing between it and your praise of him; I have told him to forget all that. What I started to say is that he makes considerable use of *The Fathers* in a study of your poetry. Isn't that right? Your book is important enough, in fact, for you to be justified in forgetting it. If it had been bad, or insignificant, not so. . . .

1. Dr. Hedwig Koenig was a longtime friend of the Van Dorens.

2. Yvor Winters, the American poet and critic.

3. Delmore Schwartz's "The Poetry of Allen Tate" was to appear in *Southern Review*, V (1940), 419–38.

4. MVD reviewed *In Dreams Begin Responsibilities* in *Kenyon Review*, I (1939), 208–11. For a discussion of the Tate-Schwartz relationship, see James Atlas, *Delmore Schwartz: The Life of an American Poet* (New York, 1977).

5. The young man remains unidentified.

To Allen Tate
ALS/NjP

March 5, 1939   *New York City*

* * *

I would recommend Schwartz for anything. Shall I write the College about him or wait to be asked for my opinion?[1]. . .

. . . Ford looked terribly feeble the last time I saw him—he was crossing Fifth Avenue on someone's arm, and as this was all he could do he didn't see me. . . .

1. Tate wanted to bring Schwartz to Woman's College of the University of North Carolina, Greensboro, where Tate was then teaching. MVD wrote in his letter of recommendation that Schwartz's *In*

Dreams Begin Responsibilities was "intellectually brilliant beyond anything of its sort I have seen in years" (Atlas, *Delmore Schwartz,* 146). The appointment, however, was not made.

To Allen Tate
TLS/NjP

March 20, 1939   *New York City*

* * *

. . . I wrote Marc Friedlaender about Schwartz immediately upon hearing from you.[1] I don't know why it hadn't occurred to me that Schwartz might want something of the sort. He had described himself as getting along on articles, and I had supposed he preferred it that way. There is something to be said for such a life, except of course that in the long run it is exhausting. . . .

A strange thing has happened. I may have told you of a novel I wrote four years ago.[2] Nannine Joseph, who never lost faith in it though I did, placed it last week with the twenty-eighth publisher—none other in fact than Holt, who is enthusiastic though he wants a few changes made if I care to make them (the contract is signed, so that I do not have to make them, and they are not forced). It will be hard to open up the book after all this time, but I started to look at it tonight and decided it was possible. I don't mean that I lost faith in the book as a book; merely as something to offer publishers. Even at that I may be sorry. Holt is not publishing it until a year from now, naturally, since the *Shakespeare* appears in the fall and there must not seem to be a glut. There is none really, but nobody would understand that. . . .

1. Marc Friedlaender was then a member of the English Department of Woman's College, University of North Carolina.

2. *Windless Cabins* (New York, 1940).

To Allen Tate
ALS/NjP

April 24, 1939   *New York City*

* * *

The Princeton move is an excellent one, not least because we shall see you oftener.[1] For yourself and Caroline it is clearly a windfall—and what new accents won't Nancy pick up? We are delighted by the news, and impressed. Impressed, for one thing, by Princeton's good sense. I hardly thought they had it in them.

. . . I am sorry your eloquence went to waste on Guggenheim. I haven't heard what happened (if anything) to my case. A week before the announcement Moe told Joe (Krutch) that I stood well.[2] Without sour grapes, I am content to be free of obligations to them next winter. We'll be pinched, but that has happened before, and in Cornwall it will signify little, since our needs there are few. It was naturally too late to recall my application for a full year's leave from Columbia etc. Once more my thanks for what you wrote, and for what I shall so long remember. . . .

1. Tate had been invited to be Poet in Residence in the Creative Arts Experiment at Princeton. Caroline Gordon would not teach and would be free to continue her writing.

2. Henry A. Moe was president of the John Simon Guggenheim Memorial Foundation.

To Allen Tate
TLS/NjP

May 15, 1939   *New York City*

* * *

I know absolutely nothing about the Guggenheim affair. A week before, as I may have said in my last letter, Moe indicated to Joe that it was certain; then it did not happen. Joe said he would inquire, but thus far he has not. I never will. Answers handed down from high places always depress me, and I really mean what I say when I say it is in some measure a relief not to have to get anything done. Also, it is better for the poem. . . .

One suspicion I have re Guggenheim is that Cowley dictates; this was suggested to me, I believe, by you and Caroline. In that case it is all clear enough, since C. always condescends to me. Some day I'll let him know how I feel about him, but right now I wouldn't for the world let him know I cared about this. Assuming, i.e., he dictates. . . .

To John Berryman
ALS/MnU

May 22, 1939   *New York City*

I am packing for Cornwall and have just remembered that you once took Vol. 1 of my Spenser. If you haven't gone to Maryland yet, and know where the volume is, I wonder if I could have it, since Cornwall is where the set should be?

P.S. I wrote also to Reisterstown, just to get the question settled.

To John Berryman
ALS/MnU

May 26, 1939   *New York City*

Don't send it now. The main thing was to know its whereabouts—and if you took it there you must have wanted to read it. Do so at your leisure, and send or bring it to Cornwall in the fall—or, if you are leaving there before that, then. Cornwall is where the set belongs, and it is a gift that I want to keep together. I wasn't really dunning you, but thought that in the late confusion you might have stored it somewhere here beyond reach.[1]

Your mother tells me one more thing about the *K.R.*—that they are proud to publish you. Shows more sense than I was beginning to believe they had.[2] I'm glad—and proud myself to point out that we'll be in the same issue, since Matthiessen's review is also scheduled for the summer.

We leave Cornwall for the West on June 6th and shall be back about the middle of July. I'll be at the Summer Session here, lecturing, August 7 to 11. If you are back from Maryland by then be sure to let me know and let me see you.

Maryland must be a bower. Good. More bower then to your pen, and may your volume grow many splendid branches.

[P.S.] Let the Hayden go—please.

1. Berryman returned the Spenser volume to John Abbote, custodian of the Bleecker Gardens, where the Van Dorens lived. On November 2, 1940, MVD wrote

Berryman: "The Spenser was still in John Abbote's bureau drawer. He had kept it only too well. But we ran right out and got it, and it was in perfect shape. So I'm glad you wrote—and I'm sorry I missed you. Yours for F. D. R."

2. Berryman's "Letter to His Brother" appeared in *Kenyon Review*, I (1939), 257–58.

To John Berryman
ALS/MnU

August 28, 1939   *Falls Village, Connecticut*

I'd love to tell you what you should do about Columbia and Wayne, but I find I can't.[1] Too many complications. I can point out that you probably won't pay your debts (be able to, I mean) out of the difference between $1000 and $1700 if you are also to be a householder (which I wish to heaven you could be); that turning down Columbia so late might queer any future chances there; that the probably vast differences between N.Y. and Michigan are to be considered—N.Y. not being quite so bad with a job; that Wayne would be no place to leave from advantageously; that you are happy out there and perhaps for that reason should stay; that—oh, dozens more, and I won't go on. The point is that I can't make up my mind, much less yours. I'm sorry to fail you, though I have written Hilberry on the chance that it might help next year if not this[2]—in case, i.e., you decided to keep Wayne as a place to flee N.Y. from. Note: Would B. like it? I can't guess.

Allen is undoubtedly not angry. He is that way—lets weeks go by without a letter, as in fact I do, and you. For instance, a card from him three weeks ago promised a long letter about my *Shakespeare* which hasn't come. I wait more or less patiently, since that above all things can't be forced. You missed your copy of the *Sh.*, of course. It was sent in May, about the time you were moving. Do you want another there, or shall I wait till you know where you are to be? Tell me frankly—I don't want another copy to go wandering. It is published October 2 but it has been out seeking praises for months—and has got some fine ones from Knight, Charles Williams, Oliver Elton, Schwartz, Cudworth Flint, et al.

I look forward to the *Nation*—bravo, and I am sure your work will have its immediate influence, not only on the *Nation* but on the general state of things.[3] It was a grand idea. You send no poems, but I am delighted that you have written more. I don't doubt for a minute that they are better too—still better, you know I mean. The move to Michigan was naturally a good one, if only for the summer.

I do nothing about the long poem but think of it, and not enough of that. It is hard to forget our trip—10,000 miles in a month, and wonderful—and now I am full of fixing over my study for the winter. There is no hurry about what is to be done there, thank God.

You amaze me with your story of my *Poems* at the *Nation*. My theory was that they had got in a roast which they were too embarrassed to print. This is more remarkable. Thanks to you, angel, for suggesting Bishop, and indeed for making the issue exist.[4] I'd rather read your review than Bishop's, but let's let that pass.

1. Berryman was to accept the position at Wayne.

2. Clarence Hilberry was chairman of the English department at Wayne.

3. Berryman had been appointed poetry editor of the *Nation*.

4. John Peale Bishop reviewed MVD's *Collected Poems* in the *Nation*, December 23, 1939, pp. 714–16.

To Allen Tate
ALS/NjP

October 2, 1939   *Falls Village, Connecticut*

*   *   *

This *Kenyon* issue depressed me for days, what with Red finding nothing to say about me and Matthiessen finding it possible only to say that as a poet I am a good critic.[1] But I have recovered, . . .

1. Robert Penn Warren (Red), in "The Present State of Poetry in the United States," *Kenyon Review*, I (1939), 384–98, made passing mention of MVD, saying only that he had a respected place in American poetry. In the same issue of *Kenyon Review*, pp. 453–57, F. O. Matthiessen unfavorably reviewed MVD's *Collected Poems, 1922–1938* (New York, 1939).

To William Sloane
ALS/NjP

October 2, 1939   *Falls Village, Connecticut*

Sloane telegraphed Van Doren that Holt had nominated Collected Poems *for a Pulitzer prize.*

Your telegram today, received as I was picking apples (I'll give you some when you come), brought blushes to all their cheeks! They hadn't known how distinguished a hand had been reaching for them. I explained that it was as much your generosity as my greatness, if not more. So they returned to their green, indifferent state. . . .

To John Berryman
ALS/MnU

October 29, 1939   *Falls Village, Connecticut*

Please don't have a conscience about writing me, and please for God's sake have none about the *Shakespeare.* That you got it was all I needed to know. It has been well received—flattering reviews everywhere, many nice letters from friends and strangers, and a sale so far of 2,500 copies, with enough orders ahead to require a second printing last week. I was glad of this, partly because it was an early chance to correct several misprints and a few slips of the pen. In a book which is all detail it is apparently impossible to avoid such things. I was glad also, of course, because I wanted the book to succeed—even be a little popular. The publisher thinks it will sell for a long time, and I won't mind that either. I must confess I like it—the book—immensely. Let's leave the matter there.

You really have a job there.[1] It sounds cruel. But it is important that you like students, and since I have no doubt that they like you I am a bit less depressed over Wayne than I might have been. And remember that the first year of teaching is much, much the hardest. And don't by any means fail to take time off—even by violence—to do your literary work. Maybe not poems for the time being, but certainly the *Nation* MSS, and the reviews. And one more thing—don't let the whole situation ever lose its reality, such as it has; that will include its funny as well as its furious sides. I'm sure there are both. It is, in other words, a human year you are living through; and don't dishonor the fact.

Didactic! Your *Nation* pages were most impressive, including Campbell's poem, and I hope you will do it again soon. Nothing could be better for the *Nation,* as I have told them.

The Tates and Schwartzes were here last weekend, and you were often spoken of with affection. I continue to like the Schwartz's [*sic*] very much, as of course the Tates. Allen scarcely knows how the Princeton job will be; but we are going there in November and should find out. Schwartz said little about his Harvard job, and I'm afraid I paid too little attention.

We are all settled for the winter, with everything to make us comfortable except enough money; and last week I made some kind of start on my poem. Nothing to tell about yet, and I might abandon it—the start. But it is a satisfaction to have been able to make marks on paper.

Please give our love to B. when you next establish communication.[2]
And all possible happiness to you.

[P.S.] Peggy Marshall writes that she has Bishop's review—long—and
will use it when she can.[3] I don't forget that I have you to thank for that.
Auden's review of the *Shakespeare*, by the way, was the best it has had so
far. (*Nation* last week.)

I never see the *Partisan* for some reason. At any rate I haven't seen "The
Statue."[4] If you have a copy, why not send it to me—merely in an envelope if you are too devilled to write?

Chiappe and Merton—and for that matter Milton Crane—have mentioned you in recent letters.[5] So you see your fame lives and spreads.

1. Berryman's teaching load was twelve
hours a week.
2. MVD is referring to "Beatrice"
3. Peggy Marshall was literary editor of
the *Nation*.
4. Berryman's "The Statue" appeared in

Partisan Review, VI (Summer, 1939),
16–17.
5. Andrew Chiappe became a member
of the Columbia faculty. Milton Crane received his B.A. and M.A. degrees from
Columbia.

To Mortimer Adler
ALS/P
November 15, 1939   *Falls Village, Connecticut*

*   *   *

Don't forget either to send me the chapter on Poesis.[1] I need it in my daily
struggle against the weakness of my pen (but read pencil). The poem is
now about 500 lines long, or soon will be; but I haven't the least idea
whether it is good. All I know is that its subject interests me—I mean
its story. Which is all to the good, and let the accents fall where they
may. My study is working out beautifully. The waterfall outside makes
fine music . . . and indoors a sheet iron stove keeps me snug even in 10°
weather, of which we have had a little. I spend half of every day over there,
in a reappointed room every inch of which reflects my handiwork (and
Charlie's). It is a good life. . . .

The *Shakespeare* has been reprinted, and has sold I believe about 3000
copies, with every indication of a steady sale. . . . The reviews have been
unanimously generous, which would not be the case in a healthier literary
situation, i.e., one in which most books on *Sh.* were written as mine was,
with the poetry as subject. The novelty of such a procedure is what all the
reviewers have talked about. And there has been nobody living to com-

pare me with or judge me against. Somebody ought to be mad, e.g., because I am wrong about some play. Apparently the art is lost. . . .

1. "Creation and Imitation: An Analysis of Poiesis," *Proceedings of the American*   *Catholic Philosophical Association* (December, 1937), 101–31.

To John Berryman
ALS/MnU

December 4, 1939   *Falls Village, Connecticut*

Allen didn't misreport you. Indeed I got the idea that you were for the volume, and I agreed with him that it might be a good idea for you to appear with a group—from whom, of course, you could shake yourself free whenever you chose, in another volume of your own.[1] Which might be easier to arrange because of this, and which could reprint all it cared to. But he said nothing of apparatus, and I must say I should prefer a bare book, without photographs or manifestoes. I hope L. agrees in the end.[2] Even if he doesn't, though, I'd stay in. Is that coverage?

Let me know when you come east, and of course you must see us— remembering merely that I am a hog about my time this year, and may root for another day than you suggest. But some day.

1. *Five Young American Poets* (Norfolk, Conn., 1940) contained the poems of Mary Barnard, Randall Jarrell, John Berryman, W. R. Moses, and George Marion O'Donnell.   2. L. refers to James Laughlin, publisher of New Directions.

To John Berryman
ALS/MnU

December 29, [1939]   *Falls Village, Connecticut*

Yes, it is better that you shouldn't come here—or to Princeton, and I hope you have a doctor you can't deceive. Lie very low, and take no chances.

I'm terribly sorry, and I'd have said so sooner if I had had your address. Happy New Year anyway—may it surprise you by being really that!

If you sent me the *Partisan* with your fine poems, thanks.[1] They are truly fine, and I yearn for a collection—with introduction by J. B. Yes, do that.

1. *Partisan Review* VI (Summer, 1939), 16–18, printed "The Statue" and "On the London Train."

Our Lady Peace
1940–1945

Just before the beginning of the Second World War, the Van Dorens spent the sabbatical year 1939–1940 in Falls Village, and Mark Van Doren completed work on the narrative poem *The Mayfield Deer*. During the spring of that year he received the Pulitzer Prize for poetry, but this event is mentioned only in passing in his letters.

Many of his former students—Merton, Berryman, Lax—were beginning to publish, and others disappeared into the army once the United States entered the war. Van Doren was much concerned with war work, especially the Books and Authors War Bond Committee. Dorothy Van Doren was also caught up in wartime activities and spent four years with the Office of War Information.

These were also times of difficulty with CBS's "Invitation to Learning," the radio program noted for its intellectual vigor. The tensions surrounding that program are suggested in many of the letters of the period.

The old patterns of the Van Doren household began to break apart during these years, for Charles and John enrolled at St. John's College and were away from home much of the time. Charles at seventeen enlisted in the air force. Dorothy's war work often kept her away from their Connecticut farm during the summer, but Van Doren continued to go there. In the midst of wartime confusion, Van Doren wrote his influential *Liberal Education*.

To Allen Tate
ALS/NjP

January 11, 1940   *Falls Village, Connecticut*

<hr>

*   *   *

My *S.R.* hasn't come, but I haven't been expecting much from it lately. I hope the Schwartz you refer to is his article on you[1]—if so, I'll read it Monday in your honor and behalf. . . .

The poem is now 2,000 lines. Sometimes I think it is good, and sometimes I don't know. At any rate it happily absorbs me. I do nothing else, literally. Wouldn't it be horrible if it ran to 8 or 10 thousand lines? It may. Of course I can cut it.

Timberlake's review of *Shakespeare* in the *K.R.* was more interesting than most, and tackled me in detail as I told you I wanted someone to do.[2] But it seemed strange to me that after agreeing or disagreeing with my judgments throughout the piece he ended with the statement that I had made few of them. I should claim that there was one in almost every sentence. But obviously he means something else by "judgment," and "criticism," than I do. I quite agree on principle that criticism involves the making of judgments. . . .

1. Delmore Schwartz, "The Poetry of Allen Tate," *Southern Review,* V (1940), 419–38.
2. Philip Timberlake's review of MVD's

Shakespeare appeared under the title "Sensitive Not Critical," in *Kenyon Review,* II (Winter, 1940), 112–16.

To John Berryman
ALS/MnU

January 31, 1940   *Falls Village, Connecticut*

I waited to thank you for reading *Windless Cabins* and finding in it just what I hoped was there until I saw Zabel's article, which Allen had mentioned too. Well, I have seen it and found it quite as depressing as Bishop's review—depressing because in neither case can the writer be waved away, even though he is discussing what I take to be a different book from mine. It is not that I mind having my limits measured. But I hang on to the belief that there is a center to which no reviewer penetrates. Doubtless this is my fault, since I made the book big. But it is their fault too, if they assume the critic's responsibility at all. Of course I may be flattering myself about that center—the word sounds overfine—and God knows I am not asking you to comfort my wounds. Nor for that matter am I wasting my own time over them. The new poem interests me to the exclusion of everything else, and that is that.

You sound more cheerful than you did before and during Christmas, which leads me to hope that the work, though still fiendish, can still somehow be taken care of. Don't bother to reread W.C. and make up your mind about the conclusion. It is the reason 27 publishers rejected the MS., and may be wrong, though it is what I started with.

If you are now engaged on the collection and preparation of your poems, I know you are both not to be envied and to be envied. For, as nothing is more impossible than to do such a job perfectly, nothing is more interesting than to try it—and try it again—and change—and change back—and learn—and decide, God damn it, to stop learning until one is older and doesn't need to.

To William Sloane
ALS/NjP

May 9, 1940   *Falls Village, Connecticut*

News that Mark Van Doren had received a Pulitzer Prize in poetry had put Sloane, his editor, in a festive mood.

Since I have a cross between baseball arm and writer's cramp (the latter from answering about 40 telegrams and notes) I won't keep you long. . . .

Your festive mood was charming. Mine since Monday has been somewhat abstracted, since I am keeping on with my poem under difficulties, particularly around mail time. . . .

To John Berryman
ALS/MnU

May 23, 1940   *Falls Village, Connecticut*

You were good to write me about the prize when it was (and is) hard to feel anything besides rage and fear.[1] Thanks for approving a decision that now seems nothing, though I was happy enough about it two weeks ago. Meanwhile—i.e., today—the news is not so black. I confine myself to the papers—the radio sickens me—and advise you to do the same, though doubtless you do already.

Steeves wrote me about you, and being here I left the question with those who were there, with the result you know. I am sorry the action was taken, but I can't regret having stayed out of it. I had pressed as hard as I could; you had seen them since I had; it was between them and you. You wouldn't have wanted to come, surely, with only one reason on the staff—and for that matter I don't know that I would have been a sufficient reason even if I had insisted.[2]

Your poems in the *S.R.* were superb, and Bob Giroux, who is at Harcourt Brace, wants you to discuss a volume.[3] But you won't answer his letters.

Why don't you? Keep things going in spite of hell. And—if you don't mind—keep most of your states a secret from such men as Steeves. They diagnose hysteria. Which doesn't help with any job. If you were free it wouldn't matter. Since you aren't, my advice is to see that it matters as little as possible. And I don't mean merely Steeves. This is no reflection on him personally, or even officially. He is the world—and you need the world, or act as if you did.

1. Pulitzer Prize for poetry.
2. Berryman had applied for a position in the English department at Columbia.
3. Berryman's "Desires of Men and Women," "Conversation," "Homage to Film," "Meditation," and "Song from Cleopatra" appeared in *Southern Review,* V (1940), 771–77.

To John Berryman
ALS/MnU

June 9, 1940   *Falls Village, Connecticut*

Thank you for taking my letter so well. I was nervous.

The fact that you did this, and that you have written so powerful—even if so terrifying—a poem as *A Point of Age* reassures me.[1] Not everything is lost when you have that much wisdom, feeling, and strength. I'll not discuss the poem in detail, but there are many wonderful places in it; indeed I think there are more such than in any other poem of yours. This is saying a lot, you know I know.

Some luck, please, and take as good care of yourself as you can.

1. See John Haffenden, *The Life of John Berryman* (Boston, 1982), 126, 137 for comments on this poem.

To Carl Van Doren
ALS/NjP

June 14, 1940   *Falls Village, Connecticut*

*   *   *

The war has made me search not only my private but the public soul—
i.e., the history of the past 25 years—and I have not been proud of what
"democracy" has done. There is of course Spain, not to speak of Czecho-
slovakia; but there is also a depression which somehow could not be
handled, and just for a symbol there is the food that was burned and
plowed under when millions of people needed it. However the war comes
out, such things probably won't happen again. Or if they do, mankind is
worse than a monkey. When the Allies win, which I hope to God they do,
in order to survive afterwards they will have to run the world in the interest of something more human than money. . . .

To William Sloane
ALS/NjP

June 20, 1940   *Falls Village, Connecticut*

*   *   *

I expect to finish the poem tomorrow, and I'll show it to you this fall.[1]
After about a month I'll make such revisions as I can then make; type it
so as to have more than one copy; and store it for other revisions next
year *et seq.* I think I like it as it stands, but I know I'll find things to
change or cut. It is about 8000 lines long—this from a prose document of
some 1500 words. I'll show you the document too if you are curious: but
don't tell me it is better. It probably is.

It has seemed indecent to go on with the poem these past few weeks,
but I decided it would be more indecent not to do so. Hitler has stopped
enough life as it is; anything we can save should be saved. It was a blessing, as you can believe, to have a single absorbing thing to do during these
days; I'll miss it after tomorrow, and maybe I'll break down with the rest
of the country. That morning sickness of yours I have had too, but not so
acutely of late. Not that I have more hope, but I have lost some of my
power to feel. Terrible, isn't it, what one man—or is it many appeasers—
can do to us? . . .

1. *The Mayfield Deer* (New York,
1941).

To John Berryman
ALS/MnU

August 17, 1940   *Falls Village, Connecticut*

Of course I am to be at Columbia again. It is necessary, and it was scheduled. But I have completed the poem, so there won't be too much grief
about going back, though as always I want to stay here. The poem is
ended rather than finished—I plan to spend a year or more in revising it.[1]
But the story is all down, and that was the main thing now. I haven't typed
it yet, though I shall do that before I leave.

Don't "rot" in Cambridge. Why not write? Laughlin was here today,
with Theodore Spencer, and reported progress on your Five-Poets book.[2]
Good luck to it, and to your health. The news from ["Beatrice"] was
most relieving—please send our love to her, and wish her every possible
safety. Any such wish must sound silly, but in this case it isn't.

Take a good rest in Windham, wherever it is, and don't anticipate too
much evil at Harvard. There may be less than you think, or, d. v., none
at all.

1. MVD's *The Mayfield Deer* was based
on Dr. Hiram Rutherford's "John Richman,
A Typical Backwoodsman." For additional
information about Dr. Rutherford, see
Willene Hendrick and George Hendrick,
On the Illinois Frontier: Dr. Hiram Ruth-

erford, 1840–1848 (Carbondale, Ill.,
1982).
2. Spencer was a poet and critic. His
book *The Paradox in the Circle* was
published by Laughlin's New Directions
in 1941.

To Scott Buchanan
TLS/MH

September 30, 1940   *New York City*

*Stringfellow Barr (Winkie) had the idea for "Invitation to Learning." The
program developed a following, but while Barr was on vacation, he was fired
and was told that Huntington Cairns, Allen Tate, and Mark Van Doren would
carry on with the program. Van Doren had met Scott Buchanan, the philosopher, in 1927, and the two had become close friends.*

*   *   *

The CBS thing has been a great embarrassment to Allen and me, chiefly
because we haven't known what was going on. We still don't, except of
course that after a four weeks' trial the powers invited us to continue
with Cairns and we accepted. We have asked Cairns and Levine several
times what happened about Winkie, but have been told substantially

nothing.[1] And until quite recently our assumption was that he was still in the background with us merely helping to carry on his enterprise. The irony in my case (probably in Allen's too) is that, having felt guilty last spring because I declined to broadcast until the poem was done, and consenting to do so in August not wholly, as you know, with relish, I started out with nothing in my mind besides a sense of duty towards Winkie and St. John's. It may sound smug, but I made my first trip with the notion that I was doing someone a favor. As things turned out, I enjoyed what I did and pleased the powers. But Winkie must know—I have never doubted this—that Allen and I were innocent of any desire to displace him or anybody else, for instance you. And the conversation at headquarters, particularly for me who drove down from Cornwall each Sunday and then drove right back again, was never about policy or personnel, but always about the broadcast to come. I want very much to discuss the whole matter with you and Winkie, and am sorry that I must wait still another week to do so. I have never known enough about it. Meanwhile my embarrassment mounts. Will you please reassure Winkie as to ourselves at any rate, and tell him that I want to hear from him frankly when I see him? . . .

  1. Leon Levine of CBS.

To John Berryman
ALS/MnU

October 2, 1940   *New York City*

I should have waited until your letter came to forward two envelopes from ["Beatrice"] which I found on my desk at Columbia last week. Having no address for you, I sent them in care of Schwartz. I hope they arrive safely. It was pleasant if startling to see B's name thus; do give her our love when you write, along with every wonderful wish.

Cambridge sounds good, and I am glad. And I look forward to the Laughlin book with more pleasure than you do. As for my poem, I am deliberately putting it away for a year. I have come to the end of any gumption I may have about it now; all perspective has been lost from peering at it steadily since June.

By all means call me when you are in New York next, and do let me take the Spenser off your hands. I can see it would worry you.

Regards to Bob, and of course to D. S.[1]

  1. Robert Jefferson Berryman, Berryman's brother, and Delmore Schwartz, who was teaching at Harvard, as was Berryman.

To Allen Tate
TLS/NjP

January 9, 1941   *New York City*

First, you are expected here for dinner Tuesday; and for ping-pong when and if we get through talking about HC and CBS.[1]. . .

I am postponing all but the substance of my reply until then. The substance is simple: If you resign I resign, and if HC resigns I do not.

You may be amused to know that the reason for my inquiring glances the other night was that I feared HC had been asking you whether I hadn't become intolerably interruptive and insultingly sure-minded. The setting is always clearly you and me vs. him; but because my manners are less perfect than yours I do sometimes jump first. The people I hear from see it as something like that: HC offering himself for the leap and the two of us leaping. They can't understand why he seems to like it. I offered Joe[2] the innocent theory that HC deliberately talks like a dope in order to provide differences. But your letter confirms my alternative theory that his leadership is going to his head and that he nobly suffers us both. In that case I wonder whether he and LL[3] shouldn't be let in on the secret of what any intelligent listener thinks of him. This would be hard to do, but it may be necessary; or at any rate it may be necessary for you and me to tell him frankly that we shall always disagree with him on the air, no matter what he asks or says. We can put it that this is an interesting difference between us, possibly an edifying one; and we can admit that we do not consider ourselves infallible. But we should be plain, and I for one am willing to be friendly. Nor am I now as one who talks behind the back; I will say all this and more to HC if you will say it with me. I still like him, though I am sorry he pulled you away for private words. When he called me at midnight to know your telephone number I asked him what the words had been. He was evasive: nothing important.

You should have been furious over the hoax. Query: have you any friend, or have I, who would do a thing like that? . . .

1. Huntington Cairns, a regular panelist   2. Joseph Wood Krutch.
on "Invitation to Learning."   3. Leon Levine of CBS.

To John Berryman
ALS/MnU

January 25, 1941   *New York City*

One of my freshmen has just written—I have the blue book before me— "Homer is a very epic poet." Why is that so funny? I wish I knew.

A Christmas and New Year card reached us from ["Beatrice"] today, and we were profoundly touched. Will you let her know, please, in your next letter to her, that we often think of her and that we particularly loved getting this card? We are very fond of ["Beatrice"], in case you didn't know.

Why not send me the 80-line poem, or don't you think I can read that many? At least I could write: John Berryman is a very lyric poet, not to say a very ironic ironist.

The labor of revision is doubly exciting: I am ashamed at things I find, but overjoyed at being able to find them where six months ago all seemed good enough. I am assuming that there is a point in this past which I can't go—i.e., that there is really a poem here, and that its skeleton is inviolable—but I haven't stopped yet, nor will I till May, when the publisher wants the MS.

I don't see how I can get to Cambridge, but if an excuse arises you will see me. Meanwhile Johnny is improving his ping-pong, and Charlie has beaten Allen.

To John Berryman
ALS/MnU

February 9, 1941   *New York City*

Thank you for the poem, which is out in front even of your others.[1] But it has given me an illumination. These ironies will some day land you in silence. And maybe that will have been too bad, for some of them didn't deserve so much wrath. That is to say, maybe the world in its badness can be taken a little more for granted. It is bad by definition, not by accident; and poetry can remember this to its own advantage.

Not that I am saying you are wrong here. Simply that your voice threatens to break, whole as it still is. And no world is worth that.

See Jack on you today?[2] He said nothing—but at any rate nothing bad.

1. "Night Club: Boston."
2. Peter Monro Jack, in "New Books of Poetry," *New York Times Book Review*, February 9, 1941, p. 18, wrote "An enterprising venture is the publication of '5 Young American Poets' by the New Directions Press ($2.50). They are as young as the average age of 28, their poetry has been published in magazines, but not till now in book form. . . . The level of writing is good, though the reader passes from one to the other without much sense of change, except in externals." Jack then made brief comments on W. R. Moses, George Marion O'Donnell, Randall Jarrell, John Berryman, and Mary Barnard. He characterized Jarrell as "slightly surrealist, Eliotish, and given to dictionary words." Jack then said that Berryman "has a similar vocabulary with a better, more modest and personal application." Jack concluded his brief notice: "One is impressed by the interest and competence of their writing, though not by its individuality."

To Allen Tate
ALS/NjP

March 20, 1941   *New York City*

Stringfellow Barr had been dropped from "Invitation to Learning," and there
were rumors that Barr wanted to get Huntington Cairns and Allen Tate
removed.

Leon is engaged for lunch Tuesday (with a publisher, Barnes & Noble,
who may become our sponsor, he says), but he insists that he wants to see
both of us in the afternoon. . . .

He also wants to see the 3 of us on Wednesday, and he wants to see *me*
alone before Tuesday. If I see him alone I promise to give you a candid
report of what we say, and to guard our double interest during the talk.
He was vague about the reason for such a talk, but did make it clear that
H.C. is not the white-haired boy with C.B.S. we have assumed he was,
and that it *may be* H.C. who is distorting the triangularity of our figure
into something too obtuse for rightness. I may have jumped to this conclusion, but I don't think so.[1]

Certainly we should not see him with H.C. The whole point is otherwise, and he understands.

1. Tate wrote John Peale Bishop on
March 19, 1941: "The situation at CBS is
getting more difficult all the time. The
backstairs intrigue is now so complex that
I don't intend to unravel it; and the interference from higher up is getting worse
constantly" (Thomas Daniel Young and
John J. Hindle [eds.], *The Republic of
Letters in America* [Lexington, Kentucky,
1981], 178).

To Huntington Cairns
APS/DLC

May 29, 1941   *New York City*

I had to rush off last night and so couldn't be unpleasant—as I hereby am.
I want to insist on having Krutch for *Walden*. After the idiotic spectacle
of J H,[1] not to mention others before him, it is high time we have a competent guest. I have never pressed for anyone else, or even suggested anyone else. Give me—& the program—a break before it kills itself.

1. Not identified.

To Allen Tate
ALS/NjP

August 2, 1941   *Falls Village, Connecticut*

CBS had informed Tate that he would be used only occasionally on "Invitation to Learning."

*   *   *

I wrote Leon (I should have made a carbon) saying that the program had been best when the 3 of us were doing it regularly, and that I advised a return to that pattern. I mean, a return to that personnel. Then I said that if he was set on having only 2 regulars, I would not be one of them with H.[1]—giving him such reasons as I thought he would understand. I said I'd be one with you as second, but never a man I couldn't talk to.

He telephoned me the minute he got the letter, professed to understand it, denied that H. was indispensable, and then gave his opinion that the program would be dropped after Labor Day, when the BOARD meets. I suppose it will, and I think I'll be relieved. He apologized for the hit-and-miss character of this summer's performance by saying that he had simply been keeping *I. to L.* alive week by week—implying that it had been noble of him to do so, as a favor to us. Of course he wasn't sure (when is he ever?) that the program would be dropped; and hinted that if it weren't you and I might be the boys. But I don't count on anything. He said you had sounded mad. I played this down, professing ignorance of your state, against the possibility of a recall. . . .

    1. Huntington Cairns.

To Allen Tate
APS/NjP

August 18, 1941   *Falls Village, Connecticut*

Nothing new Sunday, but I meet John[1] for lunch next Sunday and we shall find how things stand with us before we meet L. L.,[2] who will probably reappear on that day. Oh yes, one new thing—Miss M., who had been "running" things as you know, didn't show up either, probably offended because the week before I had refused to be run by her. So I am cooked, I'm sure.[3]

    1. John Peale Bishop, who was being asked to be a regular on "Invitation to Learning."

    2. Leon Levine of CBS.
    3. Tate wrote Bishop on August 9, 1941: "I think Cairns got me fired, as a way of

eliminating not only me but Mark, who wrote Levine a letter, after he heard I was fired, saying that he would not stay on with Cairns if he and Cairns alone were the permanent team. Levine prefers a team of two, with a guest each time. But if there is to be a team of three your presence might make it possible for Mark to stay on. It is probable, however, that you will find yourself with Cairns and a guest week after weary week" (Young and Hindle [eds.], *The Republic of Letters in America*, 181).

To Allen Tate and Huntington Cairns
TLS/NjP

September 30, 1941   *New York City*

I am sending you identical letters (one will be a carbon) about a thing I have done. And if I am brief it is not because I lack more to say; it is in order that any air of apology or alibi may be avoided.

Leon, speaking he said for the Board, asked me last week to go on with Invitation to Learning as leader, beginning November 16; a second more-or-less regular of my own choice to assist, and a guest, again of my own choice, or at any rate to be agreed upon between CBS and me, to be always third. The books, too, to be acceptable to me, and everything in general quite hunkydory.

My impulse was to refuse, partly because neither of you was to be the other regular, partly because I doubted the integrity of the promise. I mean by the latter that I doubted the possibility of any real agreement between Leon and me concerning the content of certain terms.

But when I saw him Thursday I was convinced by what he (and Fisher) said that the thing was feasible. So I said I would do it on the understanding that I would be free to withdraw at any time if the situation embarrassed me. Also, they are free to kick me out. A list of books and guests is being prepared, and for No. 2 I am starting off with Jacques Barzun [1]— and, I hope, continuing, though neither I nor anyone else knows for a certainty how he will do. I suddenly thought of him, and secretly I am sure he *will* do. Leon consented in spite of the fact that Barzun was unknown to him.

Everybody concerned, including first and last yours truly, wants both of you to be guests when you can and if you will. How you will feel about that I don't pretend to know. But the invitation is genuine; and I may add for your amusement, Allen, that Leon wants you at least four times to make up for last summer.

I am already embarrassed, of course; and aware that I may be in for something I don't like. But in that case I will stop at once. Not, I hope however, before both of you have been here to comfort me. As for my embarrassment, it is doubtless foolish. At any rate I shall compose no speeches out of the countless very subtle regrets and scruples that infest me, but beg to remain forever

> Yours in learning if not in Leon,

1. Barzun was a member of the history faculty at Columbia.

To Allen Tate
APS/NjP

October 14, 1941   *New York City*

Tate had informed CBS that he would not make five appearances on "Invitation to Learning" unless he had an advance of $250.

L L sounded milder on the phone this morning, and I think you will hear from him before long. If you don't, consider anyway that all goes well— and that you will have a real letter from me before *too* long. For some reason I haven't been writing to anybody. Where is C's novel?[1]

1. The initials refer to Leon Levine and Caroline Gordon.

To John Berryman
ALS/MnU

October 22, 1941   *New York City*

Kind to send you so long a poem? You are an angel even to dream the word. It was simply that I couldn't not send it; and that I trusted you not to punish yourself (and me) by reading it before you were ready and free. Please don't think there is a hurry.

I enjoy seeing Bob every week, though I haven't actually talked to him yet.[1] I like him, and he reminds me regularly of you.

I stupidly didn't know how to answer your letter this summer, so let it lie. I should have tried; and said that if you were thinking perhaps that your friends, including me, didn't love you as much as once you were very wrong. Know that we do, and are only waiting for an opening through that integument of despair. When that appears—what a rush!

1. Robert Jefferson Berryman, John Berryman's brother.

To Allen Tate
ALS/NjP

October 23, 1941   *New York City*

Caroline's book has come, and if you listen sharp you may hear Dot and me quarreling over which is to have it in Cornwall this weekend.[1] . . .

Dot says I should never have tried to be middle man between you and Leon, and of course she is right. The last time I saw him, which was Tuesday, it appeared that his feelings had been hurt. And still were—not so much now, but enough to keep him from writing you and saying, what does seem to be the case, that an advance remains possible. What was hurt in him was his sense of honor, which he thought you doubted. If you should write and call him a gentleman again—but I said you wouldn't, and sidetracked the whole fantastic issue by discussing with him the books you might be willing to do. If anything happens henceforth, it will happen when he invites you to do those books. You know I hope you will, but you also know that I expect you to do what you by God please. The entire subject of I to L is something I can't write you about; which is why I hope we'll see you all soon. . . . Not that I to L is, as subject, a mess. Indeed it is a fair subject. But ambiguities are too hard to avoid in a letter, and after all there are personal aspects. The general point about their policy at present is that they don't want to tie themselves up with people they might not turn out to like. They are not tying themselves, you know, to me. No contract. Why they even want to start with me (alone of us 3) is a mystery I don't examine. But there! I said I wouldn't go on about this. . . .

1. *Green Centuries* (New York, 1941).

To Allen Tate
ALS/NjP

January 22, 1942   *New York City*

*   *   *

Levine is certainly asking you for *The Turn of the Screw*, with Katherine Anne [Porter]; and today I pressed him for more. We'll see. And do come for James. He (Leon) is vaguer than anyone I've ever known, and I still don't know what to assume he will do. I suppose I am lazy about him. I should haunt him like Huntington. Yet I do value my time. . . .

To Allen Tate
ALS/NjP

April 15, 1942   *New York City*

Your review goes to my exposed spot, and while of course I am pleased by your compliments in passing, I admit the penetration.[1] You are very skilful—and you wrote a fine piece, for which best thanks.

I suppose I tried to walk an invisible line—between pedants and pukes. A dangerous game, for it is the pukes that praise you, at any rate mostly. Yet that thin line, I suspect, is where the lasting critics stand. Not that I— I fell off long ago. . . .

1. Tate reviewed MVD's *The Private Reader* in the *New Republic,* April 13, 1942, pp. 506, 508.

To Allen Tate
ALS/NjP

May 14, 1942   *New York City*

It was CBS's idea, and now I am convinced it was a good one.[1] When they sprung it on me I thought it so simple as to be silly. But a week of *The Scarlet Letter* has attached me even more to Hawthorne than I was; and the idea as such amply proves itself.

When I see you I'll tell you how it seems to be surrounded as I read by a technician, a production man, an announcer, an organist, and a black man bearing glasses of water. Hawthorne would hardly know what to make of it. You understand, of course, that *I* know.

1. To read *The Scarlet Letter* on CBS radio.

To Thomas Merton
ALS/KyLoB-M

May 15, 1942   *New York City*

Thomas Merton entered Columbia after a disastrous year at Cambridge and received a bachelor of arts in 1938 and a master of arts in 1939. As his The Seven Storey Mountain *shows, Merton was strongly influenced by Mark Van Doren. Late in 1941 Merton entered Gethsemani in Kentucky. He left his journals, his poems, and his* Journal of My Escape from the Nazis *with Van Doren.*

I have sent your poems *and* Journal to Bob,[1] who is happier at Friendship House than I have ever seen him, and who will return them to me for my archives—which are no burden to me, and no part of which will I send you until I get a definite request from you. I didn't interpret your last good letter as such a request. I am quite content to keep the MSS., which are now augmented by the *Escape,* which Miss Burton (?) at Curtis Brown sent me the other day with a note saying she had regretfully decided she couldn't sell it.[2] Too bad, but time may tell a different story, and I think it will.

Your poems are very fine. The three kings coming through the wintry trees,[3] the other trees in the other poems, and indeed all the things in all the poems have the right kind of reality at last. I was greatly interested in your Journal pages too. When Bob sends them back I'll lay them in among the others.

I am happy because you are.[4]

1. Lax.

2. Naomi Burton was an agent connected with Curtis Brown, Ltd. (London, Paris, New York). She was having trouble finding a publisher for *Journal of My Escape from the Nazis.*

3. "Carol" (1941) was written at Gethsemani and first published in the *New Yorker,* December 23, 1944, p. 36.

4. The early letters from MVD to Thomas Merton have not been located.

To John Berryman
ALS/MnU

August 16, 1942   *Falls Village, Connecticut*

I haven't known too much about your private affairs, but perhaps I have known—or guessed—enough to be convinced that the present solution is best all around.[1] I'll not say anything more than that I appreciate your telling me, that I wish you and Rusty happiness, and that I am sure the amount of this commodity which will exist depends largely on you.[2]

So you have a job, and go to it with my blessing.

As to the War, have courage. It can be had.

Boston Common is a superb poem.

1. Berryman's affair with "Beatrice" had come to an end, and several of his friends were distressed because they felt marriage would be good for him.

2. Berryman married Eileen Patricia (Rusty) Mulligan (now Eileen Simpson) on October 24, 1942. Robert Giroux had been asked to be best man but was unable to get leave from the navy. MVD then agreed to take Giroux's place. Eileen Simpson in *Poets in Their Youth* (New York, 1982), 23, writes that MVD played the role of "father of the groom," as "the father who felt sympathy and compassion for a difficult temperament so foreign to his own."

To Scott Buchanan
TLS/MH

October 20, 1942   *New York City*

Here is the latest and indeed the last bulletin from me about Invitation to Learning.

After I came back from Annapolis I went to Levine and proposed that the new series take the form you had suggested (but I suppressed your name). A panel of six or seven, including you, Barzun, Joe Krutch, Ned Miller the educated scientist, and me; these men to meet and agree upon the books to be discussed, in what order and by whom, and with whom as chairman in each case. Levine professed to find this interesting, but said that meanwhile "they" (Bryson and he, I suspect) had thought up another "experiment." Five chairmen during the year, each to conduct the discussion of six books in his "field" with persons of his and their choosing. The chairman would be Edman for philosophy, Louis Untermeyer for poetry, Harry Gideonse for sociology, Lewis Gannett for general literature, and I forget who else for what else—oh, yes, me for whatever field I wanted if I didn't want poetry. The foregoing is the language he used, and I can imagine yours. I pointed out that "fields" was the opposite of what the program wanted, that departmentalization quite killed the idea, that crossfire was the thing, that the term "general literature" (by which I found out that he meant fiction) gave his whole case away, and that his chairmen stunk. Well, he said, he would take the matter up high and let me know. He never let me know till I called him Friday. Then he informed me that the decision had gone against me and that the chairmen (those same) had already been secured and the books chosen. I had made it clear the other time that I was through if, and now I made it clearer. So I am out; after next Sunday no more.

The only thing I mind about it is that I may seem to you and Winkie to have let the program down low enough for this additional depth to be reachable. I'm not at all sure that this is the case, but I won't argue the point here. I simply wanted to make my report and assure you that I did what I could. . . .

To Allen Tate
ALS/NjP

October 27, 1942   *New York City*

*Tate had heard a rumor from a mutual friend that Van Doren had been
responsible for Tate's removal from the "Invitation to Learning" program. Van
Doren denied the rumor, commented on the person spreading the rumor, and
then announced he, too, had been fired.*

*   *   *

The one amusing thing is that now *I* have fallen. Sunday was my last performance. They suddenly were through with me. The story is this.

About 3 weeks ago, realizing that the summer series was about to end,
I went to Leon and said that I did not care to go on unless the program
could be bent back to something like its original shape—not a panel of 3,
but a panel of 6 or 7 regulars among whom the books (and the leadership) would circulate; these 6 or 7 to meet at the start and agree not only
upon the books but upon which 3 would discuss each one, with whom as
leader. The program, I said, was going to pieces now, was scattering
among "experts" and stunt men; it developed no ideas from week to
week—perfected no crossfire between known or fixed personalities. Leon
said: "But we have been considering another 'experiment'." Five chairmen to preside over as many "fields," and the books to be pastured in
those "fields" alone. When he named the fields—poetry, philosophy,
drama, sociology & economics, and "general literature"—and the
chairmen—Louis Untermeyer, Edman, John Anderson, Harry Gideonse,
and Lewis Gannett—I said: OK, goodbye. He was surprised; even offered
me Untermeyer's back lot; and is still surprised because I wouldn't play.
Of course he couldn't understand that his categories, besides being de-
structive of the idea, were idiotic in themselves ("general literature," I
gathered, meant prose fiction). At least he offered to take my plan to the
bosses and let me know. But he never let me know; I had to learn from
Gannett & Edman that he had gone ahead without me.[1]

So we are both out at last, and equal. I was tired anyway, and I am glad
to say to hell with it. Though I don't deny that Leon's foolishness is grit in
my machinery. He doesn't deserve it, but I'll never forget him. . . .

1. Tate wrote Bishop on November 2,
1942, that MVD's firing confirmed his
"judgment that CBS was acting out of
character in having people like us.—This
will be good for Mark because the program was bad for him. It developed in him
the small fraction of Van Dorenism which
he shares with Carl" (Young and Hindle
[eds.], *The Republic of Letters in America*,
195).

To Allen Tate
ALS/NjP

January 6, 1943   *New York City*

Your poems in the *Kenyon,* altered I dare say from the version of them you sent me last summer (I haven't looked into this), have grown enormously between readings.[1] The alterations may have much or little to do with this. I suspect the real reason is that they are real poems, and so grow naturally—as indeed yours regularly do. I liked and admired these then; I find them very large and powerful now. I'm not sure I wholly understand them, but that has no effect on my feeling. And to think they started (in part at least) as metrical experiments! What a wonderful thing is art, and what a wonderful artist is A. Tate. . . .

   1. "More Sonnets at Christmas" appeared in *Kenyon Review,* V (Spring, 1943), 186–88.

To Allen Tate
ALS/NjP

February 3, 1943   *New York City*

The fact that your view of this war (whatever it is) differs from mine (whatever *it* is) doesn't prevent me from hearing just about your top note in the three poems you sent me.[1] Your fishing poem—remember?—seemed to me to lack something—call it spizzerinctum—but these have all your old excitement in them again. I knew that from the first line of Jubilo and of course the second. Then the meat of it, the boy's mast, the poet's lung; then slip and glide, then snip nor glide; and at last the transfusion. The *Ode* is still better (and is, if you like, for Charlie, who apparently will be in the Air Force a year from next Friday, which is his 17th birthday). Caroline had quoted some of it to me, and of course I remembered that. But she hadn't prepared me for the last page—the wrathful peroration over Everest and the Lama. My view is not your view, but I admire this poem. As I do the *Dejected Lines,* though "worth living for" isn't quite right somehow. It is properly plain, and therefore belongs in a poem to Yeats; but it perhaps misses the distinction that ought to streak the plainness.

Now send me the Pervigilium.[2] I don't think it will be better than these, but the quatrain on your New Year's card was very fine; and you have hit on the best version yet of the refrain. If you have an extra copy, do please send it; and let me know whether I should return it. Don't send the only copy.

The news is that I am taking off this term at Columbia to write a book about liberal education. The Association of American Colleges is paying my salary through the Carnegie Corporation. But there are no strings; Holt is publishing the book; and I am accountable to no one. They are gambling on what I do. And what I will do is say there ain't no sech animal yet. If you have an idea to spare, jot it down and send it, will you? Here's your chance to influence civilization forever. Seriously, I find it interesting. The first thing I did was to reread all of Plato—Socrates being the best teacher, I wanted to start off in good company. He was even better than I thought. . . .

1. "Dejected Lines," "Jubilo," and "Ode."

2. Published by Cummington Press in 1943.

To Allen Tate
ALS/NjP

February 21, 1943   *New York City*

Perhaps you wanted me to keep this;[1] but it is a long MS., and my own distaste of copying suggests to me that you might need this copy some day.

It is—yes—the best translation. Very free—as I realized when I took down the Latin to see what had become "gangs," "girls of the farm," and "country matters." But that is what it should be, granted vigor and conviction. Which you have in beautiful abundance—abundance, without the effect of lushness which most translations haven't known how to conquer. You reduce the poem to its strict meaning, and you give it a driving shaft. When I say strict meaning, I am not semantic.

Your letter will not be shown to the FBI, but much in it will, I hope, influence my book. For me the war is a relatively simple thing. I don't talk of freedom everywhere. I talk of the German army, which since early 1940 has been something I wanted to see destroyed. That is enough to do at present. Meanwhile there are many fools in our world, and that is too bad. But to suppose that such a fact outweighs the danger of the German army seems to me to lose or miss perspective now.

The far perspective is doubtless as you say. Anyhow, I value your letter and promise you to ponder its wisdom about the liberal arts—which Conant today, by the way, seems to think means everything except science.[2] That is the vulgarity which most offends me at the moment.

This is less than you deserve in answer, but I don't want to seem to be arguing with you about principles which I share. The problem of casuistry is where we differ. And that, being almost technical, is something I would have to be either very long or very short about.

Nannine tells me she has sent your translation to the *Atlantic*. I hope they take it—with I don't know what pagan results in the New England Woods this Spring.

1. *The Vigil of Venus: Pervigilium Vene-ris* (Cummington, Mass. 1943).

2. James Bryant Conant (1893–1978)

was a chemist who served as president of Harvard University from 1933 to 1953.

To John Berryman
ALS/MnU

May 30, 1943   *New York City*

It had become increasingly obvious that Berryman would not be kept on at Harvard, and Van Doren was helping Berryman find another position. Berryman spent weeks searching for a job.

I confess I'm disappointed in my powers of prophesy. I was sure that either Tead or Finch would come through.[1] And of course it is even worse about Harcourt Brace. A time, a time! I'm not at all certain that the best thing you and Rusty could do wouldn't be to pack up and come to New York. When or if you do, please let me know. I'll be in Falls Village a good deal of the summer, but I'll be here a good deal too, and I want to see you both. I won't go any further into your miseries now, but you know I feel them.

Yes, the book is done, and I am very tired. It could be my last book. But I'll rest in the country.

Don't think a second time about the dedication of *A.T.*[2] Let that be as circumstances decide. I already consider it my poem, and it doesn't matter who else does.

Milt Halliday was here last week with his wife. And a week before that Dorothy and I heard Steve Aylward say his first high mass—at St. Agnes's.

My best to you both.

1. Berryman had thought that Mrs. Ordway Tead at Briarcliff Junior College was going to offer him a position. Finch is probably Jeremiah S. Finch of the English department at Princeton.

2. "The Animal Trainer" was dedicated to MVD.

To Scott Buchanan
ALS/MH

June 14, 1943   *New York City*

I'll be honored if you elect me to the Board of Visitors and Governors, but as for teaching at St. John's, don't you realize that the writing of *Liberal Education* taught me I wasn't competent? Now there's an irony even you couldn't have foreseen!

To Allen Tate
ALS/NjP

June 14, 1943   *Falls Village, Connecticut*

Archibald MacLeish, librarian of the Library of Congress, had appointed Tate consultant in poetry.

*   *   *

The news, of course, is your appointment by A. MacL.—between whom and you Colonel Putnam writes me he thinks there will be fur flying by autumn.[1] But I say, maybe not; for whereas M. could never have respected Auslander, he certainly respects you, and for all I know he will want to leave you free.[2] . . .

1. Phelps Putnam, the poet.
2. Joseph Auslander, the poet, was con- sultant in English poetry at the Library of Congress from 1937–43.

To John Berryman
ALS/MnU

June 24, 1943   *Falls Village, Connecticut*

Good hunting![1] I'd like to be there to hold your gun and count your ammunition, but I am here instead—though sometimes I do go down, and when I know far enough ahead of such a trip I'll send you a card about it, hoping to see both you and Rusty. It's a bad time, John, and I'm sorry you have to be a hunter. But you sound courageous, which is much, and I don't doubt you will bring down something that you can skin and eat.

Speaking of Harvard, here is an asinine letter I got from there the other day. It was in confidence, so don't tell anyone I sent it to you. I don't want it back. What a way to decide about a man! I'm telling them, incidentally, that I don't know more than two beans about Harry.[2] What's the matter with them? Are they no judges? Of course not, being without genius themselves. Or even the tenth part of a talent. I started to kid Howard Mumford Jones about this letter the other day—he was at a neighbor's house—but soon saw I shouldn't. He is a member of the committee which does this stuff, and on top of that he assured me solemnly that I should feel flattered to be one of those who were asked.[3]

You are well away from an absurd university. Anything else will be better—some meat anyway, whereas Harvard is all thick skin.

1. Berryman was not being kept on at Harvard and was searching for another position.

2. Harry Levin, a professor of English and Comparative Literature at Harvard.

3. MVD disliked the Harvard practice of assembling committees of outsiders to make recommendations on the retention and promotion of faculty members.

To Lionel Trilling
ALS/NNC

July 29, 1943   *Falls Village, Connecticut*

Your *Forster* came on a rainy day and was read at once.[1] This is to thank you for several hours of the keenest enjoyment criticism has given me since I don't know when.

I'm not convinced that Forster deserves all the good things you say, but that doesn't matter; you said them, and they are many and wise. They are more than true of F; they are true.

For instance, your whole theory of comedy—supported very well, by the way, whenever you summarize his plots, which certainly could not be souls for tragedies. The theory, if you don't mind so formal a term, is about the best one I have met, and my search for such things is constant.

My second paragraph doesn't mean I don't admire Forster. Doubtless he does deserve you, since he made himself the subject of your book. But that is my point, I guess. He is a better subject for a book than he is a novelist. He is a mind, a person, but not in the absolute sense a poet. . . .

Your inscription was generous, seeing that *you* now teach *me*.

1. Trilling's *E. M. Forster* was published by New Directions in 1943.

To Savoie Lottinville
TLS/OkU

August 6, 1943   *New York City*

Lottinville was director of the University of Oklahoma Press. Similar letters obviously went out to many commercial and university presses.

The Books and Authors for Bonds Committee has evolved a method by which books and authors are being mobilized to sell War Bonds. In the five test rallies held so far, all in towns of less than 125,000 people, more than $6,000,000 in Bonds have been sold—an astonishing record of success.

The publishers who paid the expenses of this preliminary campaign, which amounted to $1,600, or at a cost of 1/30 of 1%, seem to be well satisfied, not only by the Bond sales which everybody in a position to know considers phenomenal, but by the prestige which the rallies have gained for books. Their contributions averaged $250 a piece.

The attendance at the rallies totalled over 6,000 people, but in addition to that, everybody in town heard and read about these events—for a total of 7½ hours of radio time was given over to them, while advertising and news lineage in the local papers mounted to over 38,000 lines.

I have been present at three rallies—with Pearl Buck, Edna Ferber, Ben Ames Williams, Otto Tolischus, Clifton Fadiman, and others, and can testify not only to my own pleasure and inspiration, but to theirs. The authors have thought of themselves, not as book or bond salesmen, but as persons who were in a position at last to make a characteristic contribution to the war. They have worked hard, spoken eloquently, and, in many cases, given up their most valuable possessions, the mss. of their favorite books. The manuscripts have been, in fact, the feature of the rallies, and constitute a permanent contribution to the public library in each city.

The librarians have taken a major part in the event, but so have the book store people, as, indeed, every progressive element in the town. The community has really gone all out for us. Many citizens told me personally that no local affair had ever moved them so much.

I think you should know that these are not book fairs. They are patriotic meetings of great dignity and significance and, in my opinion, they will be of lasting effect—even, that is, into post war days, when books will continue to benefit from the prestige now secured.

The publishers who underwrite this effort are doing no more and no less than hundreds of other commercial groups. The Treasury policy is to let such groups sustain the Bond promotions themselves, in the interest of their own merchandise and of their own standing in the national community as well. Needless to say the Treasury assists such promotions with its existing facilities in every way possible.

We estimate that with $15,000—possibly less—our committee can extend the campaign over a period of a year. We have already made preliminary arrangements for a series of thirteen fall rallies. We are therefore, asking for contributions now to our fall and winter campaign. . . . Will you let us hear today, if possible, what you will contribute, for we know that you will want to be a part of a patriotic enterprise in which you can be assured of making a concrete and successful contribution to the home front.

To Helen [Taylor]
of the Henry Holt editorial staff
ALS/NjP

November 10, 1943[1]   *New York City*

You can hardly love me if I made you write a long letter when you haven't time for such.

I should be sorrier than I am that I busted out. I *am* sorry, of course, that you and Keith (if you did) took me as accusing you of mishandling me while Bill is away.[2] As Keith knows, I have been building up a theory that all of you, Bill included, think of my books as not for this world—as for the ages, etc., but not now. I am scarcely sorry that I at last said this, and seriously, just for the record.

Maybe it can be only for the record. I have to admit that my books have not sold well, and your figure on the advance for *Lib. Ed.*—2000—ought to be unanswerable. Indeed, in view of that I won't say another word about ads. I *had* hoped that a certain whoop-la upon publication would start sales off at a higher level. And I took the absence of any such thing as evidence of doubt in your minds, or at best of a notion that it is an educational book. I still think it is a trade book, as I also think the *Shakespeare* is. But to hell with the whole question. . . . My interest in *Lib. Ed.*, you see, is not personal (not vain), and is not an interest in sales as such. I simply believe in the subject, and want other people to. Of course you do too. . . .

Let's leave it at this. You know I believe in the book and believe you do—and believe that you will do all you can for it. If I got something off my chest, doing so did me more good than you. Forgive me if I used you too thoughtlessly. O K henceforth. No more of this.

1. Both Helen Taylor and Helen Stewart worked with William Sloane. John Van Doren believes this letter was addressed to Helen Taylor.

2. Keith W. Jennison was sales manager for H. Holt & Company, and Bill Sloane was MVD's editor.

To Allen Tate
TLS/NjP

November 25, 1943   *New York City*

Tate and Archibald MacLeish (then Library of Congress librarian) responded to this playful letter in kind.

Mr. Allen Tate,
  Consultant on Poetry,
  The Library of Congress,
  Hall of Echoes,
  Washington, D.C.

DEAR SIR:

As a tax-payer I take the liberty of consulting you, not about a library matter, but—if your generosity extends so far—about a private problem in composition.

I have written, Sir, the enclosed poem, and with God's help propose to publish it in a volume next year.[1] But I cannot decide whether I have done right in using the word "foison" in the third line of the third paragraph.

I first wrote "abundance," which still has to recommend it:

  a) that it is not archaic;
  b) that it balances in sound the words "sundered" and "rondures" below, not to mention "cubes" and "stubborn," and balances them significantly, since after all those heavy vocables the last line returns with more effect to the tone of the last line of the first paragraph;
  c) that it does not force the pronunciation of "centuries" in its own line as a trisyllable;

but which sacrifices:

  a) an archaism which perhaps is suited to the ancient world referred to;
  b) a word which the author, perhaps unpardonably, likes;
  c) a vocable which has its own interesting relation to "surface" in the next line, through the use in both of the letter *f;*
  d) a certain slowness in "centuries" which the trisyllabic pronunciation would promote.

My knowledge, Sir, of your own so carefully written poems, and of the assistance you have so frequently given other workers in this vineyard, as well as of the essays in which you have shown yourself a master of the word, not only as used by others but as glorified by yourself, notably in your *Ode to the Confederate Dead,* prompts the present impertinence.

Need I say that I shall be grateful for any advice you can give me, at—of course—your convenience.

1. "Berkshire Express" appeared in MVD's *The Seven Sleepers* (New York, 1944).

To Allen Tate
ALS/NjP

December 6, 1943   *New York City*

So now I have all the documents. Was ever word so buttressed?

Dot, reading proof for me last night, called out from the other room: "Foison! What's that? Misprint for poison? But you couldn't have meant poison!"

So there it is, and will be I suppose. I pulled you and Archie on her, and she meekened down at once. But think of the millions I can't cow.

Or hundreds.

Or dozens.

Well, let 'em use a dictionary.

To John Berryman
ALS/MnU

December 19, 1943   *New York City*

Berryman left Harvard for Princeton.

This will be no answer to your wonderful letter if answer means equivalent. I can only thank the dog in your throat that day for the good friend he made you be. And I can partly state my pleasure in the things you said about my book. And about Blackmur, for all of that immensely informed me concerning a man I know too little. My best to him the next time you talk, and to Gauss likewise.[1]

I gather that Princeton isn't so bad for you and Rusty (I'll keep on calling her that).[2] Good. And do call us when you come to New York. The boys are here, and our time is oddly taken; but something won't be hard to manage, and we decidedly want to see you.

I had the flu myself two weeks ago, so that I couldn't keep an appointment with your brother Bob at my office one Friday morning. He had called about this but given me no number, so I could only leave word (through a colleague) on my office door for him. I hope he saw it and understood. As it is, I'm sorry to have failed him at all. If you know what he wanted to talk about, you can tell me when I see you.

1. R. P. Blackmur and Christian Gauss of the Princeton faculty.
2. Eileen Berryman.

To Allen Tate
ALS/NjP

January 11, 1944   *New York City*

The announcement and your letter came together, and of course took our breath. We were prepared, but not *that* prepared.[1]

This must have been true for you in infinitely greater degree. What a weekend! I admire you for seeing it through, even while I sympathize with you in the loss of a daughter—and such a daughter, for you know we all love her. I particularly admire you, Allen, for turning to and performing your part with what I know was magnificent and warm grace. No one knows that art better than you, who in a world which so regularly disappoints you maintain so fairly the sweet fiction that it does not. . . .

1. Nancy Tate married Percy Wood on January 3, 1944. Caroline Gordon was away from home at the time because of the death of her father.

To Joseph Wood Krutch
TLS/DLC

February 24, 1944   *Cambridge, Massachusetts*

Almost all of Van Doren's early letters to Krutch were destroyed in a 1952 fire at the Connecticut home of the Krutches. A long letter, written after Van Doren finished the manuscript of Krutch's study of Dr. Johnson, survived the fire. Only the first two paragraphs of the letter are printed.

In this room,[1] during periods of truancy from the Harvard Committee on the Objectives of General Education with which I came on Tuesday to

confer, I have finished your *Johnson,* and now I take up my pen in something like the mood of Gibbon when he laid his down—the pleasure of
reading you lasted so long that melancholy mingles with it at this moment when I must say: There is no more of either Joe or Johnson that I
can explore henceforth as one who advances over strange, even if once
familiar, ground. I will read the book many times again, but never with
the excitement of discovery which for two weeks I have steadily and ever
more intensely felt.

Lengthy as this letter may become, I fear it will fail to tell you how
great I think your book is—how sensible, how wise, how full, and at the
same time how rich with something I can only call right feeling. Your
keeping to the mean between a simple moralism and an equally simple
scientism concerning your subject—a merely 18th century and a merely
20th century view—required more than agility. It required imagination,
and it is that supreme virtue of the soul that has given you, I suspect, the
privilege of seeing Johnson as he eternally is—a person not to be changed
by place or time, if he will permit me to quote a poet whom he did not
regularly admire. To see him thus exactly as he is—for he still *is,* thanks
to you—one has to know how to be at the same instant humorous and
serious. You are invariably both, with the result that any competent
reader will acknowledge you as unique in your authority. . . .

  1. At the Commander Hotel in
Cambridge.

To James Laughlin
TLS/P

February 26, 1944   *New York City*

*Robert Lax visited Merton at Gethsemani in 1943 and brought to MVD a
group of new poems from Merton. James Laughlin, publisher of New
Directions, expressed an interest in the poems. Laughlin was to become one of
Merton's publishers.*

Here are the 30 poems by Merton you said you would like to read.

They have all been cleared by the abbot of his monastery in Kentucky
(Trappist, I think I told you), and his friend Bob Lax has told me to go
ahead. I am more or less his literary executor now that he is out of the
world. He left all his MSS. with me when he went in—a novel, these and
many other poems, several volumes of a very interesting Journal, and a
sort of half-novel called, without much reason, "Journal of My Escape
from the Nazis." He used to be a student of mine at Columbia, and I have

always liked him. Also, I think him a fine poet. Strangely, considering the strictness of the Trappist vows, he has continued to write poems in the monastery. About a third of these, I imagine, were written there, and the abbot says OK. It doesn't seem to me to be keeping the vow of silence, but us heathen benefit whatever it is.

Merton spent his youth in England and France. He is now, perhaps, 30 or a little more. Possibly a little less.

[P.S.] I saw Delmore in Cambridge recently, and enjoyed doing so.

To Allen Tate
TLS/NjP

March 3, 1944   *New York City*

Tate had special praise for the following poems in Van Doren's The Seven Sleepers: *"The Unknown Army," "April 1942," "The Elect," "How We Shine," "Down World," "Berkshire Express," "Midland," and "Aetat 50."*

Your list fascinates me, of course, and bears its own authority. I read all of it last night except for one or two poems I had to cut out because my time was running short. But I can't conclude from your generous remarks about the others that made these possible anything but that they didn't need to be *printed*. Written, yes—as process. But why printed? I'm not putting this as a question to be answered, nor am I supposing you to mean that none others at all should have been printed. The thing that really troubles me is that others have sent me lists, and there was little or no correspondence between theirs and yours. I suspect that this has always been what bothered me. I have different audiences, if audience is not too flattering a word. Carl's list contained none of yours except Down World, and Jose Villa's contained none [1]—or Joe Krutch's, or (in conversation) Delmore's. The Elect I almost left out because no one had *ever* liked it—except Dorothy, who weakened when I challenged her for a reason; then I put it in because she had liked it once. I left out, of course, dozens that I don't regret.

Too much of this. The point is that I am very grateful to you for such a reading as you did, and secretly suppose you are my authority after all.

The reading last night wasn't much in itself, but we had a good time before and after, with dinner at Charles (6th Ave.) and everything. John Berryman and his wife came in from Princeton and were with us all the time. We missed you, and decided you must have had a rough time of it two weeks before. Nobody could understand why Williams put you with those women, both of whom you must think as poorly of as for instance I do.[2] Taggard told me the other day when I saw her at Sarah Lawrence that you seemed tired. Bored or enraged was the right word, I thought. . . .

As for a lecture there, let's see what is ahead of me at St. John's. I haven't arranged with Scott for the new term. Could you wait awhile? Of course I'd love to see you in Washington, and I don't mind working for Archie, who recently has been working for me (war bonds). . . .

1. José Garcia Villa, the Filipino-born poet.

2. Probably Oscar Williams, the anthologizer.

To James Laughlin
TLS/P

March 10, 1944   *New York City*

*   *   *

I'm delighted that you like the Merton poems, and I will answer your questions about the contract, etc., in a few days. I have written to Lax for advice. Probably the contract should be made to me as representative or agent; the royalties would go to the monastery. Would you need a letter from him authorizing me to act? But the decision may be that the contract can go directly to Merton or the abbot. There will be no substantial delay over this. I have asked Lax to fire an answer back, and you may hear next week.

And I'll send you the 200 words—to be used as yours, not mine, since in such cases the stuff ought to stand alone.

Delmore was pretty cheerful when he was here last week, reading with Blackmur and me at the YMHA uptown.[1] But one thing did upset him. His mother came to the reading. I didn't know of this till afterward, when he explained his anxiety to get out of town by saying that he had seen her there. I wish (ghoulishly) I had. . . .

1. Delmore Schwartz. James Atlas in *Delmore Schwartz: The Life of an American Poet* (New York, 1977) traces

Schwartz's difficult relations with his mother.

To Carl Sandburg
TLS/IU-R

July 13, 1944   *New York City*

Earlier in the year Sandburg had contributed the manuscript of "The American Fable of the Two Maggots" to the Book and Author War Bond Committee.

In behalf of the Book and Author War Bond Committee I want to thank you for going to the rally and for being such a wonderful addition to the occasion and for singing the songs which brought in such large sums in War Bonds. I suppose you know that the three songs brought a total of $1,050,000 in Bonds to the Treasury, and that must make you feel as pleased as we are about it.

To Charles Van Doren
TLS/P

September 7, 1944   *Falls Village, Connecticut*

Charles Van Doren left St. John's to enlist in the air force. After basic training, he was sent to Bainbridge, Georgia, where he felt nothing of importance was happening to him. He wrote his father that keeping the summer home open was important because it maintained the "tradition" of the Van Dorens' life there.

Listen. The following are worse off than you:
1) Middle-aged men like me who can't believe they are doing anything. In my case the war bond committee, the Armed Services Committee, blood donations, broadcasting for the OWI, etc., don't begin to balance what you have done and are doing. You think you are doing nothing, but that is so far false that millions envy you at this moment, dull though you think the moment is. You enlisted at 17, and at 18 you began to do what the United States Army wanted you to do; and you are still at it. Your uniform, your address, your whereabouts are badges of great honor. You are in the war, and you will never cease to be proud of the fact. Imagine not being in at all. Yes, just try that on your imaginer.
2) Me personally this summer, when I see Mama so little—she, incidentally, being right in the thick of it—and when the tradition I carry on here only sometimes seems important. Your beautiful letter, which I still after three tries can't read without crying (don't feel guilty over this, it is good for me), rebukes me for doubting the tradition, and I won't do so again. Tonight when I go out to see if anything is in danger of frost (your

letter came just in time to jibe with a cold wave with much northwest wind and blue-sky bluster) I'll have every sentence you wrote in mind, and fancy that you are there holding the lantern—or, as it has been in recent years, doing most of the work under my not too courteous or grateful direction (understatement for all the times I was an s o b). But it is true that I have not always been content to be here this summer. I have even felt sheepish. This has been aggravated by the fact that the essay I thought I would spend the summer writing for Britannica Great Books has been delayed by a lot of horsing among the committee, so that I still can't start it. In other words, I have in a way wasted the summer, except for 30 poems I wrote while Scott and Mert were here, and during two weeks after that. I had just typed them when your letter came, so I am enclosing some of them—I hope not too many. I arranged them in what seemed to me an order, but don't take that seriously. They are a present to you; I was very happy to have you ask for them. *Coming Home Carelessly* was a postal card to Mama; the others need, or perhaps deserve, no commentary in advance. *Statesman,* I will however add, was written after we saw the movie *Wilson.*

3) Johnny and other boys his age who may never get into the army. That is hard too—I know this from the other war. They never recover from it, whereas you will have nothing of the sort to recover from. . . .

To Allen Tate
TLS/NjP

October 17, 1944   *New York City*

In the summer of 1944, the Tates moved to Sewanee, Tennessee, and Tate became editor of the Sewanee Review.

You may be terribly disappointed in this[1]—I think I am. It is the best I could do in a month when all sorts of unforeseen difficulties, including Carl's convalescence from an eye operation, added to grievous domestic problems I have tried to help him solve, has turned me into a cross between a male nurse and a psychoanalyst. But all that is not offered as an excuse for the note, which may be impossibly short for you, or impossibly bad. In either case chuck it without apology and consider the incident closed. The real reason may be that I am not for criticism, etc., any more. This may have been the last gasp, taken out of water. That is what I secretly believe. . . .

1. "Poets and Trimmers, A Note,"
Sewanee Review, LIII (Winter, 1945),
52–55.

To Allen Tate
ALS/NjP

November 9, 1944   *New York City*

I have just written Red [Warren] that I couldn't make the meeting next week. Charlie suddenly came home on a furlough, which ends at the time of the meeting, and I'll be damned if I keep any engagements during that time.

I had expected to thank you down there for your nice note about my Note—I'm really very much relieved that it passed your powerful eye— and, at greater length, to tell you how much I admire the first issue of your *Sewanee*. Especially the piece by the Editor. I haven't written all this because I was electioneering; but if I had known I wouldn't see you I'd have written anyway. Your piece seems to me very important, and your use of Sandburg very telling.[1] Good Lord! . . .

1. In "The State of Letters," *Sewanee Review,* LII (Autumn, 1944), 608–14, Tate attacked Sandburg for saying in 1940 that T. S. Eliot was "so close to fascists that I am off him, to use a truck drivers' phrase; and we've got to consider the truck-drivers in the present hour rather than the intellectuals." Tate wondered why Sandburg couldn't have made his choice a year earlier and why one couldn't have truck-drivers and intellectuals.

Poems and Stories
1945–1953

Mark Van Doren wrote a full description of the years 1945 to 1953 in his memoirs. This was a time of continued artistic creativity for him, and he remained one of Columbia's most distinguished teachers. The letters of this period are mostly to old friends—Tate, Berryman, Merton, Lax; to his sons, who were often away from home; and to some new acquaintances and students, such as Allen Ginsberg. He continued his interest in world government and in the Society for the Prevention of World War III.

To Allen Tate
ALS/NjP

February 16, 1945   *New York City*

Thank you for *The Winter Sea,* which thoroughly disposes of the legend, self-circulated, that you were not writing much in the way of poems.[1] You had me fooled a few years ago—but had I counted these as they occurred, I would have been ready for the present display, which suddenly seems to me very important. I knew these, but not thus. Now I insist on taking a bit of credit for what you did with your stanza. And why shouldn't I? But seriously, I don't give anyone credit but your own excellent and mysterious muse. My salutations to her. . . .

1. Tate's *The Winter Sea: A Book of Poems* (Cummington, Mass., 1944).

To John Berryman
ALS/MnU

March 29, 1945   *New York City*

I confess I wrote "along," that being what I thought I meant, and not "alone."[1] But you and Joe give me more than pause.[2] I guess I'd better change it—to what you indicate is heard anyway. Thanks for this, and even more for the implication that you *study* me. Well, well!

And how you study Shakespeare! Don't hit, but I never thought "poorly led" was weak. I thought if anything that it was strong as understatement. But if it is wrong, it is wrong. Even then, however, you must tell me at Easter how "parti" becomes "bloody."

Of course call us at Easter. We want to see you both.

1. In "Now the Sky," MVD had written, "And knowledge sit along to count the cost."

2. Joseph Wood Krutch had noted the same "error."

To Allen Tate
ALS/NjP

April 4, 1945   *New York City*

I am happy to have you keep *Proud Song*, and happy to have you return the other one if you find it not quite successful.[1] You knew I counted on you to be frank, and I now pay you the compliment of believing that you were. I probably shouldn't have sent more poems—and I wouldn't have, to anybody else. The deal will remain as secret as you please.

Louise Bogan was good on you in the *New Yorker,* saying at length what I suppose I meant by that single word "mysterious"—if it was the word.[2] I didn't write at length because for some reason I can't do so any more. Poems are or are not. Yours are—and from a steadily deeper source. Please take this from me as meaning all I can say. It is everything.

Your *VQR* article I had read in place, but I am glad to have this reprint to slip among your works here in this room.[3] I agree with it unless it is to be taken *literally* as discouraging the hope, which I share with certain others, that the whole world may some day be brought under law. Law is what permits us to live with those who are different from us—even those who are our enemies. I want more of it in the world so that differences may be preserved—and prides, and loyalties, and local literatures. I do not assume that all people can ever love one another, and I despise those who exhort to this effect. But I am sure that without law they will destroy one another—or, what might be still worse, establish an iron unity in which there could be no soft lungs to go on breathing. I am for the differences you want, and rely on the Cynic Law to keep them going. If we still disagree, we can argue it out when you are here.

1. "Too Long Ago," collected in MVD's *New Poems* (New York, 1948).

2. In the *New Yorker*, April 7, 1945, p. 83, Louise Bogan wrote: "Once Tate's opacities were merely opaque. Now his

stranger images seem attached to some subterranean reality."

3. "The New Provincialism, with an Epilogue on the Southern Novel," *Virginia Quarterly Review*, XXI (1945), 262–72.

To John Van Doren
ALS/P

April 16, 1945   *New York City*

Happy Birthday! Seventeen has an old sound, it suddenly seems to me. We haven't any little boy any longer. But we have something still better— two big good boys, of whom you are one. Happiness to you, and if you open this on Tuesday, open it again Wednesday morning—it will still be saying that.

Your letter this morning pays every tribute to Roosevelt except the one he would want to hear.[1] He was inconceivably courageous. So let us be. Like the Athens that Pericles praised, we are greater even than our greatest men. You seem to say that we lose everything in Roosevelt. On the contrary, we gain him totally. He adds to our strength, but it was already great enough to make the addition matter. Don't forget that we govern ourselves. We really do, through such men—and now through Truman, whose speech to Congress I have just heard (did you?) and found greatly reassuring. Don't let me think St. John's is an uncourageous place, or that it is away from the center of our life. At our center we shall be strong. Don't doubt it. It's up to us. . . .

1. Franklin Delano Roosevelt died on April 12, 1945.

To John Berryman
ALS/MnU

May 24, 1945   *New York City*

Students and friends of Mark Van Doren's (including Berryman) honored Van Doren on May 22, 1945, as he was finishing his twenty-fifth year of teaching at Columbia.

Your remarks about my poetry Tuesday evening amounted to the most beautiful discourse I have ever heard about anything. Call me prejudiced if you will, I loved—well, first, your decision to talk about it at all, and then of course exactly the things you said. And nothing ever made me prouder than the way you read *Winter Tryst*.

I was thinking all the time, of course, about you and your poetry, which some day I shall insist on discussing too—but only with luck so felicitously.

This wonderful MS. of the poem about me I feel some conscience about having snatched away from you, but not much. I'll keep it and study it, noting and liking every smudge and erasure, and never missing that word "mysterious" which flatters me so dearly.

It was a shame that we couldn't talk more, about *Lear* and other matters. I do believe you now about that line. And I am very happy because you have another year for the job, if such is what you want. It is, isn't it, rather than teaching? If it isn't, I hope you will let me know.

Anna[1] said you called me here one day when I was—of all places—in Princeton. That was a conference, and there was no minute to spare even if you hadn't been in New York. We must meet soon. Eileen was never so beautiful as she was Tuesday, and that is *not* a prejudiced sentence.

1. The Van Dorens' maid.

To Allen Tate
ALS/NjP

May 25, 1945   *New York City*

At the celebration marking Van Doren's twenty-five years at Columbia, Tate's letter inviting Van Doren to have lunch at a Chinese restaurant in 1965, forty years after the two had first met there, was read to the group.

All right, let's meet there in 1965—when I'll give you a list of the things I have learned from you. You know some of them, but not all. You were good to write, and to write what you did. The party was, miraculously, not embarrassing. I'm still free. . . .

To John Berryman
ALS/MnU

May 31, 1945

The clean poem I am happy to have, but I have clipped it to the dirty one—a dossier! Unreal? I love it, and don't argue with your old teacher about the merits of a poem.

Do let me know when you are here (I won't be in Princeton), but there may be no special news about the Crane.[1] The board of editors, pleased though it is by your being a possibility, has like all boards to pull a long face and brood a long time before it speaks. Between you and me I think the sound that will come forth will be the sound of Yes, but I don't know when it will come forth. This is nothing personal, nor are you the only waiter to hear—if you *are* waiting. They have a list, and are contemplating its entire length. (You have no rival for Crane, by the way).

My love to Eileen.

1. Berryman proposed to write a study of Stephen Crane for William Sloane Associates. The book was published in 1950.

To Thomas Merton
ALS/KyLoB-M

August 12, 1945   *Falls Village, Connecticut*

Van Doren helped with the preparation of Merton's second volume of poetry.

Here they all are except for the new long ones you sent me in July, which as you suggest I am keeping for magazines—I assume you have other copies of these.

There will often be duplicates and triplicates, but I am sending everything because one text may differ from another and seem better to you. The group clipped together represents all that Bob had, so now you do indeed have everything.

If I didn't incorporate your own best changes in *30 Poems*, you are free of course to revise those pieces now. I enclose MSS. of them too, so you can see the corrections you made.

Will you send the 96 pp. of text for the new book to Laughlin directly, or through me?[1] His address if you want it is:

James Laughlin
New Directions
67 West 44 Street
New York City.

You are welcome to send them through me—I'll be in New York after September 15—but please do as you think best.

1. *A Man in the Divided Sea* (New York, 1946), being prepared for publication, included *Thirty Poems*, some of Merton's early work, and several poems written at Gethsemani.

To John Berryman
ALS/MnU

September 12, 1945   *Falls Village, Connecticut*

How good of you and Eileen to think of us when the war ended. Yes, it is wonderful—though Johnny will probably be drafted in April, and Charlie sees no chance of getting out of Florida, the hell-hole, except by going to Japan!

The best news is your prize[1]—I'll look for the story, and like it. I am here for another ten days, finishing my book on Homer, Dante, et al. It was hard, but I didn't mind. On Cape Cod last week, you will bite nails to know, Johnny and I had perfect weather, though it was on the torrid side.

Good luck to *Lear*, and my love to Eileen. Dorothy had a month off up here (interrupted by VJ) but she is back at work again.

   1. "The Imaginary Jew," published in the *Kenyon Review*, VII (1945), 529–39, received first prize in the *Kenyon* story contest.

To John Berryman
APS/MnU

September 25, 1945   *New York City*

I have the Knopf set of [Stephen] Crane (12 vol's), and never read it. May I present it to you? At your leisure you may come and get it. But don't wait so long that I won't know you.

To Allen Tate
ALS/NjP

October 4, 1945   *New York City*

                              *   *   *

The best news is your Eyre and Spottiswoode collection.[1] My advice would be yours for the asking, but you know damned well it wouldn't be good advice. I've long since decided I was no critic.

Yet what I was doing when you called was finishing a volume of criticism![2] On Homer, Virgil, Lucretius, Milton, Spenser, Chaucer, Byron,

Wordsworth, and Dante. I told you of this once. It's pretty good in places, but it probably isn't criticism. I wish I knew what it was. . . .

1. Tate's *Poems, 1920–1945: A Selec-*   2. MVD's *The Noble Voice* was pub-
tion (London, 1947).   lished in 1946.

To John Van Doren
TLS/P

January 17, 1946   *[New York City]*

Caroline Tate is living around the corner on Perry Street. She came in Sunday afternoon to announce the fact, and last night we had her here for dinner before going over with her to see her apartment—heated by a coal stove, and a bit better looking now that we have added a rug, a lamp, and the painting by Villa you didn't like for our living room (or Anna, or Ma, or I).[1] Your general opinion expressed in a letter before Christmas, I have always more or less shared, but I must say she is taking care of herself nicely now. The entire story is so fantastic that I won't try to tell it to you in a letter. . . .[2]

1. The poet José Garcia Villa.   Gordon. After the divorce, she moved to
2. Tate resigned as editor of the *Sewanee*   New York. The two were remarried in
Review in October of 1945 because he   April, 1946.
was soon to be divorced from Caroline

To John Van Doren
ALS/P

January 25, 1946   *[New York City]*

I have been thinking over one part of your letter, the part about wise men, and have collected this thought about Mortimer [Adler]. He may not be wise, but he makes other men wise; he is almost the necessary condition for wisdom in others. They resist him, correct him, soften him, relax him, interpret him, and in the process feel superior to him; but there he is all the time, furiously thinking and speaking, and fanatically faithful to the truth—and that is precious too. He has made Scott wiser—by reaction—than he was, and so I think with each of his friends. He is an angelic dope, and as such they worship him. They couldn't do what he does even if they tried. Their wisdom has a negative feel when he's around, as God's does, maybe, when he contemplates the sons of men. He is greater than they, but only they could make him know it. This, I'm sure, is one reason he loves them. Or put it this way. Mortimer alone among the men we know is irreplaceable. The rest are more or less wise, but whatever he is, he is absolutely. . . .

To John Van Doren
TLS/P

March 6, 1946   *[New York City]*

*   *   *

What follows is fairly confidential for the time being—indeed, I guess, quite confidential—but I tell it to you because being a bookseller you are bound to be interested. Bill Sloane is leaving Holt (he resigned today) to set up a new firm, probably to be called William Sloane Associates. He is taking with him all the editors I know there and like, and not a few authors, including me. Reason: a Texas tycoon has bought the company, or at least a majority of its stock, so that he may play with it and make big money with it. Bill is more interested in good books than he is in big money, so he will set up elsewhere. I had no hesitation in saying I would go with him. My old books will stay at Holt's, which doesn't matter except in the case of the poetry, which Bill assures me he can always get permission to reprint. That was the only thing that worried me. The future is more important to me than the past anyway, and there is no doubt that my future, such as it is, must be with Bill, whom I never have to explain or justify anything to. Do you approve?

To John Berryman
ALS/MnU

March 6, 1946

I was about to write *you* when your sweet letter and poem came. I was about to say that we had seldom enjoyed ourselves so much, or so simply. Your house—your wife—you are thrice lucky. And Stewart I was greatly taken with.[1]

This poem is wonderfully rich—a few lines, and there we four are, plus the evening sky and the world's evening itself. We four, of course, are there in *our* knowledge. The strange reader needn't know.

Our best thanks to you and Rusty—whom, I warn you, I am regularly more fond of. As for your work—you surely don't doubt that I respect and wonder at it.

1. Probably Walter Stewart (1885–
1958), an economist then at the Institute
for Advanced Study.

To John Berryman
APS/MnU

April 2, 1946   *[New York City]*

At Allen's request I have written the vice-chancellor of Sewanee—saying that if he didn't make you editor of the Review he was completely mad.[1]

Incidentally, Caroline tells me that there is a church at Winchester (I *think* that's it) some 17 miles away—[Robert] Lowell and his wife went to it.

"Poorly led" is of course inadequate. I think of these words often for some reason—I defended them at first, remember, for no good reason at all.

Love to Rusty.

1. This appointment was not made.

To Thomas Merton
ALS/KyLoB-M

July 7, 1946   *Falls Village, Connecticut*

*   *   *

Devin Adair is (are) at 23 East 26 street, New York, among the ruins you so powerfully describe. They might be literally that for all I have ever heard from them or Larsson.[1] May your letter have better luck. I didn't give Larsson a whole Journal, did I?

Laughlin too has withdrawn into some silence from which I can't dislodge him. The world your poems call noisy gives forth, in some quarters, astonishingly little sound. But I think you can depend on Laughlin at least to peep or warble soon.

Your new poems are very rich—sometimes too rich, I think, for the thin blood outside those walls. I mean, the phrasing runs too often in parallels, and admits too many epithets; result, a tincture of monotony. If that is heathen criticism, let it pass.

Substantially the poems are powerful. The *Duns Scotus*[2] is the best, I think, though the whole last series of Figures I like perhaps as well. Do you want me to do anything in particular with the MSS.? I suppose Bob [Lax] has copies. I'll keep these, of course, and read them many good times again, unless you direct me to send them forth soon.

I was very happy to hear from you. I hope you are happy in peace all the time.

1. "Journal of My Escape from the Nazis," finally published under the title *My Argument with the Gestapo*, had been rejected by several publishers, and Larsson was helping Merton try to get it, and perhaps other works, placed.

2. Appeared in *Figures for an Apocalypse* (New York, 1947).

To Lionel Trilling
ALS/NNC

February 24, 1947   *New York City*

In the fall of 1946, Delmore Schwartz wrote Van Doren of his interest in leaving Harvard for Columbia. The Columbia English department invited Schwartz to give a lecture, later published as "The Literary Dictatorship of T. S. Eliot."

A call from Delmore today, from Cambridge—he wants us to know that he doesn't require special status among us, he *is* willing to undertake his full share of work, he desires very greatly to come, etc. He'll be here over the weekend and I'll learn more. Meanwhile I said I would tell you this much, for whatever it might be worth.

To Lionel Trilling
ALS/NNC

March 1, 1947   *New York City*

According to James Atlas in Delmore Schwartz: The Life of an American Poet, *Schwartz drank heavily before and during his lecture on Eliot at Columbia. Atlas speculates, "Whether it was due to Delmore's erratic performance at Columbia, or to the wariness of Lionel Trilling, who had heard unsettling reports of his conduct at Harvard, the matter of a job was quietly dropped."*[1]

*   *   *

Delmore came last night and told me more about why he wants to leave Harvard. And what he wants to do here. He wants to teach, really teach; and the list of courses he showed me that he had presented to the Harvard faculty as projects was most impressive. I'm sure we would do well to consider him seriously. It's not too late, is it?

1. James Atlas, *Delmore Schwartz: The Life of an American Poet* (New York, 1977), 269–70.

To Thomas Merton
ALS/KyLoB-M

November 22, 1947   *New York City*

Thank you for a good letter and a good poem.[1]

The poem is one of your richest and best, but since you speak of criticism I will too. I don't know what you mean by "rut"—in your letter—but I can think you mean a certain habit of epithet. It is now clear to me that you could afford to reconsider some of your epithets—that is, leave them out. There is nothing of that sort to do in the last four lines of the present poem—"Homecoming" is of course necessary and fine. But working back from there, I suspect that others slow you down and obscure your power. E.g.: glossy, polished, wide, towering, full-armed, and I guess that's all. And I may be wrong.

Your letter knows its own ironies, so that I scarcely need to mention them. The desire for solitude! Now there *is* a problem—so deep, so strange, that no man in the *world* can help you solve it. I suppose there is much meaning in the very fact that you have found it, or that it has found you. You had to be searched in a unique place—your gift—for signs that you could surrender that too, or at least force it down to its true and eternal position of rest. May you succeed, yet not be silent. This is my impertinent prayer.

Of course I am happy to be in your autobiography if you think I belong there.[2]

1. "Poem in the Rain and the Sun."
2. Van Doren is highly praised in Merton's *The Seven Storey Mountain*.

To Thomas Merton
ALS/KyLoB-M

March 14, 1948   *New York City*

Your new book,[1] of which Laughlin sent me, generously, three copies, has been read again and again, not only by Dorothy and me but by our two sons—to each of whom a copy was immediately given.

It is a beautiful book, but you may not want to hear that. Well, then, it is a true book if I know anything about the truth. Some of the poems you had sent me, but not I think the last one. And of course I hadn't seen the note on contemplation. These two places in the book got all my attention at first, and still do in a degree, along with the address to Lax and Rice. Nothing has ever touched me more deeply than the problem you pose on page 110, and somehow solve on page 111.

I agree, if I may, that the good of other souls justifies a refusal to sacrifice the poet's art. But I see and respect the problem, and because you are involved in it—well, that is the immediate reason that I am moved.

Thank you and your superiors for letting this book exist. It is wonderful everywhere.

1. *Figures for an Apocalypse* (New York, 1947).

To John Berryman
ALS/MnU

March 18, 1948   *New York City*

If you are really coming in soon, then I won't try to answer your grand and generous letter in perfect kind. Do send me that card, and for God's sake don't carry on about having neglected me. I've neglected you too. Everybody neglects everybody, didn't you know that? And nobody suffers but you. What a sinner against God you are. He doesn't want you, I understand, to live in the past this way.

I want to see your book as soon as I can, or any part of it. As for mine, I have pondered everything you said about it, as I always do ponder your pleasures and your doubts. Certain ironies, as usual, appear. The only poem I "worked over" (your term) is *Back to the War*. The ones you liked better I never changed at all. Oh, I did work over the "ambitious" ones a bit. What's the moral? That I should do more of this? or less? Don't answer. We can talk it over, along with better subjects. (Meanwhile, how-

ever, please do keep the dedication to *The Animal Trainer*.[1] I'm proud of
that). Marianne Moore, lest I forgot, told me the other night she thought
Back to the War quite successful. A footnote to the irony, what?

I can't find, searching my soul, that I have much interest in writing permanent poems. If Time cares to save any, he can. But I don't contemplate
Time. Only Eternity—which means that I write for the present moment
alone.

Love to Eileen—whom please bring too.

1. Berryman dedicated "Animal Trainer"
to MVD.

To John Berryman
APS/MnU

April 23, 1948   *[New York City]*

Good news! But it can't be before 5, since I have a class at 4. To save time,
will you come to my office, 406 Hamilton, at 5—I'll be there as soon as I
can shake off the students.

I'm not promising not to mention the *Poems,* which came in the same
mail with your letter. They go with me to Carlisle, Pa., whither I'm off in
a hurry—hence this card.

To Allen Ginsberg
ALS/NNC

July 26, 1948   *Falls Village, Connecticut*

*Ginsberg was openly scornful of the professors at Columbia except Van Doren
and Raymond Weaver, and in Jane Kramer's* Allen Ginsberg in America *he
expressed some reservations about Van Doren: "He was writing in a classical
style."*[1]

First, I'll answer your last question. I'm never in the city this summer,
being busy here with my life of Hawthorne. But accident may take me
down, and if it keeps me there long enough I'll let you know so we can
have lunch or something.

Your letter was very interesting—particularly the part you thought I
might long ago have anticipated. In a sense I suppose I did, but you put it
more clearly for me now. The only thing I have ever been aware of wanting
to do in poetry is this: to give something that exists outside myself, and

this includes ideas, a form in words resembling its own in something else. You probably mean the same thing in terms proper to you. For example, I am no more impersonal than you. My idea of survival is simply to make things I see survive as I see them. You call it personality, and you should go on doing so. Perhaps it's better.

I'm sorry about Ransom. But your three sonnets should convince you that no damage has been done to the man in Ginsberg who writes poems. I too like them very much—the third, as a matter of fact, no less than the other two.

1. Jane Kramer, *Allen Ginsberg in America* (New York, 1969), 119.

To Allen Ginsberg
ALS/NNC

September 1, 1948   *Falls Village, Connecticut*

. . . I have pondered the Neff business, and decided it would do more harm than good for me to write him. But there is no reason why you shouldn't—at Westmoreland, New Hampshire. I'm sorry about that examination. It won't hurt you, though, to pull yourself out of your own hole—it will be (sermon) good practice.[1]

1. According to Jane Kramer in *Allen Ginsberg in America,* Ginsberg's career as a student at Columbia was somewhat erratic. When he was a sophomore, in 1945, in an attempt to force the maid in his dormitory to wash his windows, he wrote some pithy inscriptions in the grime. He was suspended. He was readmitted, but there were troubles once again. Kramer wrote: "Ginsberg finished Columbia at the end of 1948, under somewhat unusual circumstances." His friend Huncke, a drug addict, was released from jail and came to live in Ginsberg's apartment. Huncke was an active and successful thief, and Ginsberg and some of his friends were arrested in a car packed with some of the stolen items. Ginsberg's picture appeared on the front page of the New York *Daily News,* creating an "archetypal scandal." Ginsberg told Kramer: "Van Doren felt bad, but like he couldn't really understand it. 'What were you doing with those people?' he said. 'What were you doing with simple common criminals?' And he gave me like a big lecture. He said, 'A lot of us around here have been thinking maybe you'd better hear the clank of iron, Ginsberg. You don't seem to realize what you're doing. If you want my help, you've got to promise never to break the law again.' Which I suppose was very kind of sensible—like work within the society, within the normal structure of society. He posed the problem really very clearly, but at the same time he didn't have the right answer, because I was like saying that if you really felt that people like Huncke were saintly in some way or other, then you should be prepared to suffer for them and go to jail, or *something*." Ginsberg did not go to jail. Instead, he followed the advice of a professor at Columbia law school: "Plead insanity and go to a bughouse" (Kramer, *Allen Ginsberg in*

America [New York, 1969], 117–18, 123–28). It is not surprising that Ginsberg, like Berryman before him, was having difficulties with an examination of Professor Neff's.

To John Berryman
APS/MnU

December 15, 1948   *New York City*

I'm pretty sure we'll be in town on New Year's day, but there is a chance that we'll be with the Buchanans in Massachusetts.

You'll be here anyway, won't you? Then be sure to call up and see if we are at home (we shall be if in town) and come if so—all three of you, by all means!

To Allen Tate
ALS/NjP

February 14, 1949   *New York City*

*   *   *

I don't take the business seriously—never attend meetings, and return ballots only when I please.[1] I did attend one meeting, however, when your name was up. No effort was necessary, you are that famous and respected. I shall never attend another meeting, having got you crowned—or rather, seen it done.

Let's not talk about the damned thing.

I knew you all would like Chicago—you like every place—for a while.[2] Don't teach your head off or your heart out, and keep your telephone number dark. . . .

1. MVD was a member of the National Institute of Arts and Letters.

2. After a two-year, unhappy stint as editor for Henry Holt and Company, Tate left the publishing firm and lectured at New York University. During 1949 he was a visiting professor at the University of Chicago.

To Edward Davidson
ALS/P

May 3, 1949   *New York City*

Edward H. Davidson, then a member of the English department of Ohio University, had just published Hawthorne's Last Phase *(New Haven, Conn., 1949).*

Your letter was very moving. You are right to be concerned, as I am, about the things Condon spoke of. I am about as dangerous as, say, Hawthorne, and here this happens. I didn't answer *Life,* partly to show my contempt and partly because I knew they would do what they did in their correspondence columns later on.[1] The main job, I am convinced, is not to act scared. Meanwhile Condon and others are speaking up; Francis Biddle tells me that he is writing a book about the whole business;[2] maybe the peak is passed. But whatever we think, we should go on thinking and speaking as if we trusted the republic—which may rally and deserve the trust. May? I mean will.

Of course I'm terribly curious about your review in *American Literature,* and completely pleased in advance. I'll look forward to it gratefully. Meanwhile I hope you noted that Sunday's *Times* gave me credit for having used your *Last Phase*—my second copy of which, by the way, I gave to Lionel Trilling, who wanted it badly.

1. In an article about the Cultural and Scientific Conference for World Peace, *Life,* April 4, 1949, p. 42, published a picture of MVD (and many others) under the heading "Dupes and Fellow Travelers Dress Up Communist Fronts." The House Un-American Activities Committee had charged Dr. Edward U. Condon to be "one of the weakest links in our atomic security." Dr. Condon defended himself and was cleared by the Atomic Energy Commission in 1949.

2. Undoubtedly *The World's Best Hope* (Chicago, 1949).

To Edward Davidson
ALS/P

December 7, 1949   *New York City*

*   *   *

I have just seen your review of me in *American Literature.*[1] It gives me the purest pleasure, especially when I contemplate your knowledge of the subject. Thank you among other things for writing so well and gracefully about my book. That is the final form of praise. . . .

1. In his review of MVD's *Nathaniel Hawthorne* (New York, 1949) in *American Literature*, XXI (1949–50), 359–60, Davidson remarked, "This study is also a poet's response to a great prose-poet and a life-long debt which Mr. Van Doren here acknowledges to the romancer who has meant much to him." He called the study "among the most distinguished evaluations of Hawthorne in our time."

To Robert Lax
TPCS/NNC

January 5, 1950   *[New York City]*

For a time Lax traveled with a circus, and Mogador, a bareback rider, was a special friend of his. Van Doren had lunch with Lax and Mogador in New York. In 1953, the Van Dorens saw Mogador perform.

*   *   *

I wrote Tom about my minute with you and Mogador. Let it come again, and don't forget to tell me when and where I can see the circus next summer, or any summer. . . .

To Robert Frost
TLS/NhD

February 28, 1950   *New York City*

If you could find it possible to be in New York on Thursday afternoon, May 25, 1950, at 3 o'clock, the American Academy of Arts and Letters (of which you are a member) would be honored if you would give the annual Blashfield Address at its joint Ceremonial with the National Institute of Arts and Letters. The Blashfield Address carries an honorarium of $250 plus travelling expenses. I hope very much that you can accept and would be deeply grateful if you would communicate with me as soon as possible at the Academy, 633 West 155th Street, New York 32, by letter or telegram.

As you may know last year E. M. Forster came here especially to give the address and in previous years it was delivered by such men as Stephen Vincent Benét, Van Wyck Brooks, Archibald MacLeish, Lewis Mumford and Thornton Wilder.

We would suggest that perhaps your subject of not more than one-half hour might deal with the Relation of Society to the Arts in these Times. However, it would naturally be left to you to decide on the subject and title and whether you would present it in prose or as a long poem. It would be necessary for us to receive the text at least two weeks before the date and the title by April 1st.

May I add an expression of my own personal hope that you will find it possible to accept the Academy's invitation.

(over)
February 28, 1950

Dear Robert:

Of course you know I didn't write the letter on the other side of this. I was foolish enough to let them make me secretary of the Academy for a year, and this is how I have to seem to behave in consequence.

But I do hope you can come down and talk as requested. We all do, unanimously.

Nor do you need to talk about Society and the Arts, whatever that means! If you have ideas about that, all right. If you haven't, anything you want to say we want to hear.

How are you?

To William Faulkner
TLS/NNAL

March 10, 1950   *New York City*

I have the great honor to inform you that by a formal vote of the members of the American Academy of Arts and Letters, The Howells Medal given every fifth year in recognition of the most distinguished work of American fiction published during that period, has been awarded to you for 1950.

The presentation will be made by Mr. Archibald MacLeish at the Annual Joint Ceremonial of the Academy and Institute, to be held on Thursday afternoon, May 25th at 3 P.M.

It is hoped that you will accept the medal in person, with a short talk not to exceed two minutes in length, the text of which should be in our hands at least ten days before the Ceremonial, for publicity purposes.[1]

I hope I may hear from you within the near future that it will be possible for you to attend the Ceremonial and accept the award in person.

It would be appreciated, if for the time being, you would treat this communication as confidential since it has not yet been publicly announced.

May I offer you my warm personal congratulations upon the action of
the Academy.

1. Faulkner declined to attend, saying, "I am a farmer this time of year; up until he sells his crops, no Mississippi farmer has the time or money either to travel anywhere on" (Joseph Blotner, *Faulkner: A Biography* [2 vols.; New York, 1974], II, 1317). Later, after the Howells Medal had been mailed to him, Faulkner wrote the Secretary of the American Academy about the impossibility of evaluating a work. For quotations from that remarkable letter, see Blotner, *William Faulkner*, II, 1323.

To Kay Morrison
ALS/NhD

May 20, 1950   *New York City*

Felicia Geffen, secretary of everything at the Academy, will have tickets
for Lesley and you (glad you both can come), and now the only thing is
for Robert not to worry so much.[1] It is too late of course to tell him not
to. We'll simply hope—I, for one, that I didn't take advantage of him in
the first place when I recommended that he do this. I got the impression
he could do it easily, particularly since (if he would only believe it) there
isn't much to do.

1. Lesley was Frost's daughter and Kay
Morrison Frost's secretary-manager.

To Robert Frost
ALS/NhD

May 25, 1950   *New York City*

That was one of your best poems, and I look forward to the book in
which it can be read.[1]

You asked me if it had too much in it for reading aloud. Of course it
did, in the good sense. The worst thing would have been for it to have just
enough.

Thank you for coming and doing so well. I had felt guilty because I
asked you, but now I feel only edification, pleasure, and pride.

1. Frost's Blashfield address was a reading of "How Hard It Is to Keep from Being King When It's In You and In the Situation."

To Lionel Trilling
TLS/NNC

August 10, 1950   *Falls Village, Connecticut*

Howe's book *is* good, but until he sees your notes and mine (yours are wonderfully right) and does something about them, it won't be beautiful or splendid (your words).[1] I am astonished by his unevenness; by the vulgarity of his style and sometimes of his mind; and by his incapacity to move straight through his subject. Anderson wobbled, but his critic should not; and I don't think Howe's "two opinions" add up to a sufficient excuse. He should have had *one*—that is the critic's duty. The point surely is that Anderson had no mind. For my money Lawrence had none either—not really—and the clue may be right there: Howe thinks Lawrence is a "master" and a "genius." Oh, all right, let's let him say so, and for that matter let's print the book; but first of all you should make him understand (since you know him) that he *must* fix some of these awful places. "Values"—I vomit at the word, and he uses it inveterately. He calls a certain writer "Twain." And you weren't half hard enough on him for his Freudian argot. That alone will date the book, though it also dates itself by being written like an article rather than as a self-respecting and self-sustaining *book*. The 20's, the 30's, the 40's—good God, the temporal provincialism of this young man! No later decade (not even the 50's, maybe) will know what in hell he is talking about, at least a good deal of the time. I hadn't quite realized how completely sick his generation is with what it calls history, and with what I would call peeping at the recent past as if that were the all-in-all.

I exaggerate. The chapter on the short stories is very fine, the biography is (as you say) moving, and in plenty of places there is excellent perception. I guess it is the utterly graceless style that gets me down; it isn't like Howe's writing elsewhere—why is that, is he self-conscious about writing a book? In general there is nothing to be done about this, and of course my judgment may be crazy; but do make him look sharp at those details that you and I (chiefly you—I flatter myself it was because you were there first) have picked on.

I am sending (with the Ms.) a copy of this rather too irascible letter to Helen Stewart,[2] so that she may know what I think needs to be done. What she hoped, I take it, was that nothing would be need[ed] to be done. In spite of the tone I have taken (oh, yes, there is his infuriating word "tonal", too) I am willing to assume that the necessary revisions won't require more than a week if Howe really sits down and ponders them, and listens to the goddess of English as he does so.

Forgive my four feet. I admit I am tired.

1. Irving Howe's *Sherwood Anderson*   2. A member of the Sloane editorial
was published by Sloane in 1951.   staff.

To Charles Van Doren
TLS/P

November 3, 1951   *New York City*

*After graduate work in English at Columbia, Charles Van Doren received a
Cutting Traveling Fellowship for the academic year 1951–1952 to write a
dissertation on the English poet William Cowper (1731–1800). For his
dissertation, which he planned to write at Cambridge, he was in need of
Cowper's* Memoir, *an account of the poet's first attack of insanity.*

*   *   *

The Memoir is coming, and thereby hangs a tale. The man in Maine,
Garcelon by name, found in Boston what I had found in New York, that
the book is so rare as to have no (market) value—i.e., there is no record of
auction sales, etc.—so wrote to say that I could have it for nothing if I
would read his poems for him. It seems he writes poems and can't get
them published, and wants some stranger's opinion of them anyway. By
Johnny's advice I wrote to send the poems on, but included a check for
the book—this so that I would be under no obligation to like the poems
or help get them published. The sum I sent was nominal; I won't tell you
just how much, for the book is coming as a Christmas present, even
though I know you may already be through with it; it is thin, I imagine,
and will take up no special room in your trunk when you bring same
home. Well, Monday I got a letter from Garcelon expressing delight over
everything, particularly the freedom I would have to say just what I
thought of the poems (he had divined my motive, you see, but didn't resent it—a nice fellow), and saying that both book and poems were on the
way. They haven't arrived yet; when they do I'll read the *Memoir* and dis-
patch it to the place, or approximately so, where it was written. I guess
that was Huntington, wasn't it? But don't tell me; I don't need to know. . . .

To Robert Frost
ALS/NhD

January 8, 1952   *New York City*

---

*Frost read "How Hard It Is to Keep from Being King When It's In You and In
the Situation" on May 25, 1950.*

You know, that's one of your very best poems. Dorothy and I, having
heard it from you summer before last—and thought it no trifle then—
think it no trifle now, and neither do you, nugas or no nugas. It says all
that can be said about a people's wanting to know who or what it is. We
keep telling ourselves, or hire experts to do so, but still we don't understand—that there is nothing, new anyway, *to* understand.

Thank you for our copy, which came slowly through the Academy, and
for the inscription in it. And love to you and your winter, which I hope is
good and cold.

To Charles Van Doren
TLS/P

February 23, 1952   *New York City*

---

*Charles Van Doren, while at Cambridge, contemplated marriage to the singer
Varda Karni. A request for financial aid brought forth the following reflections
from his father.*

*   *   *

What this amounts to is the simple question whether now—and I mean
this summer, or even next year—is the time to get married. I'm not rais-
ing the question of marriage at all; only of the time to do it. You have love;
you have intimacy; but marriage is something in addition to that, and it
should be considered in its own terms, which modern life does not confuse with the first two. You say you feel like settling down, or words to
that effect. Well, that has nothing to do with love and intimacy. It has to
do with money and work and of course love too.

Speaking of work, the job you have set yourself this winter and spring
is the job of writing a book; nobody else decided you should; you decided
yourself, over my not infrequent hints that maybe you didn't genuinely
care about the career it implies. And now I hope you aren't being too
much chopped up as you try to do it. Our letters could be one set of
knives or axes descending; another set could be thoughts, quarrels, and

letters between Cambridge and Paris that have nothing to do with *The Task*. I know you are a powerful fellow, and I really believe you can survive this division. I'm only letting you know I realize it may exist, and daily pray that you can keep it down where it belongs. By the way, *The Task* isn't Cowper's only good poetry, is it? It almost is, but I'm sure there's a margin of other things to set forth the virtue of. Yes, that is the hard part, and the part that will justify the book; and I have faith that you will do it right, one sign that you will being that you recognize the difficulty. Go to it daily with my loving good wishes. I'm not doubting at all, you know, that the implied career is the right one for you if *you* think it is; or for that matter any career quite different from it, such as dancing, composing (words and music), writing, or flying about Europe in convertibles on errands for *Life,* or something still nicer that only you might imagine and effectuate. It's all up to you, and I love you; and trust you without limit, once you know you are on your own.

Mama and I have been saying tonight that you very rightly recognize your need of getting free of us. We never wanted you not to be, but we probably did all sorts of things—and *were* all sorts of things—to make it hard. Wouldn't it be an irony, though, for you to land yourself right back on our doorstep by getting married before you were in a position to make marriage an instrument of freedom?

Well, here I am adding cleavers and butcher knives. Not that I apologize, really, for trying once more to make one thing very clear, namely, the gold. You would have the right to resent it some day if I hadn't. Beyond that, however, I didn't want to go, and for God's sake I'll try to keep clear of all such stuff henceforth. As for the beautiful Monica, again my blessings on you and her, and may neither of you do childish things where childish things are out of place. *In* place I love them—for instance, when adults do them, or persons about to become adult, or for that matter children whose wishes charmingly conceal wisdom. And for all I actually know, that last describes you and Varda, and in due time you will be the happiest persons in the world—also, famous as poet and singer on at least two continents. Then how could I justify this letter? Only, my boy, by the claim that it picked out one rock on which you might have stumbled and broken a leg before you ever got started. But there! *I'm* not starting again. And forgive me, you who are so generous, for my ungenerosity—if that is how it seems.

To Charles Van Doren
TLS/P

March 16, 1952   *New York City*

Mark Van Doren was holding his breath because Charles had said in a previous letter that he and Varda were soon to be married (however, they did not marry) and that Charles would take up an academic career. Having previously given his opinion on the marriage, Van Doren did not repeat what he had said earlier, but concentrated on Charles's future career.

*   *   *

While I hold my breath let me comment on the last paragraph of your recent good letter to me. You said for me not to worry—you would embrace the academic career soon enough. This seems to mean that you think I want nothing else in your case. But not true. If you so desire, well and good; but please don't think I have any anxiety about it, or assume that it is the thing you *must* do. I thought I had remarked plenty of times that it might not be the thing you really desired; and if so, OK. It is a deadly business, this believing that one must carry out one's father's wishes, that one must live up to his expectations. Honestly, I have no such. I have only the greatest respect for you, and the sincerest faith that whatever you choose naturally to do you will do as few or none could do it. But it is your choice. The academic career has things for it and against it—it must have some of the latter, for me at any rate, or I wouldn't be considering departure from it now. It has been, is now, and always will be poorly paid; you know that of course. And it is if anything too secure; and one gets to be thought of as nothing but a teacher. On the other hand it is a good life in itself, and worth living; and within its limits it *is* secure. Beyond all this I won't go on pointing out its virtues and defects, which you know well at close range. But *don't* think that anything outside of yourself commits you to it. Me first of all. . . .

To Charles Van Doren
TLS/P

September 24, 1952   *New York City*

Charles Van Doren left Cambridge for Paris and tried to initiate a writing career. He worked on a novel, which was never published, and put aside his dissertation, though he still intended to complete it. It was his intention to remain in Europe until his fellowship funds were exhausted. Charles Everett,

*head of English at Columbia, was interested in Charles Van Doren's joining the
department upon his return from Europe. Charles did not return until the spring
of 1953; he then spent a year doing free-lance writing and did not join the
Columbia faculty until 1955.*

*   *   *

The reason for my writing at once is that Charles Everett told me today
he wanted you, Charlie, to be an instructor in Columbia College next
year or whenever after that you chose to call yourself willing. I send you
this merely as news, and perhaps as a sort of warning against some moment when a letter might come on the subject. Of course I have no official
relation to the same, and this is not an invitation. It is not advice, even.
For all I know you will have settled with *Time* by now, for a job maybe
that pays twice as much. The starting salary of a Columbia instructor is, I
believe, $3600 (it might even be a bit less) and that isn't much. Nor may
the whole thing interest you at all, now that you have a different view of
such matters, as I guess you do have. But there it is for you to ponder as
you please—an alternative anyway to *Time,* etc. Of course it is an alternative also to staying in Europe with which you are so much and so delightfully in love. Which is all the more reason for having the news now;
and so I send it. Charles, by the way, paid you the great compliment of
saying he wanted you to start (as few do) with full rank and be promoted
rapidly according to what used to be the normal course. He is tired of
little half-time persons who are not truly persons. He considers you a *person;* and that from him is no mean judgment. Don't expect to hear from
him soon; it might be the middle of the year, or even later; but his mind is
made up, and yours will have to be one way or the other. Really, Cha, I'm
not advising you to say Yes. You would have to love it to do it at all, and
the rewards, I don't need to tell you, are scandalously slight; they always
have been for teachers, and they always will be. I have enjoyed it, even
though I'm quitting soon; but the enjoyment was the greater part of
my pay. . . .

To Allen Tate
TLS/NjP

December 16, 1952   *New York City*

*In the fall of 1951 the Tates had moved to Minneapolis. Tate had been
appointed to a professorship in English, his first tenured appointment.*

Your poem in progress, of which I have now seen two parts, this one you
sent me and the one that appeared in the *Partisan* last spring, has me all

stirred up.[1] One reason is desire to have more, along with curiosity about the whole; another reason is the nature of the work itself, which dives so precipitately into regions of dark and light, and encounters so many beasts there whom I shall have to know better than I do, that—well, I wait and wonder. Meanwhile I much admire the stately way your terza rima takes you through such pits and tempests, and the truly sublime way you pay no attention whatever to anyone who might say your rhymes were (sometimes) harsh. Of course they should be; and the reader notes every one of them; and as from Dante receives them like barbs in the bosom of his mind, not to be easily pulled forth and forgotten. A strong-bitter flavor everywhere, as Cacciaguida recommended (Cacciaguida, my favorite among the great-grandfathers). . . .

The *Selected Poems* has been put off, yes, to 1954—maybe even to the fall of that year. In January Holt is publishing a volume of poems (I suspect my last, at least of size), and they agree with me that some time should elapse between the two publications.[2] So there is plenty of leisure for you to enjoy, and incidentally plenty of opportunity for you to change your mind if you like about writing anything. Please understand that nothing would pain me more than your thinking you had to do it. As for the selection itself, I shall probably end up with the job on my hands, where of course it ought to be. But it scares me too. I haven't actually seen Hemley's list;[3] I'll take it seriously, I assure you; but I must reserve my own rights too, and I guess it would be mad to suppose otherwise. I don't dream of your making a list, though when ours is submitted to you I count on you to holler at anything in it that seems wrong, or for that matter about anything that has been left out when you are sure it should be in. But as I said, no hurry now, thank heaven. One more thought, though; if it were ever natural for you to make a short list from memory (I flatter myself, I know) I'd be grateful for it to the end of doom. . . .

1. Tate's "The Buried Lake" was to appear in *Sewanee Review*, LXI (Spring, 1953), 177–80.

2. MVD's *Spring Birth* was published by Holt in 1953, followed by *Selected Poems* in 1954.

3. Cecil Hemley (1914–66), a friend of MVD's, cofounded Noonday Press in 1951. He was also an editor at Farrar, Straus. Hemley drew up a list of poems for inclusion in MVD's *Selected Poems*.

The Final Miracle
1953–1957

Mark Van Doren half retired from Columbia in 1953, teaching only in the spring and spending the summer and autumn in Falls Village. He turned increasingly to the writing of plays and stories, but he did not abandon poetry. He went on corresponding with friends such as Tate, Berryman, and Merton, and with many young writers. With friends and with unknown writers he was a special kind of critic, for he tried to get inside the work he was reading, to judge it on its own terms. Even his negative criticisms were presented in such a way as to convince the writers to go on working, revising, and improving their manuscripts.

To Joseph Wood Krutch
TLS/DLC

April 28, 1953   *New York City*

Charlie landed on a feather bed, if not two of them. The first was a commission to help Kip Fadiman compile a book of American quotations for Harper; . . . The second, better yet, is a contract for his novel. . . .

But I didn't tell you about Charlie's novel. He read the 50 pages to us the first night he was home, and we lost all self-consciousness after page 1. It was very fine—or as Johnny put it, "Hell, it's perfect." Of course he has the rest to write; but he is very clear as to how it will go, and Bob Giroux of Harcourt Brace told me that he made the deal on the strength of that plus other novels Charlie sketched out for him over cocktails at the Waldorf. Featherbeds? You see why I used the term. I only hope he doesn't think it will always be this way. But then, maybe it will. . . .

To Robert Frost
ALS/NhD

July 19, 1953   *Falls Village, Connecticut*

Your "isolationist" poem was sent us at Christmas by Ted Amussen, but we prefer this Fourth of July copy from you. Many thanks for it, and for the message that came with it. If isolationist, of course, I for one don't see why not. What are oceans for? I agree that this is a good question—and tell you that this is a fine poem.

We don't seem to get up your way any more; we travel less and less as we get older. But we never stop thinking of you, and hope to see you before too long. I never acknowledged in any way the opinion you sent Amussen of my book[1]—it was months ago, and I should have written then, except that I didn't suppose you had sent the opinion in order to know what I thought of it. I thought great things of it, and again of you, as Ted read it to me over the telephone. You do know, I'm sure, how much deep pleasure it gave me. No other opinion would really count.

Dorothy and I are here now for about twenty months. So far I have been lazy—as she has not—and it has been a good thing to be. She sends her love with mine, to you and to the Morrisons if they are there. And to Ghillie, if that is the way to spell his name.

1. Probably *Spring Birth and Other Poems*, published earlier that year.

To Thomas Merton
TLS/KyLoB-M

July 21, 1953   *Falls Village, Connecticut*

Your words about *Spring Birth* gave me the greatest pleasure. I was particularly happy to have you say you were interested in Uncle Mark; the poem is literally true in every line—and yes, we should have stayed longer.[1] But that was the summer we drove West, and we thought we ought to keep going. We should have been more like your hermit,[2] or yourself, or Grigsby Collins.[3] The world is full of such people and doesn't even know it; doesn't know, for instance, that they are what hold it in one piece. (The last word is a pun if you want to take it that way.)

Dorothy and I are up here for about twenty months. I have a sabbatical year, and after it is over I go back to teaching half-time only, in the spring sessions, so that my next class meets in February, 1955. Think of all the Tom Mertons I will miss. However, I am content to be here and so is

Dorothy, although we have to admit that it is very different without the boys, who in other such times were with us. Johnny is in the army, in Louisiana, and Charlie is working in New York. Charlie comes up most weekends, and that is fine; still, we live alone and don't always like it, in spite of the many advantages which we do thank Quiet for. Johnny was deferred from the draft until he finished his doctor's dissertation in history at Columbia; then he went, choosing nothing, and took what there was to take. So far this is hard, dull training at Camp Polk; but he writes wonderful letters about it, and we conclude that he knows how not to let it hurt him, body or soul. Charlie was to have become a doctor in English at Columbia; but he went to Paris on a fellowship, stayed a year and a half (part of the time at Cambridge), and came back with a novel partly written—no more academic life for him. Bob Giroux read the novel and gave him a contract to finish it; so, with that to do and a hack job on the side, he flourishes as a freelance these days, and I for one am glad he can do it. Both boys delight their parents with everything they do—and, being admirers of you, would want to be remembered in this letter if they were here.

You invite me to visit you when I am in that part of the country. Well, next spring I think I will be. I am going some day to write some kind of a poem about Lincoln, and although I don't really need to see his birthplace, yet I plan to do so, perhaps in March.[4] And you are close by. If it isn't Lent, I'll give you warning and come on. There is nothing, incidentally, I would rather do. Lincoln would be only an excuse.

But that is far in the future. Till then, Tom, remember that we always think of you with happiness and love.

1. MVD sent his *Spring Birth* to Merton at Gethsemani. The Van Dorens visited his Uncle Mark in Oklahoma but stayed only one night. See "The Uncle I was Named For" in *Spring Birth* (New York, 1953).

2. Probably Herman Hanekamp, a former lay brother at Gethsemani, who lived in the hills and came to the abbey for mass.

3. Unidentified. Members of the Van Doren family do not remember anyone by that name. Brother Frederick Collins was at that time manager of the Gethsemani Farms, but he was not, so far as is now known, called Grigsby. He was, too, a man of great energy and would not seem to fit the characterization of Grigsby Collins in this sentence. It is possible that MVD and Merton, in a playful mood, rechristened Frederick Collins.

4. The Lincoln poem became the play *The Last Days of Lincoln* (New York, 1959).

To Joseph Wood Krutch
ALS/DLC

October 19, 1953   *Falls Village, Connecticut*

A book a day by Joe
Makes time the better go.
But they are at an end;
So write another, friend,
And make it moral too—
The old world and the new.

That bad poem is to thank you for a second good book on something like the same subject, though its name now seems to be Reason. In either case, as a matter of fact, it could have been Wisdom or Temperance or Courage, the sum of those, as Plato tells us, being Justice, of which however the very best name after all may be Joy. Terms signify little in the longitude, old classicist, of your discourse. The paramount thing is that you insist upon the paramount—are really serious, which so few people ever are, and so are witty and sensible and reassuring too. Now I am guessing that the new *Modern Temper* will somehow gather all this in again, perhaps under an arch of metaphysical proportions. But I tranquilly await that day, in full faith that no page will disappoint me.

If *Modernism* is at all inferior to *Two Worlds* the fault is in the subject.[1] Plays are probably less important than frogs and lichens; literature is a lesser subject than life. But I don't mean by this to impute any absolute inferiority to your discussions of Ibsen, Strindberg, Shaw, Pirandello, Synge, and *les jeunes*. They were edifying and exciting too—only, I shall go back oftener to your frost crystals and your witch-hazel blossoms (which Dot and I saw in the woods today because I had read you on them yesterday; she is reading you tonight).

1. Krutch's *"Modernism" in Modern Drama: A Definition and an Estimate* (Ithaca, N.Y., 1953) and *The Best of Two Worlds* (New York, 1953).

To Allen Tate
ALS/NjP

October 24, 1953   *Falls Village, Connecticut*

Your goodness has gone for nothing. Holt, not Hemley, will publish my *Selected Poems,* and the decision is to have no introduction, either by you or by Shakespeare. This may relieve you, and I'm pretty sure it will; but please understand that I remain grateful for the willingness you expressed a year ago—also, that I won't bore you with explanations not in the least necessary. Or are they? If asked for, they will be supplied. You don't need to be told, of course, that the decision against an introduction was categorical, and had nothing to do with you—the best one to do it, in everybody's mind, if it was to have been done.

Do you still want me to send you my list (not completed yet, by a long shot) so that you can add or subtract? I'll do so only if you promise not to make a job of it—but simply to note, as casually as you please, any omissions that strike you, or any inclusions that seem horrible. And you are perfectly free to let the whole thing go. I have gradually realized that it is my job, and am willing at last—even eager—to get it done.

How are you and Caroline? We are here until February, 1955, when I go back to teach half time—spring terms only. It's a nice freedom, but I'm still having to convince myself it exists. We have fixed over the house for winter occupation by old folks: a new heating system, a fancy kitchen, and all the rest. Come see us when you can, either or both of you.

[P.S.] Your long poem, seen here and there, is wonderful.

To Allen Tate
TLS/NjP

February 25, 1954   *Falls Village, Connecticut*

You said to send you my list when it was done, and here it is, together with a preface which sets forth such philosophy as I had when I made it.[1]

But I mean it when I say to you that you should do no more than run your eye over the titles and tell me (1) if I have left out any poems you remember favorably (2) if I have included any horrors. I know you haven't the books there, and to do just this much would be doing me all the good I have any right to expect. Any further comments, of course, I will ponder most respectfully. . . .

Understand, please, that you are to bother as little or as much as you like with this formidable project; or none at all if you prefer. I make no demands on you at a time when you have, I am sure, important work of your own in the fire, and when even if you haven't there is Italy to enjoy. I'm glad you and Caroline are there, and both of us want to hear about it when you are back.

By important work I mean of course your long poem in tercets. May it prosper.

PS: The book as it stands here will be about 220 pages—one sixth (or seventh) of all the pages I have published and perhaps one fourth of the poems by title.

1. Holt published MVD's *Selected Poems* later that year.

To Thomas Merton
ALS/KyLoB-M

May 19, 1954   *Falls Village, Connecticut*

I must clear something up. You will remember that I said when we were with you I had written you about your poem on the burning of the barn.[1] You were puzzled because you couldn't recall getting such a letter, and put it down to some confusion there might have been in the monastery mails. Well, I never wrote the letter. I found yours containing the poem in the place where I had left it until the time should come for writing that we were coming—and when that time did come I proceeded as if there were no such poem, since it was not immediately before me.

So the monastery mails are absolved of any guilt, and I have had the pleasure of reading the poem again—a very beautiful one, however sad the event it relates.

Perhaps the foregoing was not required, but I am glad of a further occasion to tell you how happily we remember every minute of our visit with you, and how much pleasure it gives us to share it with others by describing it to them—Bob Lax, for instance, who you may not know is returning soon to France, where he says he will stay four years. He wondered if he should write you, and I took the liberty of saying yes.

Our love to you every day.

1. "An Elegy for the Monastery Barn." The barn at Gethsemani burned in August, 1953. Michael Mott in *The Seven Mountains of Thomas Merton* (New York, 1984), 286, writes, "When Mark Van Doren and his wife Dorothy visited Geth- semani in September 1957, the two friends talked of the poem on their walk to the site, and then of how much they both enjoyed fires, a sort of atavistic joy in the fiery destruction."

To Thomas Merton
ALS/KyLoB-M

June 16, 1954   *Falls Village, Connecticut*

Well, here's a third (don't be alarmed), to thank you for reading the stories and saying they were symbolic without intending or trying to be—

they did neither thing—and to tell you that I have now read five new works of yours with the greatest happiness while I read, and still more so remembering. You gave me at Gethsemani, you know, *Bread in the Wilderness* and two paper-bound pedagogical books. The latter I waited longest to read, not realizing the fascination they would have. When I started, I went right through them, Latin and all; and stopped very often to say to myself: How completely Tom remains himself, even when he is expounding the doctrine of others. I don't mean that a self is intruded, or even seems conscious of itself: but there it is, authenticating every lesson, as *you* were in the room we saw you in. You may remember that I exclaimed about your being your old self, and you asked, Why not? Why not indeed? It is the final proof that you exist—so that other things and persons can exist through you. Otherwise, in air.

Then *The Last of the Fathers* came from Bob Giroux; and now you have sent me the Oratorio. You are always wonderful on St. Bernard— whom I used to know in Dante only—and *Tower of Babel* is truly apocalyptic, with grim contemporary reference to our "destroying history as fast as it is made." That is terrible and true, whether I understand you or not.

My Lincoln poem has become, believe it or not, a play—written in ten days, as plays probably should be written.[1] Though now is it any good? I'll write you when I think I know.

But as I said, don't be alarmed. I'll not make it chronic; nor do you need to answer this.

1. *The Last Days of Lincoln* (New York, 1959).

To Sarah Singer
ALS/P

June 16, 1954   *Falls Village, Connecticut*

Van Doren was consistently helpful to young poets who sent him their poetry, as the correspondence with Sarah Singer shows. He would comment on particular poems, suggest ways to revise, and often point out journals or publishers which might be interested.

I like your poems very much. They are crisp, economical, and very intelligent—and intense, too, with great feeling which a certain dryness in the terminology does not conceal. The dryness is good, but I wouldn't indulge it further, for it could then become a trick (polysyllables, metaphysics, astronomy, planets, etc.). This applies chiefly to the short poems (which I have taken the liberty of marking up a bit.) The long one goes much beyond them, into flesh and blood and drama, where poetry wants to be. Lydia Pritchett is most moving, most articulate—even though it has eclipses and cycles in it too. In short, don't let me put your favorite language down. You keep it *up,* and in good living company, so that you the speaker won't grow breathless. . . .

To Archibald MacLeish
ALS/DLC

July 22, 1954   *Falls Village, Connecticut*

* * *

I have made new notes in order to preserve them all (the suggestions), and in God's good time I will carry them out. But this morning a letter came from Lillian [Hellman] offering to recommend the play to her producer,[1] and I think I'll send it to him as it is, on the practical theory that if he is interested at all he will want to consider changes from his point of view before they are made.

All right? (Don't answer.)

I even have an ending scene in mind, O Aristotle. But that too I'll keep just there until I hear from this producer. You will be amused, by the way, to learn that Lillian particularly liked the end as it stood. But you are righter. . . .

1. MVD's *The Last Days of Lincoln.*

To Joseph Wood and Marcelle Krutch
ALS/DLC

July 22, 1954   *Falls Village, Connecticut*

* * *

Don't look now, but my Lincoln Poem has turned into a play, with all the persons speaking verse except Lincoln, who speaks (my) prose. I saw Lillian Hellman (your dear friend, Joe) at an Institute lunch in May and told her about it. She asked to read it, has done so, and says she likes it well enough to recommend it to her producer. I don't know whether or not to hope that it will ever get into a theater, but that is what I wrote it for, and Archie MacLeish, who was here yesterday and insisted on my reading it to him, thinks it very actable. Good God! What if it should? For one thing, I'd be glad you didn't have to review it and say nice things you didn't mean. But I expect nothing, quite cheerfully, since it was fun merely to write. I wrote it in ten days, during a lecture trip away from books and notes, and I believe that was the way. . . .

To John Van Doren
ALS/P

September 26, 1954   *Falls Village, Connecticut*

*   *   *

I am writing 5 or 6 stories to take the places of as many weak ones in the 3rd volume I will publish someday—and then no more. But these are very absorbing, and if I am right in supposing they are better than the ones they will replace I shall be glad I wrote them. They are harder to write than any before, and take longer. Query: a sign of advancing age and decreasing strength, or a sign that only now, when about to abandon the business, I have found out what to do and (more or less) how to do it? In either case they surely are the last. Henceforth you and Charlie have the field. Me, I think I'll end up by writing nothing whatever but lyric poems— slowly, selectively, and with a kind of cunning satisfaction I already can foresee. I could speak of Yeats, Hardy, and Frost, but will not since none of them seems relevant except with respect to the matter of age and the cunning satisfaction—the deep, secret, purely personal pleasure—to which I have alluded. The job will be to say (or sing) those terribly important things which one is assumed to be unable to express as the year grows ancient. The things, in other words, one learns too late to teach; or, in other words, feels too strongly to entrust abroad. . . .

To John Berryman
ALS/MnU

November 7, 1954   *Falls Village, Connecticut*

So that is where you are. I never know—and am always happy to be told.
      And you are forty. And I am sixty. Well! Which reminds me of a wonderful sentence in a letter I got the other day from a lady who is also sixty: "Frost is in the air, and most of us are still wearing our summer

clothes." For you of course there is no frost, so you need feel no scruple for whatever clothes you may be wearing, even in cold Minnesota. I am glad you like it there, and wish you well with Dante after Christmas. The Shakespeare job at Harvard must have been tremendous; except that Sh. is tremendous too, and always pays his way.

I *have* seen the Bradstreet poem (or was it only a part?) and thought it very fine.[1] Where did I see it? You know, and so shall I when I run upon the magazine again—too carefully laid away when we moved here, as we did in June, 1953. We have had a year and a half all to ourselves, but in February go back to New York where I expect annually (for a few years) to teach in Spring sessions only. But to go back to Anne Bradstreet: you marvellously created her place, time, mind, and heart in a line whose sleepy strength immensely moved me. Congratulations upon it, and thanks for sending it if you did.

My best to Allen[2]—*our* best, I should say, and of course to you, and ultimately to Caroline. It gives me great pleasure to hear that my Civil War poem still works for someone.

1. "Homage to Mistress Bradstreet."
2. Both Tate and Berryman were teaching at the University of Minnesota.

To Thomas Merton
ALS/KyLoB-M

November 15, 1954   *Falls Village, Connecticut*

Of course you are free to use the poem *If They Spoke.*[1] You always have such freedom, but in this case I am particularly delighted by your gloss, which of course I could have expected. A melancholy fact, Tom: almost nobody these days talks that way about poems—i.e., about their subjects. It is the only way, if critics but knew; and then they could be interesting writers, which as a tribe they certainly aren't, at least for my dime.

We are still here. The sabbatical is over, but now I am a half-time teacher, meaning spring sessions only. . . .

You write of rain. We didn't have a dry summer especially, but the fall has been wet enough to please the greediest farmer, who as I understand him hates to go into the winter with dry frozen ground which when it is spring again won't ooze and gush and run with rivulets suggesting deep, damp roots. Of course he is right. But even apart from all that I love fall rains; there is a good excess about them; they can't hurt; so I have been happy, at least weatherwise.

I don't remember telling you (if I did, forgive my doing it again) that the Lincoln poem turned into a play about the last three weeks of his life, with everybody else speaking verse but he, of course, prose (my prose). The Theatre Guild is interested in it—very much so, judging by their letters, though I don't count on this continuing. The theater has become a chancy place—on, then off again. I wrote the play in about a week last May. It is about Lincoln's plan for the South, which died with him. But it is about other things too. I found that I seemed to know him very well, after years of reading and considering. He talked readily for me; and when I rewrote some scenes in July, there he still was, saying just what I hoped he would say, in language better than mine, though his is in a way mine too.

My best to Fr. Matthew, whose interest in my poems pleases and moves me. We never asked his name in the world; perhaps it is not for us to know.

And to you our ever continuing love.

1. Merton wished to use the poem in a book he was writing published under the title *The New Man* (New York, 1961). In his gloss on page 82, Merton wrote that MVD remarked in his poem "that the animals are not at all conscious of having been named and classified by men." Merton then notes: "The poet goes on to remind us that the animals 'simply are' and he comments that if they spoke they would tell us that the same is true of ourselves. The information might prove so disconcerting that our objectivized knowledge of ourselves would collapse along with everything else in the 'end' of our intentional world."

To Joseph Wood Krutch
ALS/DLC

December 11, 1954   *Falls Village, Connecticut*

Now I am rewarded. The *Selected Poems* (incidentally, I suggested it to Holt, not they to me—how's *that* for egotism?) has been something of a flop. Ignored, faintly praised, or contemptuously dismissed (I'm old-fashioned. I don't live in these times). Usually called "quiet"—a term which makes me loud in wrath, though nobody hears. Well, your letter quite sets me up again. Many thanks for your large words, which I believe and love. . . .

To John Van Doren
ALS/P

July 3, 1955   *Falls Village, Connecticut*

*   *   *

A letter from Thurber says they were taken to a night club in Paris by Zabbie and Schillie and among other things there was a strip-tease act; but nobody thought of mentioning this to Jim, so that he knew nothing of it "till the girls were dressed and gone home."[1] . . .

1. Dr. John Zabriskie and Dr. John Schillinger were two New York friends of James Thurber and MVD. By 1955, Thurber was almost completely blind.

To John Van Doren
ALS/P

July 20, 1955   *Falls Village, Connecticut*

I have just written Mira [Jedwabnik] to say one simple thing which circumstances (or, more likely, my own absurd and I fear selfish habit of saying first things last) kept me from saying simply over the weekend. I am very happy that Mira and you are getting married. You must know this, but let me tell you something—it is now five days since you released the news, and though it began by being the best news I could imagine it has miraculously become more and more so. The more I take it in the better I like it. In other words, it grows and grows. For one thing, I don't suppose two nicer persons ever did marry each other. And for another, each of them separately is a joy forever. Just to think that I shall have me such a daughter! After 27 years of such a son, I know I don't deserve it.

Mama thinks all this too. We are both happier every minute, and speak of few things else.

To Thomas Merton
ALS/KyLoB-M

October 14, 1955   *Beaune Cote-d'Or, France*

Dorothy and I are on the move again—probably for the last time in our lives—and yesterday, believe it or not, we called on Lax at his seminary in

Corps. I called from a neighboring town to make sure he was there. He was, and the next morning we arrived by car to spend two very happy hours with him, mostly in a little visitors' room where we had coffee in bowls about the size of your head, but also, just before we left, in the garden where Bob knew the names of all the vegetables and flowers. He named them like Adam, then photographed us standing among them.

He is in a fine state, I think, but fears he will have to go back home before too long. Apparently he could stay there forever, looking at the mountains and the trees. You will see shortly, I suppose, a little book of poems which he has just published, all of them (save one) about the miracle of trees.

We have driven through England, Scotland, Ireland, and France, and Monday we take a train from Paris to Athens. Then home in November, to stay there, as I said, probably for the duration. Meanwhile we find traces everywhere of your fame. On a boat to the Aran Islands we talked with a Franciscan friar who knew your books, and one evening in a restaurant at Cannes we overheard some American sailors speaking of *The Seven Storey Mountain* and *The Waters of Siloe*. I couldn't help going over to their table and boasting of our visit to you last year.

We never forget that visit, of course, though I believe I did neglect writing you about your last book, received long before we left and profoundly enjoyed.

I wonder if you were ever at La Grande Chartreuse. We drove up there yesterday, on the way here from Corps, and I must tell you that nobody has ever exaggerated the grandeur of the scenery thereabouts. The mountains look like cathedrals at the top. They really do. And the gorges look as deep as any place in Dante. The monastery, properly enough, was not to be visited, but we walked around it a little . . . and naturally thought of you and your brothers at Gethsemani, in a different order to be sure and among less grandiose hills, but possessed of equal quiet.

May all be well with you in every way, inner and outer. We both send you our best love, for always.

To James Thurber
ALS/P

December 20, 1955   *Falls Village, Connecticut*

Your alphabetical sedation piece is all the joy I can use this Christmas, so I may call off any further festivities.[1] This will be a surprise to the children, and at first a disappointment; but I have faith that by the time we have memorized your entire text we shall be happy enough, in the solemn way you prescribe, to last us throughout our remaining lives. . . .

1. "The Tyranny of Trivia," *New Yorker*, December 17, 1955, pp. 30–35.

To Allen Tate
ALS/NjP

January 5, 1956   *Falls Village, Connecticut*

I never hear from you and this is my fault, since you never hear from me. But it could be Henry Holt's fault if you failed to get the copy of my *Selected Poems* I asked them to send you. I have just learned that several other copies never left the office, and am prepared to raise some hell if yours didn't—yours, of course, more than any other, in view of your relation to it, abortive though I made that be. If you did get the book, no comment is solicited. I only want to know if I should raise hell. . . .

To Thomas Merton
ALS/KyLoB-M

January 12, 1956   *Falls Village, Connecticut*

ONCE IN KENTUCKY

(To Thomas Merton)

In our fat times a monk:
I had not thought to see one;
Nor, even with my own poor lean concerns,
Ever to be one.

No. But in Kentucky,
Midway of sweet hills,
When housewives swept their porches, and March light
Lapped windowsills,

He, once my merry friend,
Came to the stone door,
And the only difference in his smiling was,
It sorrowed more.

No change in him, except
His merriment was graver.

As if he knew now where it started from;
And what the flavor.

He tasted it, the joy,
Then gave it all to me:
As much, I mean, as I could carry home
To this country,

To this country whose laughter
Is a fat thing, and dies.
I step across its body and consider,
Still, those eyes.[1]

This is your poem if you want it. I wrote it the next day after Bob's, in the middle of December, but hesitated to impose it on you at Christmas. I hesitated anyway, yet here it is as a kind of answer to your recent letter. I thought you might not mind knowing how you *looked* down there, and of course still do. Such things as *looks* can be important facts, not discoverable except through others. I am terribly interested in what you tell me about your wrestling over solitude again. I don't pretend to understand it all, but with your suffering I have, believe me, the fullest and tenderest sympathy. And I can doubt that you are washed literally of everything. You couldn't be, and I dare to say shouldn't be. For instance, of your created person. Which is why I send the poem—to show that someone saw that person.

1. The poem is typed. For an account of
the meeting with Merton, see MVD's *Autobiography* (New York, 1958), 330–32.

To Allen Tate
ALS/NjP

February 14, 1956   *New York City*

After a month my book has come from Holt, and it goes to you today.[1]

Your own book, the essays, came today also.[2] A most agreeable coincidence, considering the pleasure your new preface gave me. A strange pleasure, for you out-Adamsed Henry Adams; but a pleasure nevertheless, and one of a high order because of the taut way in which, with lips all but closed, you spoke the truth about confession and criticism.

I repeat: you need not comment on *Selected Poems*. I know you will find it too long. But it is yours, to do with what you like. . . .

1. *Selected Poems* (New York, 1954).   *World: Selected Essays, 1928–1955* (New
2. *The Man of Letters in the Modern*   York, 1955).

To Thomas Merton
ALS/KyLoB-M

March 18, 1956   *New York City*

Thank you for finding what you did in my poem about you, and thank you for those two poems of yours, which I have read many times and keep rediscovering. They seem to me very fine, though *A Landscape* is difficult for me because it is almost too good: the child, the window, the Personage, the cornflowers, the sun, the mother are so true that I don't know what they mean.[1] Not that I want you to tell me. I think I do understand. But you have been such a good painter—a real religious artist, to remind you of your lectures—that the poetry is almost a by-product. And poetry is really best that way. In other words, I think this is a great poem and I shall live with it as long as I do with anything. *Spring Storm* blows in among the woolen hundreds and scatters them among the four walls so that they are visible in a new, touching, troubled way that again seems wonderful to me.[2] If you wait this long and then write two poems and they are as good as these—well, waiting itself was good.

But who knows that better than you? We are here now, for my one term at Columbia, and we wait for Cornwall again, though this is all right, too. It has been two years since we visited you. I don't know if or when we can do it again, but if we ever can, we will.

1. "A Landscape" appeared first in   2. "Spring Storm" appeared in *The*
Western Review, XII (Autumn, 1947),   *Strange Islands* (New York, 1957).
30–31.

To Allen Ginsberg
ALS/NNC

May 21, 1956   *New York City*

*   *   *

Now you know I can't say anything about the poems that you want to hear.[1] But I got them and read them—and have no shred of influence with the *H.-T.* toward a review for them.[2] The long line *is* good, I agree, because it lets you say what you want, and furthermore I agree that you have said it. So!

1. Probably *Howl for Carl Solomon*, the mimeographed pamphlet, 1955, which contained "Howl," "A Supermarket in

California," "Sunflower Sutra," and "America," plus prose.
2. New York *Herald-Tribune*.

To Elizabeth Sergeant
ALS/ViU

July 6, 1956   *Falls Village, Connecticut*

*   *   *

I'm not sure that I could add anything to your knowledge of Robert Frost.[1] I myself know remarkably little about him personally. We get along well, it may be too well; we have never even argued, let alone fought, and I don't need to tell you how much one learns of him by doing that; or so at any rate his theory goes. What I have to say about his poetry, which between you and me is the only thing that matters, I have said in half a dozen scattered pieces which I take it you have seen. . . .

1. She was at work on a study of Frost.

To Charles Van Doren
TLS/P

September 10, 1956   *Falls Village, Connecticut*

Charles Van Doren spent the summer at the family farm; when he returned to New York in September to teach at Columbia, Mark Van Doren sent him the following letter-poem.

LINES WRITTEN IN IMITATION

OF

WILLIAM COWPER, ESQ.

He has driven away, and with him has gone
More even than summer, though that is as much
As I look for this morning; and see on the lawn—
Look, leaves fallen, and dry to the touch.

More than warm green, than lazy long growth,
Went down the cool hill with him only last night.

I am here, he is there: it is each, it is both
Things sicken me now with their secret delight;

As if it were good to devour an old heart,
As if it were pleasure to leave in its place
A little dry mind whose meagerest art
Will be to remember his hands and his face:

How he did this, and how he said that,
And how he was angry for part of one day;
As if it were better to sit where he sat
Than to have him still here and deciding to stay.

To Allen Ginsberg
ALS/NNC

October 6, 1956   *Falls Village, Connecticut*

*   *   *

Thanks for the new work,[1] which I like better than *Howl*, I believe,
though when 2 copies of that came last week I thought it was good too.
You've found a natural idiom and line for yourself, and with their help
you'll be able to say anything. Which is as it should be.

[P.S.] Some traveller.

1. Probably *Siesta in Xbalba and Return
to the States* (Mimeographed pamphlet,
July 1956).

To Allen Tate
ALS/NjP

March 3, 1957   *New York City*

We'll expect to hear your sweet voice on the 20th of June or thereabouts,
and to have you come and see us for as long as you like.

Now don't fail to do this. It *has* been long, and heaven knows how
much there might be to talk about.

Johnny teaches at Brandeis (this is his first year), but he and Mira, his
wife whom we consider our own, will pretty surely be in Cornwall when
you come. He may even be able to give you a few tips.

Charlie staggers us too, and so does his fame. I for one never knew anything before about that.[1]

1. Charles Van Doren was appearing on "Twenty-One," the television quiz show.

To Joseph Wood Krutch
TLS/DLC

March 21, 1957   *New York City*

Charles Van Doren's appearances on "Twenty-One" brought him to national attention. He won $129,000 before being defeated by another contestant.

* * *

We haven't answered or even acknowledged the good letters you and Marcelle wrote us about Charlie, the chief reason being that the situation was always changing—also, we heard from so many people that we were almost as overwhelmed as he was. Of course that last is an overstatement: his correspondence has been mountains of letters daily, so that he finally had to get a secretary. . . .

Your diagnosis of the ending phase is of course correct. He couldn't stop; he had to be beaten, preferably by his opponent's stopping; and the only question was, by how much? We were all delighted by the way it ended, and so was he, for he was more than ready to get out. There is no new program for him yet. Hundreds have been suggested, but all are phony, and he may end up by retreating altogether from the field, which he is strongly tempted to do. . . . What strikes us more than anything else is the good sense he has shown. He doesn't pretend that nothing has happened, but he does seem to have kept his head. The whole thing was pretty crazy, and he knows this too. But such fame! I never saw anything like it. . . .

To Thomas Merton
ALS/KyLoB-M

May 1, 1957   *New York City*

On this perfect May Day, high and blue, with cool air hiding in corners to surprise the warm air just when it thinks it is king, we thank you for the dedication of your beautiful book to us, with its woollen hundreds running under storms of spring.[1] New Directions had sent no copy before yours came, so our first news—after the letter—was the inscription inviting us to Gethsemani again. We'll come if we ever can, but meanwhile we shall have these fine poems, most of which, as you say, I for one have already seen, but it is vastly better to have them in a book, *Babel* and all (a great play that).

Charlie has gone through something, certainly. About 15 million people have fallen in love with him—and I don't use the word lightly, nor did money have anything to do with it. Such letters I have never seen—quantity and quality, with not one peep of envy or malice. So much good will was (is) overwhelming. One thinks quite well of the world in consequence.

Don't worry about not writing. Of course I know you don't. You will again, you know.

1. *The Strange Islands* (New York,
1957) was dedicated to Mark and Dorothy
Van Doren.

To Thomas Merton
ALS/KyLoB-M

August 21, 1957   *Falls Village, Connecticut*

Believe it or not, I have written an autobiography, to be published next year by Harcourt Brace, and it appears that I must ask you whether you have any objection to my quoting:

1) Several first lines from *Thirty Poems*.

2) A sentence or two from the letter you wrote for the 25th anniversary party given me in 1945.

3) A sentence or two from *The Seven Storey Mountain*.

If you do object, please say so and nothing will happen—cheerfully. Or if you want to see the texts of what I quote, I'll send them. You may believe I don't traduce you. Quite the contrary.

Then there is this. Dorothy and I are taking at the end of September the same trip we took in 1954, at least as far as my brother's in Illinois. We expect to be driving through Kentucky (your part) on (I think) September 28th, and would love to stop and see you if you are free. If you won't be free, once more I tell you to say so, and it will be all right. I feel some hesitation in suggesting that the experience of three years ago, so perfect for us, be repeated. But you have urged us to do something like this, and so I write as now I do. . . .

To Thomas Merton
TLS/KyLoB-M

September 12, 1957   *Falls Village, Connecticut*

A confession. I was careless about my dates, or rather about my times. We can reach Gethsemani on Saturday the 28th, but not in the morning. I had supposed that a lecture I was giving at Hampton Institute, Virginia, on the 26th was in the afternoon. But now I find it is in the evening, and since it is 650 miles from there to you, and I am not as young as I once was, I can't drive fast enough to hear the conventual mass and see you at nine. The earliest hour I am sure of is 2 p.m.

And Saturday afternoon may be an altogether different matter with you. If it is clearly out of the question, simply say so and we'll manage better some other year. On the other hand, if you would still have an hour or two free, then we'll stop by. But please be frank in any case. Of course you know we want to see you if it is conformable to other things; but only if.

My autobiography has no movements in it. Quite the contrary. It is the story of how I have learned to stand still. I'm afraid it is innocent of history altogether. It is chiefly about my friends, who don't move either, though they change. But I'll not say any more about it; of course you'll get a copy sometime next year, and you can see for yourself. Lax is in it a good deal. I found that he was always somehow there, either in person, or in notes he sent me, prose or verse. Right now, as I'm sure you know, he's in St. Vincent's Hospital with a variety of ailments. He has been very funny about them, but I don't suppose they were funny at all. After he convalesces for a month at Olean he will come up here for a further rest. I think New York is not the place for him, and he says he thinks so too.

The lecture at Hampton, to Negroes, is about Homer. I like the prospect as well as I can like the prospect of any lecture.[1]

Don't go to Nicaragua before the 28th.

P.S.: We *might* make it by 1 p.m., but I don't promise—unless you say it is necessary, and then I do.

1. Michael Mott, *The Seven Mountains of Thomas Merton*, 587, quotes from Merton's journal for September 29, 1957: "I was happy to have had him [MVD] stand in these rooms, so wise a person, and lean against the bookshelf in the Scriptorium and talk about some things that had come up when he was at Hampton Institute the day before. The English Professor there complained that his students had no preparation to face Shakespeare and Mark said everyone is prepared to read Shakespeare by the time they are 18. They have been born, they have had Fathers, Mothers; they have loved, feared, hated, been jealous, etc."

To Robert Lax
ALS/NNC

December 11, 1957   *Falls Village, Connecticut*

These have been read and reread—the poem for the third time, since Tom had showed it to me at Gethsemani, and for that matter the play too, which I don't understand, do you?[1]

Many thanks for all of it again. The letter is wonderful, of course—you bring out the deepest and craziest in Merton, and it ought to be brought out, for if it stayed in the walls of Gethsemani would sure tumble some day.

1. Probably *The Tower of Babel* (New York, 1957). This verse drama appeared in *Jubilee* and was collected in *The Strange Islands* (New York, 1957).

The Last Years
1957–1972

Mark Van Doren's *Autobiography* (New York, 1958) ended in 1957. Beginning in that year, Charles Van Doren, an instructor at Columbia, was much in the public eye because of his appearances on the television game show "Twenty-One," on which he won $129,000. In 1959, however, there were charges that "Twenty-One" and other game shows had been rigged, that Charles Van Doren and other contestants had been provided the answers to questions. After the charges were made, Charles Van Doren wrote in a statement read to the Special Sub-Committee on Legislative Oversight of the House of Representatives in Washington, D.C., on November 2, 1959, that he had a hard time deciding to tell the truth. "I was beginning to realize . . . that the truth is always the best way, indeed it is the only way, to promote and protect faith. . . . My father had told me this, even though he did not know the truth in my case. I think he didn't care what it was so long as I told it" (New York *Times*, November 3, 1959, p. 22). Charles did speak about his part in the episode, and there was a nationwide furor over the revelations.

Mark Van Doren retired from Columbia in 1959, and the Van Dorens sold their New York house and lived at their farm in Connecticut. He continued to write, lecture, and give poetry readings. The deaths of Merton, Berryman, Krutch, and other friends diminished his life, but he continued to work. He had a new volume of poems ready for his publisher at the time of his death in 1972.

To James Thurber
ALS/P

February 2, 1958   *Exeter, New Hampshire*

William G. Saltonstall, principal of the Phillips Exeter Academy, invited
Thurber to be a Visiting Fellow. Thurber was unable to accept and suggested
Mark Van Doren. Thurber's letter to Saltonstall follows this letter.

I finally begged from Saltonstall's secretary a copy of your letter about
me—people kept talking about it, for it had been read in chapel before I
came—and now I must tell you that I want the whole text of it carved
on my tombstone. I know that will be expensive, for those fellows are
chisellers, but I won't be able to lie quiet without it.

You are a wonderful man. I'm proud to know you and be known by
you. You should hear all the questions I am asked about you. Your works
are frequently read in chapel here, and the boys have a just idea of your
greatness. I find that it is a deep pleasure to describe you.

The week has been strenuous but good. It would have worn you out, I
think. Maybe I'm worn out, but it doesn't feel that way. Back tomorrow,
though, to the simple life of New York.

Johnny and Mira are coming up today for lunch with the Saltonstalls
and me. Two bits we'll discuss Thurber.

Love to you and my girl Helen.[1]

1. Mrs. Thurber.

James Thurber to William G. Saltonstall
TLS[1]

January 20, 1958

I realize you know all about Mark Van Doren's literary and academic career, one of the most distinguished we have. Nearly fifteen years ago I attended a banquet in honor of his 25th year as a teacher, I think it was.
Among those present were his famous former student, Clifton Fadiman,
and many of his friends and admirers, including Rex Stout, Louis Gannett
and their ilk, if they have the same ilk.

Mark has just finished his autobiography, which Harcourt, Brace is
publishing. Two years ago he wrote a fine play and verse about the last
three years of Lincoln's life, and it was praised by the Theatre Guild as one
of the most interesting plays they have read in years. Casting and production are difficult for such a play and it has not yet been put on. Mark is a

great student of Lincoln and of almost everything else, perhaps the best read man I know and he is interested in everything that happens to Mankind and to men. Much of what happens to them moves him to poetry, short stories, novels, reassuring letters and personal visits, and neighborly kindliness. The world knows all about his son Charles, and certainly your students do. His younger brother Johnny teaches at Brandeis and is as likeable and as intelligent as his brother. They learned to consult dictionaries and other sources from Mark's example. "Don't waste time arguing about a fact," he told them, "Look it up." He has rarely been at my house, or I at his, that we haven't looked up some word or words. (In the same week we both discovered "emmenagogue," but your boys would not be interested in that yet.) Like all the rest of us he enjoys a drink or two and is trying to cut down on cigarettes. He still writes poetry and its excellence is well known in the country, since he is a Pulitzer Prize poet, for one thing, and because some people read poetry anyway, prizes or no prizes. In the spirit of liberal education about which he has written a standard book, he is intelligent without being pretentious about it, and is gentle on the surface, and tough underneath, when he has to be. He can fascinate as well as be fascinated, and of course he likes boys and girls and men and women. He will play word games with them, or discuss catalysis or toss cards in a hat or play Run Sheep Run. He and his wife Dorothy, a well known writer novelist, and good neighbor met when they both worked on the Nation in the twenties, and since then have met and charmed everybody.

Mark came to the wedding of my daughter four years ago this Valentine's Day, along with other men friends of mine, and Rosemary (who likes to be called Rosie) said to me "If you pass out at the last minute and can't lead me down the aisle, I want Mark to do it." That ought to give you an idea about him. I know you and the boys will have a wonderful time and he will too.

1. Published with the permission of Helen Thurber.

To John Berryman
ALS/MnU

July 20, 1958   *Falls Village, Connecticut*

How nice to hear from you about our granddaughter[1]—whom her mother's little nephew, unable to talk plain, calls "Littlebit," an appropriate and somehow touching name. It may stick.

Of course we love having her in the world, but the delight her parents take in her is a sweetness I hadn't sufficiently foreseen. You know about this, with your aged son—whom I salute. I am glad that you are happy, with him, his mother, and Shakespeare. *Not* with the State Department—no—nor with the condescending English.[2] Who called E. D. an English poet?[3] It's hard to believe.

The buried news in that part of your letter seemed to be that Faber & Faber are doing your *Collected Poems*. Wonderful, if so. *Homage to Mistress Bradstreet* can't escape being in it, I assume—which reminds me that I sent word to you only through Bob Giroux of my admiration for *HMB*. At the moment I had no address for you. I *remember* the poem all the time, and bless you for writing it.

I'm afraid I don't know Ralph Ross.[4] But I await your Vermont volume with great pleasure,[5] here in Cornwall where Dorothy and I happily spend most of each year—after next June, all of every year, except for trips.

1. Charles's daughter, Elizabeth. Charles Van Doren had married Geraldine Bernstein.

2. Berryman, under the auspices of the United States Information Service, made a lecture tour in India in 1957. He found the tour taxing and criticized the administrators of USIS for their officiousness and the State Department for its poor organization.

3. The review in the *Times Literary Supplement*, May 30, 1958, p. 296, of

T. H. Johnson's *The Letters of Emily Dickinson* began : "Emily Dickinson was one of the great English poets."

4. Ralph Ross, Berryman, and Tate published *The Arts of Reading* in 1960. For a discussion of the Berryman-Ross relationship, see John Haffenden's *The Life of John Berryman* (London, 1982).

5. John Berryman, *His Thought Made Pockets & the Plane Buckt* (Pawlet, Vt., 1958).

To Dan Wickenden
TLS/NNHB

October 27, 1958   *Falls Village, Connecticut*

Dan Wickenden was an editor at Harcourt, Brace and Company.

*   *   *

Tom Merton has written me a marvelous, funny letter about the book,[1] and he ends by talking about Robert Lax's poems, which says have got to be published. I agree with him—indeed, Lax spent three days here in July while I made selections from them. He couldn't do this himself, and I can only hope mine was right. Now I don't know what (if anything) he is doing about said selection, but it occurs to me that H B might like to see it. It is very fine in my opinion. Perhaps you saw Lax's circus poems in a recent volume of *New World Writing*. That would be another book.[2] Both ought to see daylight soon. . . .

1. MVD's *Autobiography*.
2. Lax published some of his circus

poems in *The Circus of the Sun* (New York, 1959).

To Robert Frost
TLS/NhD

July 16, 1959   *Falls Village, Connecticut*

There by the way is my one and only address from now on.

I haven't seen my son since he asked you to discuss love on television, so I don't know what your answer was. I suspect it is too big a subject to discuss at all; I don't know a bigger, or for that matter a better, but it is best treated as you have been treating it from the start, in poems and (by way of Poems) stories. Those were of course the reason he asked you, and I suppose you would have been within your rights simply to remind him and the audience of what you had said for good on hundreds of occasions.

But I can't be sorry the correspondence took place, since it provided a chance for me to hear that you had liked my stories. Someone told me you had; then you said so yourself. This gives me the greatest pleasure, be sure of that. The prison one happened in fact; the warden of an Illinois penitentiary, at Chester, told my brother Frank about it, and I changed no part of what Frank told me. As for the Lincoln play, it only touches on Mrs. Lincoln and Anne Rutledge; rather more on Mrs. Lincoln, since she is in it; but the reference of the whole thing is elsewhere, in the war and the way it ended.

You survived Trilling as you have survived all of your commentators. I assume you know he was praising you; Donald Adams made some think it had been an attack. The only trouble was the tone, and the highfalutin business about Lawrence. His praise was for your strength in the face of reality, a good thing to find in anybody, but he leaned too heavily on the word "terrifying," which I fear is a cant word nowadays. It was an article, not a speech, and a *Partisan Review* article at that; between you and me, I can't abide such articles.[1] This one depressed me so much that when I got home that night Dorothy looked at me and asked at once what the matter was. I found it hard to say, and I still do. For Trilling did do his best to prove that you are a poet of great depth, importance, and truth. And so you are, yet there are more beautiful and simple reasons than he found.

However, you are bound to survive even the cleverest of your admirers. If I were you I wouldn't give any of them a further thought.

1. Trilling spoke at a dinner celebrating Frost's eighty-fifth birthday and called Frost a "terrifying" poet. J. Donald Adams attacked that view in the *New York Times* *Book Review*, April 12, 1959, p. 8. Trilling's talk was published as "A Speech on Robert Frost: A Cultural Episode," *Partisan Review*, XXVI (1959), 445–52.

To James McCartin
ALS/P

September 13, 1959   *Falls Village, Connecticut*

I'm honored that you wanted to review the *Autobiography,* and did.[1] I assume I may keep the review, which of course interests me greatly. Doubtless the book should have been written by another fellow, but since he didn't show up I did it myself—concentrating not on myself as subject but on almost everything and everybody else. I guess I should have confessed a few sins, described a few agonies and attacked a few enemies. But it bored me to think of them, with the perhaps too bland result you now have.

As for the styles of my brother and myself—or the style, if it is one—I know what you mean, but think I'll continue if I can to commit the fault of saying more than I seem to. It tickles me to do this; also, it seems to me to be what any artist should try for. A commoner complaint is that I say too much too briefly. I like that too, and wish more people did it—if I do, for I'm not claiming the virtue, I'm only noting that you attribute it to me, without calling it a virtue. . . .

1. "The Values of Mark Van Doren," *Audience,* VII (Winter, 1960), 118–21.

To Allen Tate
ALS/NjP

October 12, 1959   *Falls Village, Connecticut*

Of course we had heard your news—nothing travels like vital statistics— and we do wish you well, both of you, singly and together.[1] As for November 6th, we probably won't be in New York then; this is now our only and permanent address, since we have sold the house on Bleecker Street; but why not come up here if you can?. . .

Welcome home in all ways. You were very good to read the *Autobiogra-*

phy as you did, and to speak of it thus. Don't be deceived, though: I've changed too, some days I suspect for the worse.

1. Tate and Caroline Gordon were divorced during the summer of 1959, and Tate married Isabella Gardner on August 27, 1959.

To Joseph Wood and Marcelle Krutch
TLS/DLC

November 21, 1959   *Falls Village, Connecticut*

I could (I mean should) write you a long letter about Charlie, but I won't. It is too big a subject, and must wait till we see you. And if by that time it is too *old* a subject, all right. I'm sure you will understand this; indeed I know you will, remembering your own fine letters and remembering you.

The chief thing we have learned from it, apart from things about Charlie and ourselves, has to do with the people of this country. They have overwhelmed us with the most remarkable, the most thoughtful and humane letters; not one of them has been bitter; all have been, as I say, thoughtful, as if each writer had dived down into his own person and found out a few things for himself.[1] The Congressional hearing began this, I guess; it was like a church service, with the most exquisite courtesy being shown by the members of the Committee (save one) to the young man before them. Since then, these letters from strangers, by the hundreds and the thousands; sermons in pulpits; discussion hours on radio (of course we haven't heard those); and in general a sort of universal soul-searching, not sentimental or foolish but really serious. It is enough to make Charlie stagger under it, though he has not done that.

He is getting along pretty well, considering. He has his low moments, but they are not all the time. The correspondence is of course a burden, but I think it is good for him to hear what people (not the newspapers) think and that they do think. I don't mean that they all think the same things. The range itself is impressive.

One of our own discoveries is that we love him more than ever. It was a terrible month, and each of us lost about 10 pounds, but now we are OK, and so I am sure he will be. . . .

1. Later, the tone of the letters was to change.

To Margaret Clark
ALS/P

November 29, 1959   *Falls Village, Connecticut*

Margaret Clark, a former student, was then in England in an Anglican religious order.

Two beautiful letters from you, and the second one about Charlie—who was the reason I didn't answer the first when it came, since it came at a time when neither Dorothy nor I could think of anything but him. It has been a terrible *and* wonderful time. I don't know what you have heard or read about it there—you have more serious concerns, not I mean than him but than quiz programs—so I'll not write you a book, though I could (and never shall). The thing for you to know now is that far from being destroyed by what finally happened he has been created by it, and made free and happy for the first time in years. I went with him and Gerry, his wife, to the hearing in Washington where he read his statement; and I have seldom been more moved to love and admiration. We love him more than ever, you will easily believe. You see, he was in a special pit—of fame—and never could decide how to climb out of it. He actually thought for a long time that he owed the schoolchildren who adored him—*owed* them, mind you, an obligation not to shatter them with the truth. Whereas the truth, when it did get stated as he stated it, was precisely what they desired. The letters that have come—thousands, I guess—say this with so much courtesy and love that all of us have been overwhelmed. We have learned about ourselves, and others have learned about themselves. It is amazing, how many of them write *their* confessions to us. Scott Buchanan, now in California, says it is true there; and indeed it goes on everywhere, in sermons, even, of which a number have been sent us. The result at this date is that we can't really be sorry it happened. So you need have no further anxiety of the sort I know you felt, and you know we felt.

This is all too brief, but I count on your love to make you understand it as for instance Tom Merton did. His letters have been wonderful beyond words. Of course I wish you had written Charlie the letter you thought of writing; and yet I suppose he wouldn't have been able to take your advice, for he wasn't ready yet. He was leaving today (after Thanksgiving) just as your letter came, and of course I showed it to him. (He remembers you perfectly, by the way.) What he said confirms my belief that nothing could have helped him till he had to help himself. But Margaret, he found your whole letter beautiful, and sent thanks to you for the message it contained.

On December 7th I shall pray for you as you desire. It is good to know that you will then become a novice, and so be on your way to the vows you went to Holme Eden to take. It was a profound relief to hear that the place had no handicaps for you this time. In fact, both of your letters make it plain that you find it both good and beautiful. Let's say it *was* a hazelnut you picked up that day. And may the winter not be too harsh, after so dry and warm a summer. But even if it is harsh, I count on you not to mind too much, since summer is inside you now. . . .

To Allen Tate
ALS/NjP

February 29, 1960   *Falls Village, Connecticut*

Your letter about the poems filled me with such pleasure as I haven't felt for years.[1] It's your gift, of course, to do just this. There is no such reader, no such praiser, no such friend. And not the least of my pleasures was hearing that you accepted *your* poem. I should have sent you the whole thing when I wrote it, but I preferred to have you find it here, chancy though that was. If the little it says about you seems true, good. There are volumes more, not I suppose to be written, at any rate till I know how. . . .

1. MVD's *Morning Worship, and Other Poems* (New York, 1960).

To Elizabeth Sergeant
ALS/ViU

July 2, 1960   *Falls Village, Connecticut*

You said you wanted to know what I thought of your book.[1]

Now that I've finished it, I consider it less a book than an experience—indeed, a life, which I've lived through moment by moment with the very anxiety, alternating with serenity, that distinguished Robert as he went along. To give readers experience is what a writer is for, but it happens so rarely that I like to reserve out such books as yours for special gratitude, hardly in fact expressible. . . .

1. *Robert Frost: The Trial by Existence* (New York, 1960).

To Thomas Merton
APS/KyLoB-M

August 9, 1960   *[Falls Village, Connecticut]*

If there were anything left to say about the solitary life, you said it in this beautiful book.[1]

As a matter of fact, everything was left to say. And you said it for the first time.

I should be silent, but I send you this.

1. Merton's *Disputed Questions* (New York, 1960) was partially concerned with solitude.

To Margaret Clark
ALS/P

October 10, 1960   *Falls Village, Connecticut*

                              *   *   *

Your news is only in measure surprising. I'll not claim that I knew you would return to the mixed life, or that I even thought you would; but now that you have, and looking back, I think I can understand it.[1] For one thing—and it's the main thing—you were always in the mix; both here and above; both woman and contemplative; so there is no real change, and the more I reflect on it, there should be none. I believe you have every right to be at peace wherever you are; and I look forward to hearing of many happy works that you will do. At the moment I am glad you are with your brother, and send my hope that he will recover in a better climate. . . .

Charlie has been doing excellent work in the way of memorandums for a foundation, and better yet, he is in a good firm state which, looking on it at my distance (never great), I profoundly admire. I don't see how anybody, given the circumstances, could have behaved better than he has this past year. Thank you for inquiring about him. I told him, and he was gratified and touched. . . .

1. Margaret Clark had entered an Anglican religious order, but had withdrawn from it.

To Thomas Merton
ALS/KyLoB-M

December 2, 1960   *Falls Village, Connecticut*

---

*   *   *

Lax has just left with his beard after three good days during which he agreed with everything I said, and as usual I said plenty. Someday I may startle him with a heresy, but so far I never have, nor Dorothy either. We love having him here, nor do we wish he would disagree with us. His favorite topics are always you and Rice. I must know Rice better—only once have I seen him, at *Jubilee.*[1] He is a legend merely, but believe me, a rich one. Bob's beard, if you must know, is quite French and quite distinguished—not long and square, but pointed like a 16th-century poet's, or a savant's of any time. Only two white streaks in it suggest that 25 years have passed since I first saw him.

I took my time with *Disputed Questions,* as you can see;[2] but now I have read it all and want to tell how living a book it is, from Pasternak on to St. Bernard. The Pasternak pieces were valuable to me because of all they straightened out. I had been disappointed in *Zhivago* as a novel, though I hadn't missed the singular sweetness of the man. But you put both book and man in a powerful perspective, and I find myself agreeing with your vision of them. So does Charlie in his own fashion. Charlie, by the way, denies calling you politically naive; or if he did, retracts it.

The rest of the book—on solitude, on love, on sacred art, and on the particular persons or orders you deal with—is just as strong. Indeed, as I said to Bob, you can't write about anything without lending it your own terrific life. May it last almost forever.

1. Edward Rice, Merton's friend and baptismal sponsor, was a founder of *Jubilee.*

2. Thomas Merton, *Disputed Questions* (New York, 1960).

To Thomas Merton
TLS/KyLoB-M

March 19, 1961   *Falls Village, Connecticut*

Look here, young man, you're going to talk yourself out of Gethsemani. I don't really mean this, but how come you know so much about the so-called world and Them who think they run it, and in a measure do? *Letter to an Innocent Bystander* lifted my white hair; so did *A Signed*

Confession and—yes—*Prometheus*,[1] not to speak of *Original Child Bomb*.[2] My question is of course rhetorical, and does not wait for an answer. If any is to be given, it will be given by me, and will run this way: It vastly comforts me that you feel wrath and fall to raging. Let there be even more of that, and from Gethsemani, where you never forget what is true even though almost everybody else does.

The Behavior of Titans, I'm feebly saying, is a terrific book, for the aforesaid reasons as well as others. For instance, *Herakleitos*, and the *Atlas* in its best form. I had seen others, but this must have been what you most deeply intended. Atlas as you do him is done to stay—just read page 25 again and see if this isn't true—and the fatman is so funny that he isn't funny. Meanwhile I keep hearing that dim bell.

As for the desert fathers, I like them even better in this new book. *They* are funny in the sweetest possible way. They help me at last to see what wit is. It is what one utters when one has truth by the whip end, but doesn't know how to spell whip.

I want to see your little house and hear your birds. When I simply don't know, but in this life, but in this life.

We have had a wonderful winter here, one so implacable that we have lost our power to imagine anything else. All our thoughts are white. Should be a little color; but none.

You ask about Charlie. He is in an excellent state, working hard, and in my opinion very wise. The legal business, over which he has no control, doesn't seem to bother him at all. I mean, he doesn't bite his nails, and neither do we, largely at his bidding. I could go on about this, but won't; except to say that he never seemed stronger or better.

Every now and then Dorothy asks me: Why are you grinning? and I say: Because I'm going to receive the medal for Tom on June 6th.[3] I am both touched and tickled: proud for you and for Columbia, and at the same time blissfully amused for some reason I don't even try to understand. I really can't wait. I am so pleased that you suggested me for this office. I take it you did.

1. All three titles were included in *The Behavior of Titans* (New York, 1961).

2. New Directions did not publish *Original Child Bomb* until the following year. Merton had sent MVD a mimeographed copy.

3. Columbia awarded Merton the Medal of Excellence.

To Russell Miles
ALS/IU-Ar

April 13, 1961   *Falls Village, Connecticut*

Russell Miles, professor of music at the University of Illinois, asked Van Doren to write the foreword to Johann Sebastian Bach: An Introduction to His Life and Works *(Englewood Cliffs, N. J., 1962).*

You honor me by thinking I am competent to write such a foreword.

Since you do, I'll humbly accept—on condition that it be indeed brief, say a single page. When I get started it may run over to another page, but I'd rather rest on the prior assumption. You see, I dare not expose myself at length!

If this isn't satisfactory, please don't hesitate to say so. Otherwise I'll await your text with pleasure.

To Thomas Merton
ALS/KyLoB-M

June 14, 1961   *Falls Village, Connecticut*

Dorothy and I went down last week as guests of Columbia while you were given the Medal.[1] You were more visible in that vast place, I hope, than I was. The crowd was happy to hear your name, and the citation made them see you if they had eyes to see. I stole a look at it—also at the Medal—before it was sent on, just to make sure that in the excitement of standing up for you I had missed no word. They were fine words, I thought. . . .

I was very pleased, amused, and proud to be your ghost. I shall ask for no greater earthly glory.

    1. MVD accepted the Medal of Excel-
lence for Merton.

To Thomas Merton
ALS/KyLoB-M

September 9, 1961   *Falls Village, Connecticut*

Yes, I'm to be in Louisville (Bellarmine College) December 1 and 2. And since I am due in Milwaukee on the 4th, I have the 3rd to spend with you—or as much of it as you should, can, or wish to spare.

Looking at the calendar, I see that December 3 is Sunday. That bad? I hadn't thought of this. Don't scruple to say it's impossible. I hope it isn't, for it would be a joy to see you.

Your Auschwitz poem is terrific. That last line! After, I mean, the others. It's like the little reptile in *Inferno,* Canto XXV.[1]

1. Probably a reference to "Chant To Be Used in Processions around A Site with Furnaces." The last line of the poem reads, "Do not think yourself better because you burn up friends and enemies with long-range missiles without ever seeing what you have done."

To Thomas Merton
ALS/KyLoB-M

November 13, 1961   *Falls Village, Connecticut*

I have learned that I have lectures (readings) to give both Friday and Saturday nights in Louisville, so I can't come down Saturday evening as you suggested. . . .

But Sunday is free (I don't leave Louisville until Monday morning, for Milwaukee). May I find my way down somehow and see you when I can? For instance, I'd dearly love to look at the hermitage, preferably with a wood fire going in it.

I learn too that I may see you at lunch in Louisville on Saturday. Good—and let's see that we're not placed at opposite ends of a long table.

You asked me about Thurber, and now you know he is dead. Poor man. Poor me. I'll miss him. We can talk about him when I'm there.

To Thomas Merton
ALS/KyLoB-M

December 7, 1961   *Falls Village, Connecticut*

For all your lovely deeds and words, much thanks. I shall never forget that day, at the retreat, in your class, and on the Abbey walks. I'm sure you gave me time you didn't have; but I think I'll keep it. I've been telling Dorothy all about everything, and have phoned the boys to tell them. They severally rejoice and send their love once more.

It was wonderful to have lunch with the abbot, whom I'm afraid I didn't thank eloquently enough. But he is so good to be with that one does not think of such things at the time—I mean, thank yous. He is his own reward.[1] So are you, even though I thank you.

I'll be thinking of you in your little house—but not so little either. I was impressed.[2]

1. MVD was apparently not aware of the often difficult relationships between Merton and Dom James Fox, the abbot. For excellent accounts of Merton and the abbot, see Monica Furlong, *Merton: A Biography* (New York, 1980) and Michael Mott, *The Seven Mountains of Thomas Merton* (New York, 1984).

2. After a long struggle with the authorities of his order, Merton was finally permitted to move into a small house away from the main buildings at Gethsemani. Furlong in *Merton: A Biography* and Mott in *The Seven Mountains of Thomas Merton* give many details about this episode.

To Thomas Merton
ALS/KyLoB-M

January 26, 1962   *Falls Village, Connecticut*

Merton was extremely concerned about Charles Van Doren, and he wrote two supportive letters to Mark Van Doren which brought this response.

Your first letter came by chance after the second, but no matter: the whole thing is over for Charlie, and he and we are gladder than can be stated in prose. When he called, after leaving the court room, I found myself unable to speak, so that he kept saying "Dad, are you still there?" The judge didn't even lecture them, and they left after a few minutes.

Both of your letters were sweet to read. Your concern is the right concern, of course, and it did me great good to know about it. Charlie, as you say, has long since got beyond hurt; still, it is wonderful that no further attempt was made to inflict it. Quite the contrary, if I understand his Honor. Charlie even says he has learned so much during the past few years that he is almost glad they passed as they did. That, I think, is what could be called a generous view of adversity, or whatever it was.

Thank you for the new things, all three of which I found most moving. Yes, war is the only winner. Success to your peace book, here and in heaven.

My deepest regards again to the abbot.

To Thomas Merton
ALS/KyLoB-M

February 4, 1962   *Falls Village, Connecticut*

PROPHET[1]

He did not say anything utterly strange,
At any rate to a thoughtful person.
Why then do we honor him, and call him prophet?

Because he said what we had always understood
When we were alone, when we were thoughtful.
We honor him because he made us remember,

Why, that we ourselves were serious once,
That we were children, and loved peace.
He gave us again the quietness of our minds.

The only strange thing was, his wild look.
But of course it was terrible to be where he had been:
To have dug those utterly simple sentences out of the soul's grave.

Your last two pieces, on Christian Action and Father Metzger,[2] came just as I was about to type this poem, which (believe it or not) it has taken me years to finish. I send it to you because I know now whom it fits. You.

[P. S.] Whom, I mean, among the living. Live forever.

---

1. Although the letter is handwritten, the poem is typed.
2. "Christian Action in World Crisis," *Blackfriars,* XLIII (June, 1962), 256–68, collected in *Thomas Merton on Peace*

(New York, 1971), 219–26, and "A Martyr for Peace and Unity: Father Max Josef Metzger (1887–1944)," published in *Thomas Merton on Peace* (1971), 139–43.

To Robert Frost
ALS/NhD

April 2, 1962   *Falls Village, Connecticut*

I gave this to Al Edwards to give you, but he let the reporter take it for copying.[1] She has returned it to me, so here it goes again.

Many happy returns of the evening we all had in Washington. Dorothy and I wouldn't have missed it for anything.

Our warmest love to you.

1. MVD had given a copy of his talk on   Building in Washington, D.C., to Edwards,
Frost given at the Pan American Union   president of Holt and a friend of Frost's.

To Thomas Merton
ALS/KyLoB-M

April 4, 1962   *Falls Village, Connecticut*

I languished a whole day without the poems you promised.[1] Here they are now, though, and I roll and revel in their pity and their indignation. I don't know the occasion for the Ladies' Jail one, but of course I know the other occasion—and incidentally, I detected no flaw in its technology. Wot's the odds? He was up there, wasn't he? That's enough for your purposes and mine.

Space. I abhor it—or rather, the talk of it. To think that one should ever be made sick of the stars. Of course I'm not, of them. Unless they are five-pointed, and pollute the banks of the Potomac.

Be angry, in St. Thomas's good way. The pines will be witness, and the distant freights will make the necessary music. How I love distant freights. You're always wonderful about them.

P.S. I enclose the latest communication from Lax. Words seem to fail him.

1. "There Has To Be A Jail for Ladies"
and "And the Children of Birmingham."

To Thomas Merton
ALS/KyLoB-M

May 30, 1962   *Falls Village, Connecticut*

Trips and other silly things delayed my reading of your *Letters*.[1] I'm sorry for myself, now that I've finished them in late afternoon on the lawn, considering as I did so the difference between the peace about me there and the peace you say is just, just possible in this madly indifferent world. I'm sorry, I mean, that I didn't listen to this voice before. It says everything that must be said. It deepens the darkness, then lets in the light of angry hope. For all this, Tom, much thanks. May the anthology thrive, and may your voice, whether or not you personally use it, be the one that carries the burden. It has to be borne, no kidding.

Of course I knew who R. L. was (is),[2] but most of the others were only initials to me. No matter, you covered the ground. And with what speed, as when you said we felt threatened by girls bearing placards, not by bombs. What speed, and what terrible, telling straightness of aim. A good wrath, I call it. And a deep love.

1. Merton published many "Letters" in prose and poetry; it is not clear which ones MVD had been reading.

2. Robert Lax.

To John Berryman
ALS/MnU

July 6, 1962   *Falls Village, Connecticut*

Your letters along the way brought us joy—assurances, too, that you passed safely through Bennington at least. . . .

Your visit was excellent to have. Stop again, so that we may see both you and your saint[1]—whom we adored in silence because *she* was silent. But adored.

Full professor—wonderful! You should have told us. What you did tell us (about Charlie, about your Songs, about Allen) was rich to hear, but it would have been good to know that Minnesota is not a land of bastards altogether. . . .

1. After divorcing Eileen in 1956, Berryman had married Ann Levine. That marriage also ended in divorce; in 1961 he married Kathleen Donohue, called Kate.

To Robert Lax
ALS/NNC

November 14, 1962   *Falls Village, Connecticut*

No news of Tom except an angry poem during the Cuban crisis—perhaps, perhaps, perhaps outdated now. . . .

Don't you like the Greeks? The women especially? Women are always more likeable than men, for reasons nobody knows but men. . . .

To John Berryman
ALS/MnU

January 5, 1963   *Falls Village, Connecticut*

Hail, Martha;[1] Hail, Kate; Hail, Father John.

Since you didn't seem to get my other letter, I'll make this short. But it is full of joy because of Martha's coming and because of your recovery from everything.

The Book containing "Dunce Songs" comes under separate cover.[2]

1. Martha was the first of two daughters born to Kate and John Berryman.

2. The "Dunce Songs" appeared in

MVD's *Morning Worship and Other Poems* (New York, 1960).

To Joseph Wood and Marcelle Krutch
TLS/DLC

February 12, 1963   *Cambridge, Massachusetts*

*   *   *

Everybody is very good to us here, very polite, very flattering; but sometimes, for instance now, I could wish I hadn't come. I find I don't care a damn for teaching any more, not the slightest damn. I'll just be going through the motions. Plenty of those, though, since one course I'm giving now has 600 students in it; I lecture with a microphone around my neck, and have six readers (excuse me, graders) who will read the papers when they come in. It is a course I enjoyed at Columbia; we read the Odyssey, parts of the Old Testament, The Castle, and Don Quixote; and I even enjoy it here, but would just as soon not be doing it. The second course is a writing course for 10 students, whom I meet tomorrow for the first time and set going on their little masterpieces. Of course they are all too young to be bothering with—why didn't I realize that before? Sour, you see. . . .

This Sunday we go to Amherst, where a memorial service will be held for Robert Frost. I am to read some of his poems, and a bishop is to speak, also the president of Amherst, and if Kennedy comes from Washington, Kennedy. (He probably won't come, they think.) The thing of mine about Frost you read to Joe, Marcelle, must have been the obituary I wrote two weeks before his death. The AP called and asked me for it, and of course I hesitated; but they said I might be glad to have done something not under pressure, and the event proved them right. Actually, once I got over the feeling that it was a ghoulish thing to do, I enjoyed it. There are few subjects I like better than Frost, and of course few or no poets, living or dead. As for him, he had lived so long and rich a life that nobody can feel depressed or gloomy about his ceasing to be visible. One couplet of his I won't read Sunday, but you may like it—from his last volume, on a page by itself with no title:

Forgive, O Lord, my little jokes on Thee
And I'll forgive Thy great big one on me.

Harvard is a great place for forms to fill out. Within the present week I am instructed to take a loyalty oath, to go for a TB test, to say whether I smoke cigarettes, and if so how many a day, and for how many years; also, to send someone the maiden name of my wife, the date of my marriage, the place and date of my birth, my citizenship, and God knows what else. Nothing yet about my prostate or my immortal soul, but doubtless that comes in March. I may even have to put down a list of my friends; if so, your names will lead all the rest. . . .

To Arthur Wang
TLS/P

May 2, 1963   *Falls Village, Connecticut*

Hill and Wang had become MVD's publisher.

*   *   *

I am deeply moved by your program of promotion—scared a little, too, since I can't be sure that it will work, and then you would be disappointed. Also, if it did work, I don't know how I could adjust to that; I'm so accustomed to unpromotion and unfame that I might blink foolishly in even the feeblest light. . . .

Sales figures follow. I can't guarantee their completeness, since when we moved here a number of records got misplaced; but they must be about right. I hope they won't disappoint you.

Collected Poems, 1939 (out of print since 1957):	3610
Selected Poems, 1954 (still active):	3730
A Winter Diary, 1935:	1400
The Seven Sleepers, 1944:	3340
New Poems, 1948:	1593
Spring Birth, 1953:	2380
Morning Worship, 1960 (still selling):	3572

The first two of these had limited editions, but they didn't sell; I don't know how many copies were made. The figures:

Collected Poems:	36
Selected Poems:	58

This may indeed be incomplete, but in any case I doubt that sales were gratifying. If you try it with the new book, I certainly wouldn't overprint. Of course I'll autograph anything. . . .

To John Berryman
ALS/MnU

June 15, 1963   *Falls Village, Connecticut*

Ramparts—man, like Henry is my last friend in the world, holding on to everything, even though his teeth chatter, till the great globe start turning nice and still again.[1] Educational material—not ha ha, but here here. I'm taught, I'm caught, I'm fraught with my friend Henry, whom I love as I do you, old Bones, old brilliant begetter.

Thank you for *Ramparts,* and for the inscription. And thank you for your delicious letter to Wang, whom I told to use it as is, and Wang will.

It doth appear that it is Congdon Street. Pray you get this, with love in it for Kate and Katelet.

1. *Ramparts,* II (May 1963), 9–13, published several of Berryman's "Dream Songs." Henry was Berryman's persona in *The Dream Songs.* Berryman wrote: "Henry both is and is not me, obviously. We touch at certain points. But I am an actual human being; he is nothing but a series of conceptions—my conceptions" (John Haffenden, *The Life of John Berryman* [Boston, 1982], 4).

To Thomas Merton
ALS/KyLoB-M

July 28, 1963   *Falls Village, Connecticut*

Long time no write, no see, but plenty often think about. And now comes *The Early Legend,*[1] in six splinters, all of which, flying off, have entered plenty deep. Blood of Mexico, smoke from the ghats: beat one drum in honor of right. Good, good.

The other evening we saw the Andrewses (Shaker people) and loved hearing of their visit with you.[2] And last week Scott Buchanan was here, and with him too we talked of you. . . . Lax, too, . . . sends us some of your letters, to be passed on to Olean.[3] He talk Merton all the time. Him Greek now, him gone for good, except he'll be back, with no difference visible. How could Lax look like anything but Lax? Don't want him to.

You may not know that we spent three months this spring at Harvard, where I was visiting professor. No more of that now, but nice for a notion.

People there were very sweet to us—many of them because you are our friend—but the end result is that I write different English henceforth, if any, if any. . . .

1. Published in *New Directions*, XVIII (1964), 1–9.
2. Merton wrote the introduction for *Religion in Wood: A Book of Shaker Furniture* by Edward D. and Faith Andrews (Bloomington, Indiana, 1966).

3. Merton taught at St. Bonaventure University, Olean, N.Y., and the university library has holdings of Merton papers. Lax's letters were being sent to the library.

To Thomas Merton
ALS/KyLoB-M

September 7, 1963   *Falls Village, Connecticut*

Paeans to you for your wonderful words about my giant book.[1] I had feared it was too big, but if it's a world, better it be big—unless it is full of dead leaves and unborn worms. Thank you for all you say in those sentences of yours that take my breath.

When you collect *your* poems—which do—yes, be fair to those who love the ones you don't. You're no judge, really. Neither are they, but poems belong to readers, not to writers. You're only the writer, and you know what kind of a nothing that is. Remember what Don Quixote said to Don Lorenzo as he rode away: "Be governed by other men's judgment more than your own."

All of us here have read the three truly wonderful pieces you tore out of the mimeograph machine and sent me. The one on prayer comes out at the only right place: of course the two identities of Christ are simultaneous and inseparable. The one on the sanity of Eichman[n]—ah![2] That cuts through and in—And the one on the Negro (I don't give the titles because all three are in Charlie's house down the road) says more than anything else I've read. The wonder is that you know so much—more than most of us—about what happens or doesn't happen *here*. But the knowledge that operates in this case is of still another kind, and you could have it in a cell, and it is the only kind that matters. "The Negroes are trying to tell us something"—I go everywhere saying this, and maybe that will help. I mean, you will. Actually, Tom, more people than you might suppose are with you as to all this. They know nothing, but they are troubled—I hope, because they *don't* know. And I like to think they are learning. Fast enough? Another question. I like to believe—yes.

1. *Collected and New Poems, 1924–1963* (New York, 1963).

2. Probably "A Devout Meditation in Memory of Adolf Eichmann."

To Allen Tate
ALS/NjP

September 28, 1963   *Falls Village, Connecticut*

I suppose I have read your review six times, always with a growing sense of uncanny wisdom at work—as, for example, when you confront perception with form and catch me out at wishing only for another chance to knock their heads together. Nobody else will say so many sharp, true, and (of course) generous things. If I had known the *Herald-Tribune* was to ask you for a review I'd have begged them to let you off; but how can I be sorry now? For one thing, I live—have always lived—for your good word; and for another, I can take your reservations as I would take the gush of any other man. And believe me, I will study and restudy your lists, if only with a backward-gazing eye.[1]

Your remark that I do not disclose whatever self I possess reminds me of Hardy's line by way of epitaph: "He was a man who used to notice such things." For me the noticer is less important than the thing noticed, and indeed can be defined, if definition is desired, only by the totality of the things he has noticed. So I rest there—only asking you, in response to your aside, to take a minute some day and read, among Late Poems, "The First Snow of the Year." Now of course I never *noticed* all that, but it is quite as if I had. . . .

1. In his review of MVD's *Collected Poems, 1924–1963* in the New York *Herald-Tribune Books*, September 29, 1963, p. 4, Tate noted that MVD's large number of poems and the formal metrical patterns helped explain why MVD had not been closely read. Tate argued it was a mistake to put MVD in the rural tradition of Frost. He wrote that MVD "is immensely aware of the modern world but he is not *in* it; yet he is not above it; he moves a little to one side and gazes at it. He is as committed as anyone but he is not directly involved." Tate felt MVD was a "formalist who is not trying in every poem to write a masterpiece; he is day by day the whole man who submits the whole range of his awareness to the forms that he has elected to use." Tate added a list of poems he thought successful, and ended by calling MVD "a great poet in the minor modes."

To Thomas Merton
ALS/KyLoB-M

January 7, 1964   *Falls Village, Connecticut*

Emblems of a Season of Fury[1] has been going off daily, nightly, by my chair in the living room—pop, roar, hiss, bang, fire, fire, fire. It is like one of those Vesuvius Fountains we used to have on the Fourth of July—always more smoke, more fire, more better. It is a wonderful, wrathful, and sweet work. I wish it were going off everywhere, and maybe it is. Much of it of course I knew before, but that didn't matter; or rather, it was all to the good, for thereby your rage was more entirely summed up. Your sweetness too, however. The juxtaposition of *Hagia Sophia* and the *Letter Concerning Giants* is terrific—"the diapason closing full in man" (Dryden).[2]

And we are just now finishing the Gethsemani ham we sent for to furnish forth the Christmas table while our children and grandchildren were with us (all gone now: dark, quiet, cold). You scorn those products, but the ham we got was very, very good. . . .

1. Published as a New Directions Paper-   2. "A Song for St. Cecilia's Day, 1687."
book in 1963.

To Thomas Merton
TLS/KyLoB-M

March 17, 1964   *Falls Village, Connecticut*

Your last letter (not owed; letters aren't owed, any more than breaths are, or smiles) followed me to California, where I didn't answer it (letters don't have to be answered either, any more than thought does, or praise) because I was writing a play. The Huntington Hartford Foundation had invited Dorothy and me to come out there and live for any period up to six months, in a small house in a canyon, and write or anything else we liked. Well, Dorothy wrote a children's book and I wrote a play, my third to date; the second was a dramatization of my novel, *The Transients,* which you may never have seen—don't know. This one is all in verse (the other two were half and half), and I don't know what to think of it yet. It has murder in it, and bastardy, and madness; and in the end it has forgiveness—which Johnny, who has read it, says I don't get away with, and maybe not. But it was exciting to write, and I wrote it in a month; we stayed five weeks altogether, in an earthly paradise where we had nothing whatever to do but work, being fed like children of God and taken care of in every conceivable way. You may like to hear how I got started with the play, which was not in my head at all when I arrived. I sat for three days and looked at the blank wall in front of me (I avoided the window; too interesting) until, out of that wall, I swear, the people all came, and their pasts, and their presents, and their songs and their words (songs: at the center of the action is a ballad sung by a mad girl, Dinah). Zen? I suppose so. But now I'm for blank walls. The writing, compared to this wrestling with pre-Creation chaos, was a pipe; hard enough, of course, but exciting every minute of I guess a month. Then we flew home, as we had flown there, and now I am writing you while snow outside makes like March; won't last. . . .

Your *Message to Poets* is wonderful;[1] did they say so down there? Solidarity, yes; it's our secret, and it's also the secret of those sweet people who read us and don't write about reading us. They're in it too, those readers with the minds of angels who understand instantly what we mean and don't mean—what, in fact, we simply see. . . .

Lax's poems will be a job to edit. I tried it once, with no luck for Lax, who said he liked my selection, but I wasn't sure he did, nor could I be sure myself that I had done it right. The job in your case will be complicated by the existence of what I call his raindrop poems, among which I simply couldn't choose. I have told him I wasn't strong for these, and maybe I hurt his feelings. They produce a queer result for me: instead of brevity, loquacity. Long drawn out indeed. So it is—isn't it?—with most devices to reach ends quickly: device conquers, and the end retreats into a dim distance. Now I admit that some of them have seemed better than others; but for the life of me I couldn't say why, and I don't intend to grope for reasons. Lax is a fine poet, naturally, and I rejoice that you are undertaking this work; but it will be work. Good luck—and actually, if you ever have specific poems that you want to trade views about, by all means let me have them. There are few books I'd rather see than Poems by Lax, even if (looking back) I don't sound that way. I do, I do. . . .

1. Merton had sent MVD a mimeographed version of "Message to Poets," ex-   tracts of which were printed in *Americas*, XVI (April, 1964), 29.

To John Berryman
ALS/MnU

April 28, 1964   *Falls Village, Connecticut*

You there, Mr. Bones? This avenue and number right for you?

Just sent Dolly Guinther some words about the *Dream Songs*, which I been reading off and on for weeks. A stern, brave, terrific and funny book, your book, nobody else's. Makes me want to be brief, so won't carry on; but it's it, and I'll never be the same again. You cover the ground, also the sky, and hell down there while you're at it. Also, Berryman's heaven.

Come by and see us, you and Kate,[1] to whom (both) my love. Did you get your copy of my big book? Some didn't arrive.

1. Berryman's third wife, Kathleen Donohue.

To Russell Miles
ALS/UI-Ar

May 9, 1964   *Falls Village, Connecticut*

＊　　＊　　＊

I'm more pleased than I can say that you read my poems as you do. But don't always blame yourself if they are not clear. I consider this to be my fault; nor do I take refuge in any such thing as "underlying symbolism." What's that?

To Thomas Merton
ALS/KyLoB-M

July 23, 1964   *Falls Village, Connecticut*

I break the silence of your summer (if silence) to say that Ted Andrews, our Shaker furniture friend, died suddenly a few weeks ago. You may not have heard this, so I tell you. Faith, his wife, was here this afternoon and gave us the merciful particulars: in his sleep, with none aware.

She also said that *if* you had heard of his death you might suppose that the book for which you were to write a foreword was not to appear. But it is, for he had finished it and (I think) it is even now being put into type. So your foreword is as dearly desired as ever. Nobody is pressing you—certainly not I—but them is the fax. Of course you have nothing to do but write forewords.[1]

Greetings to your woods and to you among them; and to you at home among your brothers, novices or not. I could speak of politics and civil rights, but won't—this time. I haven't heard from Lax for months, doubtless for the good reason that I haven't written him. I wonder about his poems that you're selecting. I may have sounded harsher than I felt about the extremely narrow ones; yet I leave the question where it was. A tough question, and I wouldn't know how to settle it. . . .

1. The book with Merton's foreword was published under the title *Religion in* *Wood* in 1966. Merton was at work on the foreword when Edward Andrews died.

To Thomas Merton
TLS/KyLoB-M

January 3, 1965   *Falls Village, Connecticut*

I shouldn't answer your last letter so soon, but tomorrow we go away for six weeks and I don't want to wait that long. It seems I have a knee that needs treatment in New York—by the doctor who took care of President Kennedy's back, so I trust him. I sprained the knee in Texas last spring (Charlie tells me to keep out of Texas, and after this I will); I walked on it wrongly; and now the muscles are all bobbled up. I'm on crutches, believe it or not. But in six weeks all is supposed to be well.

Rain and the Rhinoceros is lovely.[1] Yes, rain is its own excuse for being, and the same goes for everything else. As I read your pages I heard, felt, smelt, and believed the rain; for which, humblest thanks. I was reminded, perhaps vainly, of the many poems I've written about rain myself. I'll mention only two in the vast book I sent you last year:[2] After Long Drought, p. 420 and What We Wanted, p. 439. But you don't have to read either of them. Simply sit there and listen to the next rain that comes, and as you do so, think of me a little bit.

Seeds of Destruction, a good deal of which was familiar to me, is terrific.[3] I read some of the Negro parts to Charlie and his wife Gerry the other evening, and all of us agreed that the future had better be what you recommend. I don't know anybody that sees it more clearly, or sets it forth more powerfully. The Diaspora part was new to me (wasn't it?), and there again you have the high, bright voice we need to hear. The letters at the end, including the one to me, were a wonderful way *to* end the book. May the whole work produce earthquakes, beginning right here on this farm.

Which reminds me: we'll be away most of the spring. In March I'm having a new play produced (can't describe it) at Florida State University in Tallahassee, and I must be there all the month for rehearsals and performances. Then in April the Lincoln play is to be done at the Library of Congress and in Springfield, Illinois (different auspices), and I must be at those places too. Anything you write me will be forwarded, but you see I'm telling you. . . .

1. Appeared in *Holiday,* XXXVII (May, 1965), 8–16.

2. *Collected and New Poems, 1924–1963* (New York, 1963).

3. Published by Farrar, Straus and Giroux in 1964.

To ⸺

TLS/P

May 8, 1965   *Falls Village, Connecticut*

Mark Van Doren's letter to a member of the Hill and Wang staff might well be compared with Thoreau's angry letter of June 22, 1858, to James Russell Lowell concerning deletions in "Chesuncook." Thoreau wrote: "The editor has, in this case, no more right to omit a sentiment than to insert one, or put words into my mouth. I do not ask anybody to adopt my opinions, but I do expect that when they ask for them to print, they will print them, or obtain my consent to their alteration or omission."[1]

The galleys and the manuscript have arrived, and I have given the galleys one reading, to be followed by a second reading this coming week. The week after that I shall be in New York, and I'll bring everything in to you on the 17th, 18th, or 19th.

The galleys are not quite as clean as you thought. Several lines are missing, and several others are here twice: in their uncorrected and corrected forms. There are further typos too: not many, but they stuck out.

I considered the queries you had cued on the galleys and responded according to my best judgment.

But you didn't say in your letter that you had silently rewritten me in other places, without cue or query. You changed my punctuation, you omitted or transposed words, and sometimes you destroyed my sense. In most such cases I have restored my text, which Arthur [Wang] once promised me would not be tampered with in this way. Questions of printer's style I leave of course to you, but otherwise: I write, you print. That is my motto, and if it is not to be honored at H&W I will send no more manuscripts there. In a few cases, as where I had omitted words, you of course were right; but even then you should have favored me with a query. You should always have done that, and I resent it that you didn't. I have the unclean feeling that this is no longer my book. You may think I'm making a fuss about a few minor things. They are not minor to me, and they are not so few. They certainly are not minor when they change my sense or weaken it—which is how I came to be aware of your tinkerings: reading, I was puzzled, and reached for the MS. to compare. It would have been so simple to take me as I came. Cheaper, too, since some of my restorations will involve resetting. I avoided this whenever possible, but it was seldom possible. I still feel unclean, and all the more so because I suspect that further inspirations of yours lurk unseen in the MS. I'll try to find them all in my second reading.

As to page proofs, yes, I want to see them; but only the pages that involve corrections from the galleys. Many will not, and so the bulk of what you have to send me will be much diminished. The MS. pages need not come; but I want the pages and galleys where corrections were made. I promise to return them swiftly.

1. Walter Harding and Carl Bode (eds.),
*The Correspondence of Henry David
Thoreau* (New York, 1958), 515.

To Charles Van Doren
TLS/P

September 3, 1965   *Falls Village, Connecticut*

The reference is to President Johnson's picking up one of his beagles by the ears.

I can't wait to tell you what someone has just told me, namely that Proverbs 26:17 reads as follows:

He that passeth by, and meddleth with strife not belonging to him, is like one that taketh a dog by the ears.

As the final word on LBJ, isn't that compendious, isn't that inspired?[1] Even gets the beagles in. Tell Gerry[2]. . . .

1. MVD had ample reason not to think kindly of President Johnson. As one way of quieting opposition to the Vietnam war, LBJ had sponsored a White House Festival of the Arts on June 14, 1965. Mark Van Doren, Saul Bellow, John Hersey, Edmund Wilson, and Robert Lowell were to represent literature. Edmund Wilson refused to attend; Robert Lowell was to give a poetry reading, but decided to decline. Mark Van Doren did introduce the literature section.

The whole festival ended in controversy, and MVD remarked: "I have been troubled as to whether I should speak [of Lowell's absence]; I do so now, after several previous attempts merely as honoring the scruple of a fine poet who, in his own terms, was 'conscience-bound' to stay away." For a detailed account of this episode, see Ian Hamilton, *Robert Lowell: A Biography* (New York, 1982), 320–27.
2. Charles Van Doren's wife.

To Thomas Merton
ALS/KyLoB-M

October 8, 1965   *Falls Village, Connecticut*

I'm fine, thank you. Hospital? I've never been in one—yet. True, in January I had a traumatic arthritic knee which I took to New York to have treated (I had wrenched it, I guess), but it is nearly well now so that I don't think of it much any more. I take exercises morning and night, and probably always will.

What's this about the hermitage? Is the exile voluntary? I suppose so, in the interest of (at least) two books—which I await. Doubtless you mean by hermitage the little house you let me see. A wonderful retreat; I can see it now, as if I were there. All peace and blessing to you in it, and keep the logs off your feet.

We watched the Pope all day last Monday. A sweet, sweet man; we couldn't turn away. (T V, of course I mean.)

Charlie and his family have moved to Chicago, leaving us quite devastated. He will be with Mortimer Adler in the Institute for Philosophical Research, which Mortimer wants him to take over as director in two years when he, Mortimer, retires. A good job in every way, and apparently he will enjoy it, and we want him to be there, that being true. But we must study how to get along without them all. They are inexpressibly dear to us. For several years, incidentally, Charlie has worked for Mortimer in New York; now he will be on the ground, and of course that is sensible.

Today I had a birthday message from Lax (my birthday is in June) and a long thin poem about how the sea moves like a dancer. It does so move in the poem; but I appreciate your problem, in case you haven't solved it yet.

To Allen Tate
ALS/NjP

December 28, 1965   *Falls Village, Connecticut*

Ghost to ghost—this because I've just given Columbia your letters to me. Feel stiff in the joints? Queerly, I do.

Certainly I'll join you in nominating Jack Wheelock for the Academy; so send the form. His last book was very fine, I thought; but he belongs in anyway. . . .

To Thomas Merton
TLS/KyLoB-M

February 16, 1966   *Falls Village, Connecticut*

I have hesitated to intrude upon your retreat, which even the New York *Times* knows about, but I have a question to ask.

First, however, let me tell you that J. Laughlin has sent me your Ghandi [*sic*] book and the Chuang Tzu one,[1] and I have been reading them as if they were a new bible, which in a sense they are: two testaments, neither one old, neither one new. They put this mad world to rest, and without burying it either. They are wonderful. If they are your farewell to politics, what a farewell I say.

The question has to do with two volumes of a Journal Lax has been keeping on Kalymnos. He sent them to me; I have read them; and when I asked him what I should do with them, if anything, he said he didn't care, but perhaps they might go down to you. Do you want to see them?

They are very fine in my opinion. He walks about the island, talks to the sponge fishermen, looks out at the sea (he never tires of that, as it never tires of being there), goes to hear singing and watch dancing, gets concerned about the fishermen who may not return from their perilous voyage to the waters off Africa where they dive for sponges and sometimes die in the act, sleeps, thinks, writes poems, and tells himself he will probably be there forever, as perhaps he will be. He also mentions pretty often a very handsome girl (he has sent me pictures of her) who lives with her mother and weaves rugs on a loom. I have no idea what his Greek is like, but clearly he communicates with this girl (no name yet), and he even claims he has told her about me, though I doubt that he tells her I tease him about how I think he will end up by marrying her. He says if he does marry her it will be only so I can come over there and kiss her. Well. Do you want it? I didn't mention another incessant activity: photographing. He has shot every person on the island, I imagine, over and over, as well as the little white house where he lives. Kalymnos (Calymnus to the Romans) has never been so visible before; images of it go fluttering over the Aegean like so many butterflies, never perhaps to rest again.

1. Merton (ed.), *Gandhi on Non-Violence, Selected Texts from Mohandas K. Gandhi's Non-Violence in Peace and War* (New York, 1965), and Merton's *The Way of Chuang Tzu* (New York, 1965).

To Thomas Merton
ALS/KyLoB-M

March 6, 1966   *Falls Village, Connecticut*

From Gethsemani, Father Louis, as Merton was called there, sent Van Doren some tales of the Desert Fathers—including Nasrudin.

Thank you for telling me how you live—I know you live—and for the Tales of Nasrudin, who henceforth is one of my boys. . . .

Here is Lax's *Kalymnos Journal* (it might be called that), and I hope it can be published—with as few editorial tidyings as possible. Typos, yes; but the hesitations, the vaguenesses (not really that), the gentlenesses, the Laxnesses—keep those, tell Doubleday. You might be tempted to write a preface, and include a few mad letters.[1] But I'll not make any more suggestions. (It also could be called, I suppose, *The Sponge-Divers: A Journal from Kalymnos,* or some such thing.)

Charlie seems to be happy in Chicago. Did I tell you, however, that he had to get away for a week and so flew out here with Gerry and the children (Elizabeth, 7, and Johnny, 3) and they left the children here with us while they skied for a week in Vermont? We had a priceless time renewing our own youth. Once when I was having trouble with the zipper on Johnny's snow suit I cried out: "What the hell's the matter with this thing?" He said: "Daddy says that sometimes, and it doesn't make me feel very good." "Sorry. I won't say it again." "Oh, that's all right. When I get to be a big man I'll say 'shit' and 'God.'" I made no remark. So wags the world, my masters.

1. Merton's letter to Lax about the journal is included in Thomas Merton and Robert Lax, *A Catch of Anti-Letters* (Kansas City, 1978), 79: "It is the great book of each evening it was come from Mark Doorstops with encomiums too far short of the truth. It is the Everest of Journals."

To John Berryman
ALS/MnU

July 16, 1966   *Falls Village, Connecticut*

Why should I be surprised when a letter comes from you, and a beautiful one to boot? There is so much logic in it that I should be outraged when none came at all. But the fact is that words arrive from you on waves and waves of surprise and delight.

You ask how my "fine work" is going. Well, after 4 years of no poems I am writing some—so simple-minded that you might complain if you saw them, which you won't just yet; perhaps I'll inject some dubieties, some inner defeats [d e f e a t s][1] and contradictions, before I disclose them to your generous yet exacting eye. Fact is, I've been writing plays, and 3 of them are to be published this fall in a volume called—guess what?— *Three Plays.* All in verse, by golly, and I took an unholy joy in that. They're not closet plays either; I'd like to see them produced; and may never.

A year in Dublin—that is wonderful. Henry will talk brogue? 259 Songs, you say; the number staggers and entrances me. Cut to 84? That is massacre. Do you *have* to do it? Keep them all, of course; for these Songs are *it*, and I rejoice to hear that Germans and Italians agree. I heard about your sweet sentences concerning me at Columbia—I think not from you—and I wish I could have been behind the blackboard. I'm proud, Sir, I'm proud.

Does Kate go with you to Ireland? And the young?[2] However it is, enjoy Dublin; and if you do any travelling, drive across to Galway. Dorothy and I loved doing that in 1955. Also Connemara, also the Aran Islands. We should have gone south to the Lakes, they say, and north to I don't recall what; but the middle suited us abundantly. Oh, we did go far enough north to see infinite miles of bog. I'll never forget that.

Thank you, John, for (again) a beautiful letter. And love, love to all of you.

1. Brackets in original.
2. Berryman did take his wife and daughter with him to Ireland.

To John Berryman
ALS/MnU

September 3, 1966   *Falls Village, Connecticut*

Yes, I read of Delmore's death—alone in a room with no one to call—and felt as you did. So did Dorothy, who remembers as I do how Gertrude used to say his name: as if no one else in the whole world had a name.[1]

The dedication? Of course; I'd be so pleased. But if as time goes on to March you get to thinking that it ought be for Delmore entirely by himself, this would be more than all right.[2] Meanwhile, bless you for the thought.

May all Ireland now be yours, and may the new *Dream Songs* go as you most desire they should. The 114 sonnets, too—I didn't know about those. Print 'em print 'em.

I have no carbons to send because I never type poems till I'm sure—well, pretty sure.

1. Gertrude was Delmore Schwartz's first wife.
2. Berryman's *His Toy, His Dream, His Rest* (New York, 1968) was dedicated to MVD and Delmore Schwartz.

To Allen Tate
ALS/NjP

January 6, 1967   *Falls Village, Connecticut*

Tate divorced Isabella Gardner in March of 1966. In July he married Helen Heinz.

> For better, for worse,
> You took a nurse.
> I'm certain it's better,
> So here is this letter
> To say to Helen:
> Be glad that it's Allen;
> And likewise to Allen:
> Be happy with Helen—
> Whom bring to see us,
> O, son of Aeneas,
> As soon as you can.
> You're not an old man,
> And neither am I—
> Thank you. (Oh, my!)
> Memoirs? Can't wait
> For the story of Tate.
> But I'm sorry as hell
> You won't be in St. Paul.
> I had thought we could chatter.
> Yet no great matter,
> We'll do it anon
> When you visit us—when?
> Next summer, Why not,
> Say I, and says Dot.

To Allen Tate
ALS/NjP

September 11, 1967   *Falls Village, Connecticut*

Your news was grievous, and though I don't pray, I now will, for you and Helen and the babies—both of them, but particularly of course for Michael.[1]

May things go well in all ways. You must have seen in May how much Dorothy and I liked Helen. . . .

1. Twin sons were born to the Tates on
August 30, 1967. This letter indicated
Michael was not thriving soon after birth;
he died in an accident in the nursery
in 1968.

To John Berryman
ALS/MnU

September 20, 1967   *Falls Village, Connecticut*

I kissed both of Dorothy's cheeks for you, much to her surprise and pleasure—she sends her love—and here is the small book of mine I mentioned. If the other copy turns up, give it to somebody you like.

It is a trifle compared with your 384 sonnets, which I can't wait to see. Once more, I am happy about the dedication, and wish Delmore could be happy about it too—I mean, be present, and perhaps he will be, and then I know he will be happy. Nonsense? No.

It was wonderful to talk with you today, King Lear, old friend, good student (why not the best?), and now so high among living poets, and high anyway in my opinion. All power forever.

I've written Bob Lax on Kalymnos (a sufficient address), and if he doesn't write you, write him. I'm not sure I should have spoken about the rug girl, but then I did, didn't I? Use your judgment about speaking of her yourself. He's shyer than ever, you know. He's writing poems and keeping journals: both very fine. He lives among sponge-divers.

Our best love to you and Kate, plus by all means Martha.

To Robert Lax
ALS/NNC

November 2, 1967   *Falls Village, Connecticut*

*   *   *

The Emperor of Beard[1] called me the other morning at 7 here, at 6 there, and said he hadn't gone to bed yet. Is publishing next year a volume of 384 Songs & Sonnets, and insists that I help him reduce the numbers, saying Yes—No. Want the job?

[P.S.] *Life* says he drinks a quart of whiskey a day.

1. John Berryman.

To John Berryman
TLS/MnU

November 17, 1967   *Falls Village, Connecticut*

I can't do it, and furthermore I think it shouldn't be done. I'm sending a copy of this letter to Bob, who I hope will publish the entire book[1]— minus, I guess, #193, which you had doubts about and manifestly you were right. It doesn't scan with the total context.

My reason for refusing is put perfectly by you in #366:

These Songs are not meant to be understood, you understand.
They are only meant to terrify and comfort.

I think I do understand them, and I *know* I am terrified and comforted. What a vein you opened when you found Henry: a vein leading back and down into the very bowels of existence. I wonder and bow down. Cervantes had the same luck (if luck) when he opened *his* vein and felt the whole world pouring through. Every artist dreams of this, and damned few of them ever draw blood. You do, out of your own heart and mind, and out of all us others who are strangely like you as it happens. This book is a tremendous trip through everything. You leave bits of your flesh on thorns and out-jutting stones: so many bits, in fact, that I marvel at your surviving to call me as you did the other morning when by rights you should have been Orpheus Fragmented. Your strength is a miracle. It is what *makes* this book, which it would be an impertinence even to try to cut. Cut where, cut what? It's a testament, and I say, leave testaments alone. The Delmore group is wonderful, but so is every other group, which being the case, what then? Nothing, I answer.

Of course you know how swollen with pride I am over my half of the dedication. It could have been to Delmore only. If between now and publication you'd rather do that, by all means do it. Yet I'll bleed.

Love to you and Kate and to the little girl you helped over the fence.

1. Robert Giroux (Farrar, Straus and Giroux) was Berryman's publisher. Berry- man's *His Toy, His Dream, His Rest: 308 Dream Songs* appeared in 1968.

To Thomas Merton
APS/KyLoB-M

February 26, 1968 *Mexico*

Heavy footed, for heavy weather. Ponderous Gods down here. We are on a two-week trip to Mexico. How are you?

To Thomas Merton
TLS/KyLoB-M

March 15, 1968 *Falls Village, Connecticut*

I shouldn't answer you so quickly, but the fact is that I was about to write you to say that I had got *Cables to the Ace;*[1] . . . . The *Pond* is a wonderful act of generosity, to several good poets, and doubtless too it was fun for you.[2] "North" is very fine, as the Cables are, and as the piece on Mont Albán is.

We didn't get to Monte Albán . . . only to Chichen Itza, Uxmal, and neighboring cities, and then at last Mexico City—where Montezuma took his revenge on me the last day I was there; I barely got home, and now two weeks later am still wobbling. So it will be a long time before I can remember Mexico with pleasure, though there is much to remember, I know, and of course knew then. As for the gods of all that world: pretty hideous, I'd say, and deserving of their deaths. The people were (are) different. I'm all for them, particularly the Indian babies: such utter staring quiet, so intelligently maintained, such patience, such beauty.

I haven't been writing you either, and as you say, haven't come to see you. Sometime I will, or we will; there is nothing we'd like better. . . . Lax will come down, surely. . . . Your letters and his—what's the matter with your regular publishers doing them? It will be a wonderful book whenever it appears; they should know that, those publishers. I hope the not quite despairing fellow comes through and does it right.

And the *Journal of My Escape from the Nazis*[3]—yes, the world will have caught up with that. Good. Go to it.

We live quietly on the whole, reading and writing and simply living here, which after all is the best thing. This fall I publish the third volume of my *Collected Stories* (no more then), and next year when I'm 75 I'll publish a volume of new poems. Not anti-poems. Quite the contrary. The most pro I can manage. It's daring to do that these days.

1. Published by New Directions in 1968.

2. *Pond* was the journal being edited by Merton.

3. Published as *My Argument with the Gestapo* (Garden City, New York, 1969).

To Thomas Merton
TLS/KyLoB-M

April 16, 1968   *Falls Village, Connecticut*

Merton wanted to publish Van Doren's poem "Merton's Wood," but wished to retitle it, for it might have been politically unwise to use the original title.

Use the poem of course if you really like it, and entitulate it as you see fitulate. I know they're not your personal woods; I guess I was thinking in such terms as Shakespeare's Rome or Shakespeare's England. For me that day they were yours—mine too, maybe.

Lax is only a few miles from where I was last month—Yankton, South Dakota, where I lived for two days and nights in a convent (Mount Marty) and had many talks with the sisters about how the Church is throwing too much of itself away. I see this everywhere, and am troubled. Pope John didn't mean, I take it, when he suggested that everything be questioned, that all the answers should be NO. There are at least three answers: NO, YES, and THINK IT OVER. The Church should be like a strong man stirring in his sleep, even feeling the bed shake; not like a sick man saying might as well die now and be done with it.

And now here is your Easter Letter indicating that the malady has reached the monasteries—got there first for all I know. Your discussion of it is wonderful; leaves nothing to be said; so be it; amen; Selah. . . .

To Thomas Merton
ALS/KyLoB-M

June 22, 1968   *Falls Village, Connecticut*

Monks Pond No. 2 is even better—maybe my favorite is "Projections 23,"[1] p. 13, but then I have others too.

Swamped yet with letters and Mss.? Don't answer. I know the answer.

My advice is not to use "Merton's Woods," or whatever its new title. Not enough of an anti-poem. Dull, could be. Give it to the squirrels, not that they don't deserve something nuttier. . . .

1. The poem is by Halvard Johnson.

To William A. Sutton
ALS/IU-R

July 26, 1968   *Falls Village, Connecticut*

Sutton, professor of English at Ball State University, circulated a letter to a large number of contemporary American writers. Sutton's premise was that writers often had reservations about the way their works were taught in classes, and he asked the writers for suggestions about ways to teach their poetry or fiction.

Sorry to disappoint you with such simple answers, but I have never thought it was my business to tell people how to read *or* teach my work. It is for them, not me. I agree that teaching is often bad, but this will always be the case. We can simply pray for good, careful, generous reading and hope for the best.

To John Berryman
ALS/MnU

September 26, 1968   *Falls Village, Connecticut*

Well, I gaze and gaze at my name and Delmore's—bless his memory—in your wonderful book that came last week with your compliments.[1] Nothing ever pleased me more, and I know how true this would be for Delmore too if he only—hell! No more of that, what *am* I saying?

The book, I repeat, is wonderful. I've done nothing but read it since it came, recognizing and not recognizing what I read: Not recognizing, because there are wonders here I missed before, and I know this will happen with every future reading. The thing that overwhelms me this time, if you want to know, is the tirelessness of your mind and heart—busy with all the world all the time, noticing everything, remembering everything, and forgetting—at a guess—absolutely nothing. You've been everywhere, including heaven and hell. Here it all is, dreadful and ridiculous and beautiful and real and terrible and sweet in one long breath, which you know how to hold.

1. Berryman dedicated *His Toy, His Dream, His Rest* "To Mark Van Doren, and to the sacred memory of Delmore Schwartz."

To Thomas Merton
ALS/KyLoB-M

November 29, 1968   *[Falls Village, Connecticut]*

In 1968, Thomas Merton traveled to India, stopping at Honolulu, Tokyo, Hong Kong, Bangkok. In November, at Dharamsala in the Himalayas, he had three meetings with the Dalai Lama. In December he returned to Bangkok, where he was accidentally electrocuted on December 10.

I never expected to hear from you in those parts, and when you said the Monastery would forward mail I'm sure you didn't expect a piece of it that had to come by mule or camel train. But here this is, with apologies to Gethsemani for the burden and expense of forwarding it, if they charitably do. I didn't know what postage to put on.

Anyway, I rejoiced in your card from Darjeeling—unbelievable, of course—and in all the news you managed to pack in. Please now contrive to have a wonderful journey through unimaginable places. What a change all this is—I tremble to think what is building up in you as a consequence. Himalayas on Himalayas arise, and Indonesia archepelagates.

Love to you from us both, and down with entero-whatever-it-is. We flourish mildly. Have been invited to Israel in April, and may go. But that is nothing at all, compared to this trip from which you may return so rounded that you will roll.

To Robert Lax
ALS/NNC

December 10, 1968

Tom dead in Bangkok.
    The Abbot just telegraphed me
        —no details.
    I never felt so bad.
    I'll never get over it.
    And I know you won't.

To Robert Lax
ALS/NNC

December 30, 1968   *Falls Village, Connecticut*

We drove down today to a memorial mass for Tom at St. Patrick's, with Father Ford celebrating it.[1] Father Ford looked terribly ancient, but his voice reached the whole audience, which filled the cathedral. Afterwards we saw him for a minute, then went to Schrafft's for lunch with Bob Giroux and Ned O'Gorman.[2] We talked much of you—did you hear us? Did Merton hear us? Maybe.

For some reason I felt better when Ned suddenly blurted: "I'll miss that cat." Probably the best way to talk about him.

Yet only one way. *America* asked me for a piece about him, and I made it up mostly out of his last letter to me (July), talking with great joy about the trip he was to take. Heartbreaking now, and yet because it was so funny—almost like his letters to you—it somehow preserves him without loss.

Loss, though! God.

I wish I could be with you, and possibly I am.

[P.S.] I'll send you the *America* piece.[3]

1. Father George B. Ford was the counselor to Catholic students at Columbia. In October of 1938 Merton had told Father Ford that he wished to become a Catholic.
2. Giroux was Merton's Columbia friend who became one of Merton's publishers, and O'Gorman was a poet and teacher.
3. MVD's "Thomas Merton," *America*, January 4, 1969, pp. 21–22.

To John Van Doren
ALS/P

January 23, 1969   *Falls Village, Connecticut*

You are exactly right—as usual—about Merton's death. And I'm glad the little article said nothing to contradict you.[1] I've written another one for the spring issue of *Columbia Forum* which makes it even worse, for it quotes a lot from a paper Tom wrote in June on "The Future of Monasticism." He should have lived to make his promise good.

Meanwhile poor Lax talks of continuing to send him letters—not literally, of course. I think his loss is greatest. . . .

1. MVD's "Thomas Merton," *America*, January 4, 1969, pp. 21–22.

To Allen Ginsberg
ALS/NNC

May 5, 1969   *Falls Village, Connecticut*

Your letter came at the very moment when Arthur Wang, my publisher, was asking where you were. So I told him, and so you'll be invited to something on June 13 that you may not be able to or care to attend. Don't if neither; but if you do, I'll rejoice to see you. I can hardly count how many years since the last time. Too many, of course.

What Gods am I worshiping? Maybe just one: Himself. If Wang also sends you my new poems, you'll see (at the end of the book) what I mean.[1]

I'm sure you had a good time with Joe Krutch—some subjects, those. He's my oldest and closest friend. I don't see him enough either.

I'm going to be quite well, I think, thank you. No pain, much ease.

1. *That Shining Place: New Poems*
(New York, 1969). The reference is to the
psalms that close the book.

To Joseph Wood and Marcelle Krutch
ALS/DLC

August 8, 1969   *Falls Village, Connecticut*

Dot got ahead of me—wrote you about your letters (1924–1969) while I was in Georgia. And she probably said all that I would have said hereinafter. But no matter; both of us are full to overflowing with memories stirred up of those 45 years, and if either of us wrote all night there still would be plenty left unsaid. The main thing, as I believe Dot told you, is the record here of your two great selves: of Marcelle, for instance, remarking that if only animals could read Joe would be a best-seller. Well, he is anyway. And both of you are people very precious to us—never doubt that, even when you hear that we have given your letters to Columbia, where we can only *hope* the right readers will some day come along. At least we assume it to be a safe place for them—if any place is, now that the moon itself has a litter problem. . . .

To Robert Lax
ALS/NNC

September 2, 1969   *Falls Village, Connecticut*

*   *   *

Have you seen Merton's "My Argument with the Gestapo," formerly
"Journal of My Escape from the Nazis?" Now out, and wonderful; but no
more wonderful than all his letters to me, which I've just given to Columbia for safer keeping than this here. I read them all, and almost decided
not to send them; then did. Peace be.

All the young are now in Chicago. Where's that?

To Robert Lax
ALS/NNC

November 17, 1969   *Falls Village, Connecticut*

Guggenheim—yes, though sometimes it seems that I'm a Jonah with
them. However, I've got out the boxing gloves and will take on any Gug-
ger comer whose hands are tied behind his back. . . .

We went Sunday to have lunch with the Laughlins in Norfolk and met
John Howard Griffin, whom I suppose you know. One thing I wanted to
discuss—if I could—was whether he's a good choice for Tom's biographer. Well, I think he is. I liked him very much—liked the way he talked
about our friend, never pretending to know everything (who does?—
except you) but always eager (lovingly so) to know more than he now
does. He had hundreds of photographs that Tom had taken in Alaska and
the Far East—magnificent things, which he (Griffin) had developed. He
said Tom was one of the great photographers, and I can't doubt it.

PS: Griffin, you know, is the official biographer—there's a Foundation
(at Bellarmine) that has so decided.[1]

1. For reasons of health, John Howard
Griffin was unable to complete the official
biography of Thomas Merton. Michael
Mott was then appointed to be Merton's
biographer; Mott's *The Seven Mountains
of Thomas Merton* appeared in 1984.

To John Berryman
ALS/MnU

November 24, 1969   *Falls Village, Connecticut*

When our connection broke—when *was* it?—I didn't call you back at once because I thought your nerves, or whatever, might have acted up again. Perhaps it didn't matter much, for I had made it clear, I hope, how firmly I am against the notion of your coming in April solely to introduce me. And I assumed you were against it too—of course, of course. Let's let that subject rest.

Here's another one. The custodian of Special Collections at the Columbia Library wants your papers if you haven't arranged to place them elsewhere. He has mine, and is nice to deal with. (Kenneth A. Lohf, 301 Butler Library, Columbia, NYC 10027.)

So there! I've sent you the message. How's your neck? God love you.

To Joseph Wood Krutch
ALS/DLC

May 22, 1970   *Falls Village, Connecticut*

Van Doren wrote this letter the day of Krutch's death.

Do you remember Frank Calhoun in Cornwall? He's our bird man—that is, we call him when we want to know what bird we've just seen or heard. The latest case was one of hearing, not seeing, though as it turned out I had often seen the little fellow in winter and spring. I called Frank and described his song: one long, low note, then three higher ones on the same level. "Oh," he said, and whistled four notes into the phone. "That it?" "Yes! What is it?" "The white-throated sparrow." Remember him, Joe?

The next morning, early, and every morning since I have waked up early enough to hear those notes over and over again. Early morning bird talk is the best, I've decided, for me as well as for Chaucer.

To Jack T. Ledbetter
ALS/NNC

December 13, 1970   *Falls Village, Connecticut*

The poet J. T. Ledbetter, professor of English at California Lutheran College, was an admirer of Van Doren.

Dylan [Thomas]. You'll be shocked to learn how little I know about him. I met him only once—briefly—when some Columbia students invited me to dinner with him before a reading (I couldn't go to the reading), and he suffered so much from their failure to provide whiskey for him that he almost died, he said. They got some beer, and that helped—a little. Whenever they asked him a question (sitting in a semicircle) he responded by telling a story, usually with no connection that we could see. I always understood his last days in New York were miserable—incessantly drunk, incessantly sad. But I'm no authority, as you may perceive. I liked him that hour I was with him, but he didn't know—or care—where the hell he was.

To Robert Lax
ALS/NNC

January 12, 1971   *Falls Village, Connecticut*

*   *   *

Have you seen *A Hidden Wholeness* yet?[1] I asked Houghton Mifflin to send it, and they said they would. Meanwhile Rice's *Man in the Sycamore Tree* is out; and I'm not sure what I think of it.[2] Much new information (to me new), and many ideas about Tom that I'm glad to see stated, true or untrue; but something about the book bothers me. I guess it's Rice's omniscience about Merton, as if he and only he had all the answers. Jay Laughlin can't abide the book. I can, but still I'm bothered. (Don't let this bother *you*. Who am I that I shouldn't be?)

1. John Howard Griffin, *A Hidden Wholeness: The Visual World of Thomas Merton* (Boston, 1970).

2. Edward Rice was Merton's friend.

To Donald L. Keene
ALS/P

February 25, 1971   *Falls Village, Connecticut*

When Donald Keene published this letter in the Mark Van Doren issue of Voyages V *(1973), he commented: "He remarked once in class . . . that no action was more specifically human than to praise. In his letter he praised my book in terms that gave me intense pleasure, as you will easily understand, and in so doing revealed to me once again his generosity and his deep humanity."*

Two precious gifts from you: your beautiful letter of January 29th, and now the *Twenty Plays*.[1] Would you believe it, I have read every word of that, notes and all, pretty much without stopping, day and night, so that I am under a spell which I pray will not leave me soon, or ever. I think it never will; for the intensity of these plays is a thing quite by itself, and the beauty, and (often enough) the sadness—all those people caught like birds in nets of tragedy, and singing after death as they had not been able to sing in life. I know I shall never see any of these plays, but that doesn't matter too much: I *do* see them, with the precious help of you as editor and of your students (bless them) as translators. I do see, hear, and feel them, and I'll do so many times again. You have brought an entire theatre to life, you have saved it pure and strong for people far away. That is wonderful. Thank you.

1. Keene's *Twenty Plays of the No The-atre* (New York, 1970).

To Gladys Ely
ALS/P

March 20, 1971   *Falls Village, Connecticut*

Van Doren had worked with Gladys Ely to prepare The Selected Poems of Rosemary Thomas, *with an introduction by Van Doren, published by Twayne in 1968.*

About Frost. There is only one thing that matters: he was a wonderful poet. All the rest is biography and balderdash. Just think: before Thompson gets through he will have published nearly 2,000 pages, and the net effect of these, on people who read them as *if* they mattered, will be everlasting confusion.[1] There ought to be a law.

Frost should never have been allowed to say so many times in public (in these volumes) that he was a terrible man. Of course he was, but he enjoyed too much the telling of it. The rest of us are equally terrible, and have too much pride to confess it. In Frost, though, it was fear as well. Incredibly, he never seems to have known how good a poet he was, and so had to play games with fame, and with rotters like Louis Untermeyer. He shouldn't have cared what people thought of him; he should have known what *he* thought; but he didn't, and so was as nervous as a child just learning to walk and talk. He feared every living poet, and needed to fear none. It wasn't jealousy; it was terror. And maybe there is something grand about the spectacle; but I think there isn't.

I exaggerate. In my case he was always generous, always affectionate. In 1937, in fact, he made all the difference to me. Mr. Thornton, of Henry Holt, invited me to lunch one day and said he wanted to publish me—said Frost had suggested it. Well, within the next two years Holt published *The Last Look & Other Poems, Collected Poems,* and *Shakespeare;* not to speak of other books later on. It was like a fairy tale. When Thornton called me I had just been told by Macmillan, who had published *A Winter Diary & Other Poems,* that they were dropping me—I didn't sell. There I was, sprawled on the ground, and it was Frost who picked me up and dusted me off (not that he knew about Macmillan). Nothing he ever did in the way of malice and spite to others—and Thompson is all too ready to show him at it—counts for me against the foregoing. . . .

1. Lawrance Thompson was Robert Frost's authorized biographer.

To Russell Miles
ALS/IU-Ar

March 23, 1971   *Falls Village, Connecticut*

*   *   *

Forget the *Literary History of the U.S.* I'm used to that. I scarcely exist in the minds of such.[1] And I don't give one good God damn (or I *think* I don't).

1. MVD is not discussed as a poet in this literary history by Spiller and others, but his *Liberal Education* is given passing mention.

To John Berryman
ALS/MnU

June 18, 1971   *Falls Village, Connecticut*

Of course I wanted to write National Endowment about you, and indeed I have already done it, and the document is on its way, with my fervent wishes for your success folded into its most intimate, most vulnerable recesses.

I didn't tell NE what I'll tell you, namely that you will never finish the Sh book. There will always be metal more attractive: poems, novels, a memoir, a collection of pensées—God knows what else. You have this illusion you're a scholar, but you know damn well you are nothing of the sort, any more than I am. Scholarshit is for those with shovels, whereas you're a man of the pen, the wing, the flying horse, the shining angel, the glittering fiend—anything but the manure whereunder scholars have buried the masterpieces of the world. You're for the masterpieces, and you know that nothing else matters one tiny little bit, one pitiful little jot, one tit, one tittle.

Of course I didn't tell NE this, and now you may confound me by finishing *Sh's Reality* after all. If you do, God bless both you and it. But I can't forget that if you had been going to write this book you would have written it long ago. Maybe I'm daring you to do it now. If so, then *be* it so.

Meanwhile here is Sarah, and glad I am that she has come—with lynx ears too, the better to hear what she will hear. I love the name, and already I love the child. Greetings to her from Dorothy and me, and love to Kate who bore her Sunday night—not yet a week in the world, and here she is getting messages from old friends of the family. Ah, well-a day, calloo, callay, I chortle in my joy.

Meanwhile too there is your mother, whom I confess I've been afraid to ask you about in recent years. Our love to her, if she is in a state to receive such a faraway gift. I hope she can be with you more than a little while.

The three poems you enclosed make me impatient for the volume they'll be in—particularly "Old Man Goes South Again Alone" and "King David Dances." Very fine, Dr. Berryman, Sir, all three, all three; but especially those two.[1]

1. For Berryman's response to this letter,
see Haffenden's *The Life of John Berryman*, 402–403.

To John Berryman
ALS/MnU

July 15, 1971   *Falls Village, Connecticut*

More power to you against all pipsqueaks—march at them, to them, through them to the music of Psalm 26. Lord, how I'd like to have been there when you executed him with your voice, destroyed him with your loathing. Down with all pipsqueaks, clerical or lay.[1]

OK then, you're a scholar. But remember: it's a secondary thing to be, and you know what's primary, or if you don't you're not my John any more. You do though, of course.

I can't second Bellow because for me he's not a natural novelist[2]—don't make me explain, except by saying he bores me, fatigues me, instead of refreshing me, which by God fiction still should at least try to do—nor Erikson because I haven't read him.[3] Sorry on both counts.

Love, however, to Kate and Sarah—and wait a minute, your others— and to old Scaliger himself, whose last letter was wonderful beyond telling.

1. During the last year of his life, Berryman returned to being a practicing Catholic and attended a Minneapolis Catholic church. One Sunday in June of 1971 he was provoked by the sermon of a young priest who said he could imagine leaving the priesthood. Upset by this manifestation of what he considered a permissive society, Berryman spoke up against the views of the "pipsqueak" and created quite a stir. Berryman later felt some sense of wrongdoing until he read Psalm 26.

2. MVD is referring to the nomination of Saul Bellow for membership in the American Academy of Arts and Letters.

3. Erik Erikson, author of *Young Man Luther* and other psychological studies.

To Sholom Kahn
ALS/P

September 13, 1971   *Falls Village, Connecticut*

Sholom Kahn, a former student of Mark Van Doren's, was teaching in Israel.

Yes, I knew Schwartz—a nice good man with terrible problems, chief of which was permanent insomnia (you probably know of this). Also, he latterly developed a sensibility to imagined slights and affronts—very strange, since everybody who knew him liked him—couldn't help it. But a very good poet, I think. . . .

To Gladys Ely
ALS/P

March 1, 1972   *Falls Village, Connecticut*

John Berryman jumped to his death from the Washington Avenue Bridge over the Mississippi River on January 7, 1972.

*   *   *

You know of course how thoroughly I agree with you about tools and knowing how to use them.

Berryman did too, as you very brilliantly say. I knew him from the time he was a student in Columbia College; even then living was hard for him, and it got worse and worse, until the memory of his father's suicide really outweighed all other memories; or he despaired of ever abandoning the bottle; or—well, who knows? Allen Tate's letter today says he "had been committing slow suicide for years. God knows why." I'm sure there's no knowledge in this field. Tate was his colleague at Minnesota for perhaps 15 years, or so; so if he doesn't know, who indeed does? I'm certainly sorry. I'll miss him. Over the telephone, long distance, he *screamed* sometimes, in rage or joy; I can still hear him. And in 1938, when he was visiting the Tates here in Cornwall, one day he shut himself in a closet and barked like a dog, life even then being, he explained, too much for him. . . .

To John Haffenden
TLS/P

July 15, 1972   *Falls Village, Connecticut*

John Haffenden was preparing his biography of John Berryman and wrote to Van Doren asking for information.

This reply to your good letter of May 28th will probably disappoint you, but it is the best I can do.

My knowledge of John Berryman was never as intimate as you may have assumed it was. He was my student, yes, and he was always my friend; but with me he was not confessional, and since your letter I have been wondering why. My guess is that for the very reason of his devotion to me (your word, whether or not I deserve it) he seldom or never showed me any of his weaker sides. He confessed in public, as of course you know; but when I gave him hell for several poems in *Love and Fame* he wrote back that I was doubtless right: the book should have been called *Love and Shame*. How serious was he then? I really have no idea.

For a good many years I was pretty much out of touch with him—for the most important years, in fact. Our letters were few though affectionate, and most of them antedate the period of his maturer accomplishment. Incidentally, all of his letters to me are among my papers in the Library of Columbia University, New York (Special Collections). I have no other documents bearing upon his life.

After his graduation from Columbia College in 1936 he went to Cambridge for two years on a Kellett Fellowship, and returned with an accent so fantastically British that many of his friends, including my wife, chided him for it; he abandoned it more or less, but always spoke, I thought, a bit unnaturally—with just a touch of the synthetic in his accent until the end of his life. I don't know why I speak of this, but you see I do. Forget it, please, and read on.

John never relinquished the notion that he might become a tremendous Shakespeare scholar. Latterly I sought to discourage him from this, saying that poetry was more important, but he steadily assured me that his ambition was scholarly as well as literary; the relevant fact is that most of his projects in this field were unfinished, whereas he always finished his poems. Shakespeare, incidentally, was not his only "subject"; but you know this, of course.

I know nothing of his insomnia or his hallucinations. Alcoholism, yes, though even here my knowledge is sketchy. I do remember telephone calls from him in Minneapolis when he screamed rather than talked, but I was never with him when he was drunk. A note from him a year or so before his death assured me that after a recent term in a sanatarium he was certain he would never drink again; and perhaps he never did, though his wife Kate said to my wife in New York this last May, when several of his friends, myself included, read from his work under the auspices of the Academy of American Poets, that in her opinion (Kate's) he killed himself because he missed alcohol so much—her point being that either on or off was impossible for him. This sounds likely, but I cannot vouch for its truth. If truth, how terrible however.

John's mother, on this same occasion, remarked to me that he had tried suicide as many as forty times. Hyperbole, I suspect, though again I don't know. It is a subject he never discussed or even mentioned to me.

He was a charming man who never ceased to seem young to me—or generous, or impetuous, or frank, or amusing, or serious too. I was very fond of him; his death was and still is a shock from which I reel. . . .

To Arthur Wang
TLS/P

November 10, 1972   *Falls Village, Connecticut*

---

*   *   *

Early in 1973 I'd like to send you the manuscript of my new book of poems, entitled (probably) *Good Morning*.[1] It's for 1974, when I'll be 80 if I live. Not that I want anything made of that, but it's why I pick the date. I seem to be assuming that you still want the volume. The last one that you so generously brought forth has been the occasion of wonderful letters to me, even if (I guess) it hasn't sold especially. Queer, that. I'll never understand. . . .

1. The volume appeared posthumously under the title *Good Morning: Last Poems* (New York: 1973). MVD died on December 10, 1972.

Index